THE
MONTESSORI
POTENTIAL

How to Foster Independence, Respect, and Joy **in Every Child**

PAULA LILLARD PRESCHLACK

CHICAGO

Copyright © 2023 by Paula Lillard Preschlack
Foreword copyright © 2023 by Virginia McHugh Goodwin
All rights reserved
Published by Parenting Press
An imprint of Chicago Review Press Incorporated
814 North Franklin Street
Chicago, Illinois 60610
ISBN 978-1-64160-892-3

Library of Congress Control Number: 2022946311

Cover design: Jonathan Hahn
Cover photographs: (top) Anna Silverthorn / Adobe stock,
(bottom left) author's collection,
(bottom middle) courtesy of Forest Bluff school,
(bottom right) John Dickson
Typesetting: Nord Compo

Printed in the United States of America
5 4 3 2 1

To Paula Polk Lillard.
You are an inspiration to me and to many with your strength,
spirit, and clear vision.
Thank you for being the wind under our wings.

And to all the children who show us the way in
Montessori classrooms and around the world.
This is your story!

I repeat and insist: I did not wish to originate a method of education, nor am I the author of a method of education. I have helped some children to live, and I have set forth the means which I found necessary. And if these means of help are a method of education for children of this age, then all aids to the development of humanity are also methods of education. This is not a method like other methods, but it is the beginning of something which must grow and which is in no way bound to any personality that may appear as the author, but is solely allied to human beings who develop in freedom. It is a history of liberty.

—Maria Montessori, *The 1913 Rome Lectures*

CONTENTS

Foreword by Virginia McHugh Goodwin   ix

Introduction   What Should Education Be?   1

1. Montessori in Action   15
2. The Framework That Makes Montessori Work   47
3. An Effective Model: A Montessori School   89
4. Authenticity: The Quest and the Challenge   124
5. Benefiting All: Public Montessori Schools   153
6. In the Heart of Things: Embracing
   the Approach   188

Conclusion   A Revolution in Thinking   221

Epilogue   "Why?": Curiosity Drives Learning
for Life   229

Acknowledgments   233

Notes   237

Bibliography   251

Index   253

FOREWORD

WHILE TRAVELING FOR TWENTY-SIX YEARS in my role as executive director of the Association Montessori International / USA, I was often asked by fellow travelers about my occupation. It's not an easy question to answer, so I generally replied with a question of my own: "Have you ever heard of Montessori?" This often elicited a long pause, followed by something like, "Yes, but I don't know much about it." It became apparent through the ensuing conversations that most people had different perceptions and misconceptions. That misinformation has dominated the public's impressions of what I held to be an innovative and progressive educational approach. Despite my best efforts leading a national Montessori organization, the impressive success stories of former Montessori students, such as Sergey Brin and Will Wright, had not reached the American people.

Paula Lillard Preschlack comes from a family of Montessorians. Our paths were bound to cross—which they did decades ago during a school visit. Her uncommon distinction of holding AMI Montessori certification for multiple age groups, from fifteen months through twelve years, along with her persuasive communication skills, instantly attracted my attention. Whether it was a podcast, webinar, or presentation, her message was always clear and compelling, and this unique perspective has driven her growth through the years from teacher to head of school. I encouraged her to think big—to reach out to a wider audience using her skills, experience, and ability to explain Montessori education in concise terms while capturing the essence of its integrated plan.

Paula's desire to see Montessori thrive ignited the fire for her to author *The Montessori Potential*. It stands out among Montessori books by virtue of the added breadth and depth of her experiences. Her extraordinary gift to communicate in combination with the extensive research and interviews done in preparation have produced a magnificent contribution. It is masterfully written—a book of hope and opportunity!

While many books have been written about the what and why of Montessori, this author has chosen to focus on its potential, its capabilities. Her singular approach makes this a valuable source for parents, current and future teachers, education support staff, researchers, professors, people who want to learn more about how children learn, and those wanting to effect educational and social reforms. Paula's well-organized chapters lead you through the key facets that distinguish this educational experience from all others. The reader is given a remarkable overview of Montessori theory and practice with its pedagogical orientation on the different stages of human development. The key foundations of an authentic Montessori classroom are clearly articulated: an environment created around the child's needs, a trained Montessori teacher, and the paradigm of freedom with responsibility. When all three are optimal, every child has the opportunity to reach their potential.

Throughout the book Paula shares recent research and stories from both private and public Montessori schools, indicating that Montessori benefits all children, even those with higher needs. Her observations and discussions with public school leaders and teachers present the realities with both challenges and effective solutions. Paula highlights a school that implements a complete and authentic Montessori program and includes practical suggestions for building successful partnerships with staff and parents; this chapter is especially beneficial for schools.

Montessori comes alive as you see it in action through Paula's experienced eyes. She tells the stories of diverse groups of children, demonstrating clearly that children's different backgrounds, learning styles, and cultures build the foundation of Dr. Montessori's concept of the *universal child* and validate the flexibility of this education model that allows for individual differences. She includes testimonials from graduates, delightful stories of her time teaching children—from toddlers to preteens—and observations from her visits to myriad schools. Her style is dynamic, engaging, readily understandable, and flows beautifully. Her sense of humor carries weight, for as a parent herself she knows the challenges and joys of parenting. The author brings it all *home*, addressing Montessori's view for parents and the support that is available.

I have been involved with Montessori my entire adult life as a teacher, head of school, consultant, coach, and ultimately executive director of AMI/USA. Dr. Maria Montessori professed that children are the hope and promise of humankind. She believed that only through improving the future of children would society achieve progress and peace. Her life's work revolved around this conviction. Looking at our society's landscape today, this book is more relevant than ever. Consider the tensions gripping our culture today: racial injustice, the pandemic, and a mental health crisis among adolescents that has our nation in a stranglehold. The loneliness, depression, and anxiety of our youth must be addressed.

My thirst was for a book that expresses what education could be. It would clarify authentic Montessori in simple terms and dispel the Montessori stereotypes and misinformation. *The Montessori Potential* presents a clear and compelling affirmation that Montessori's method will prepare children to adapt, to be resilient, and to meet the challenges and demands of their future confidently, independently, joyfully, and with a strong motivation to learn and explore. With Montessori in the mainstream, the ultimate goal of accessibility for all children will be realized. We need to embrace Dr. Maria Montessori's revolutionary approach and accept a new mind-set about education. It's a recipe for success.

I am grateful that Paula has written *The Montessori Potential*, elucidating Montessori and inspiring us to know that it holds the power to change education—to change the world!

Virginia McHugh Goodwin
AMI/USA Executive Director Emeritus
Wildflower Foundation Partner

Introduction

WHAT SHOULD EDUCATION BE?

OUR CHILDREN FACE UNPRECEDENTED RATES of change and an uncertain future. Rather than be paralyzed by anxiety, this next generation needs to adapt. For this, they must develop necessary skills, knowledge, and traits. On this quest, education plays a vital role.

When I ask parents, educators, employers, and business leaders what abilities children need for the future, they tell me that children will need to think creatively, to innovate, to collaborate, and to solve problems effectively. They give descriptive words like *persistent, resilient, confident, compassionate,* and *intellectually curious.* People recognize that young adults need to cultivate their abilities to learn new things, to view failures as learning opportunities, and to persevere with lifelong passions. In essence, the next generation needs to foster their adaptability for anything that comes their way.

Considering this reality, we must ask ourselves whether the current educational system helps children. And if so, how? If grades and scores drive progress in our schools, how do children learn not to fear failures? When children are stopped midthought to leave one subject of study and change to another every fifty minutes, how do they develop focus and get deeply engaged? If units of study end after six weeks and students cannot dive deeper into a subject, how can they pursue

1

their curiosity, develop passions, and practice the courage to persevere? If they are restricted from interacting during class time and taught to compete with each other to be winners, how can children learn to truly collaborate? And after they are told what information to acquire, and when and where to apply it, how can children develop creativity, independence, and resourcefulness? If such traits are the goals of education, then schools are failing.

The Pendulum Swing of School Models

The most recent attempts to reform education in the United States have been the No Child Left Behind Act of 2001 under President George W. Bush and Race to the Top in 2009 under President Barack Obama. Each of these efforts used testing aligned with curricula to improve outcomes. Many educators argue that these changes have caused more problems than solutions for children in classrooms.[1] The recent reform movements do not address the main obstacles in education today. In fact, American educators have been working with two extreme systems, both flawed at the core, for more than 150 years.

On the one extreme is the common model, which stems from the premise that children's minds are like buckets to be filled with knowledge. In this model, we assume that children are passive by nature and that teachers must be active to make children learn. This idea means that we adults must stuff and mold children's minds. Such an approach was based on the behaviorist theories of John Locke (1632–1704) and was developed further for educational practices by Edward Thorndike (1874–1949). From this foundation, American educators adopted the belief that children must be prodded into learning by various forms of rewards and punishments, such as grades and external rankings. The behaviorist theory has been treated as truth, despite observable evidence to the contrary and mountains of research conducted in fields of psychology and education suggesting otherwise.

Relying on this premise of children's minds as buckets to be filled, most schools adopted a factory-style schedule, imparting information in a highly organized fashion of dividing knowledge into discrete subjects. A different teacher taught each subject, and children moved from room to room to acquire the information. This model was created during the Industrial Revolution to educate masses of immigrants and to prepare workers for the factories they would enter after school. Such a model necessitated textbooks, time limits, and letter grades. The goal was to prod children to acquire the same knowledge at the same rate, times, and ages, regardless of interest or readiness. This model became the norm and remains what most schools practice. For this book, I will refer to this model as *conventional* schooling.

This conventional system has become tightly aligned with testing, to the point that school systems design curricula around tests, which are decided not by those working with children but by politicians, textbook publishers, and policy makers. This test-driven school model is not preparing our children for an innovative, rapidly changing workforce that differs so completely from the factories of the past. And yet parents and educators are entrenched in the familiar. If we take a step back, most people willingly agree that children are active learners who need to move their bodies, use their hands, try things out, explore, and converse in order to absorb and retain information. However, as a society, we struggle to create a model that fully takes these needs into account.

Enter the progressive school models, based on the idea that children construct themselves. Beginning in the early 1900s, *constructivists* such as John Dewey (1859–1952), Jean Piaget (1896–1980), and Jerome Bruner (1915–2016) spread this concept. American educators have been experimenting with this idea ever since, with several progressive movements in education. A parent looking for a progressive school for their children today might look for an innovative model like High Tech High (featured in the 2015 documentary *Most Likely to Succeed*) or choose a Waldorf school, a Sudbury school, or an AltSchool, as examples.[2]

Progressive schools as a whole, however, have not found ways to impart a structure of necessary knowledge without losing the free-flowing aspects of lively classrooms where students follow their interests to drive their own educations. In such schools, many children do not get the help they need to develop their focus, their organization skills, and their executive-functioning skills. Progressive models typically lack a reliable or consistent curricular plan. With no formal curricular plan, progressive schoolteachers are left with the gargantuan task of deciding what to show children and how to steer them through the labyrinth of human history and its accomplishments. Without guided presentations of a coherent body of information, students may not develop organized, effective ways of thinking or the skills to carry out their ideas. Allowing children to do whatever they wish on a daily basis and to be active in any way they desire proves to be insufficient.[3]

The reaction to this dilemma is often to return to the more rigid, conventional school approach, resulting in a school that appears progressive in some ways but that is still rooted in conventional practices, such as dictating to children what they must learn and do and when to work on each subject. In the United States swinging trends in education toward looseness (progressive) and then back to rigidness (conventional) have been repeating for decades; they are nothing new.

Most parents and educators argue that their modern schools combine the best of various techniques to produce the most child-centered learning environments. Many reputable schools *claim* that they are teaching children the skills and traits they need to succeed—abilities to innovate, think creatively, and problem solve independently—but they cannot show *how* their students learn these skills, much less prove that they actually do. For instance, students may do a group project, but they are told what group to join and what to do the project on, and students are directed by the teacher to the point that the children are assumed to be passive. A contrary example might be that students are allowed to come up with a problem to solve, are given free time to do it, and are encouraged to be creative, but the approach rests on a permissive style that lacks the organization that children need for success. By taking a close look, you will find practices that reflect the belief that children's minds are empty vessels to fill or, conversely, that they should be left to do whatever they wish. American educators still revert to these two flawed bases.

The result is that our schools *thwart*, rather than enhance, the development of necessary traits. They discourage the very traits that lead to success in a workforce that rewards innovation, creative problem-solving, effective organization, collaboration, and engagement in one's own learning. Whether a person works in a warehouse or a laboratory, with computers or directly with customers, these skills are the building blocks for adaptability and human progress. Classrooms are the very places that must prepare children for life in the real world. Education must be designed not for progressing to the next level or grade within a school but for life outside it, in society.

Montessori's Unique Perspective

While Dewey, Piaget, and Bruner were developing the theory of constructivism, Dr. Maria Montessori (1870–1952) saw that children have a natural propensity to form themselves and recognized a problem in treating education as the act of the educator imparting knowledge. Instead, child education must account for, study, and align with the natural process of self-construction already occurring within children. Adults must create an education that takes children's self-forming *fully* into account. Educators must go *all the way* into the details of the format, the manner, and the content to reflect this paradigm. Dr. Montessori then designed an educational approach to reflect the concept of children's self-formation. This is why the Montessori approach differs from both the conventional and progressive models. Dr. Montessori's view was—and still is—a revolution in thought and practice.

Dr. Montessori's revolutionary approach to teaching began with close observations of children. Through her observations, she found recognizable behaviors that indicate how children learn. When Dr. Montessori identified what behaviors she was seeing, she looked for the real purpose each might have in human development. Developing on these behavioral findings, she proposed educational environments and practices that deliberately employ children's most positive learning characteristics at each age, freeing children to reach for their full potential throughout development.

Dr. Montessori recognized that the inner drive to discover the world begins at birth and progresses throughout childhood in distinct stages. She illuminated the importance of seeing each child's life as a whole and a continuum, proceeding from birth to maturity at approximately age twenty-four. She then examined and discovered how education can align with human development in its successive stages on this continuum and meet individual needs along the way.

Dr. Montessori championed what she called the *universal child*: children all around the world—born in any time, culture, or place— have the same underlying developmental characteristics and tendencies. They respond to their environments in similar ways, and they need the same kinds of support to develop fully. This means that Montessori education can be applied anywhere and anytime because the goal of this educational approach is to foster human qualities of adaptability. In the process of adapting to their culture, time, and place, children become their unique, individual selves, able to incorporate their impressions of the world around them into themselves. Dr. Montessori had the foresight to see that in all ages, adaptability must be the goal of education.

What the constructivists who came just after her and the related progressive models of schooling missed is how deeply Dr. Montessori aligned her approach to these discoveries. The architects of progressive methods did not take this final step. Dr. Montessori created a complete curriculum that reflects the characteristics and developmental needs of every stage of childhood, in succession. She figured out how to demonstrate abstract concepts with concrete representations by designing specific learning materials for the children to manipulate with their hands. Through these carefully constructed materials, Dr. Montessori found a tangible way to help children discover—and to fully comprehend—truths and concepts that can be logically applied. This process frees students from relying so heavily on the teacher and allows them to explore and learn more independently. She also scripted her curricular plan to give teachers the flexibility to respond to children's individual learning styles and paces. Finally, rather than separating the subject areas of study, she preserved the interrelation of topics. This allows children to naturally discover relationships between subject areas and understand the context in which all knowledge interrelates. These qualities of Dr. Montessori's curriculum support the exploratory style of learning that comes so naturally to children.

The Montessori approach for education, therefore, differs from any other at the outset, as well as in every aligned detail and style of execution. Montessori does not incorporate, add in, or tack on innovative teaching strategies to help students solve problems, think creatively, or collaborate the way that other methods do; instead, these techniques are inherent in the very core of the approach. It is cohesive. Nothing needs to be added or changed in order to adapt to changing times because the approach itself considers that "*Adaptability* ... is the most essential quality" for human beings.[4] Enhancing traits for adaptability is what this education does.

Inspired by Children

Where did Maria Montessori's foresight come from? She grew up in Rome in the late 1800s, and she developed her approach from the early 1900s into the early 1950s. Her ideas grew out of a strong foundation of intellectual work, infused by a wide network of thought leaders in various fields and decades of her own observations of children's behaviors.[5] Dr. Montessori studied mathematics, engineering, science, the humanities, and eventually medicine at the University of Rome. She was a voracious learner and one of the first women to graduate from the university, and then the first to graduate from its medical school.[6] She went on to practice medicine but returned to the university for further studies in anthropology, psychology, and philosophy; she continued to study and work until the day she died at age eighty-one. Dr. Montessori's decisions and pursuit of education were, of course, most unusual for women in her day. Her life's work reveals a determined, courageous spirit and a highly intelligent mind.

Dr. Montessori's first professional task with children was to discover ways to help disabled children. She was put in charge of the physical and psychological development of young patients in a psychiatric institution in Rome. Simultaneously, she studied the works of other scholars who had experimented with children with similar needs, such as the French medical doctors Jean-Marc Gaspard Itard (1774–1838) and Édouard Séguin (1812–1880). Dr. Montessori began using some methods and concrete learning materials that such pioneers had found successful. She altered and added to these materials extensively, based on her own experiences and those of her colleagues working with children under her direction. Crucially, she approached her work in just this order:

observing children, consulting the work of other great thinkers, collaborating with teachers, and then implementing systematic experimentation.

In the early 1900s Dr. Montessori attracted international attention when "mentally defective" children she had been assigned to work with passed the same state educational tests designed for Italy's neurotypical students.[7] Instead of agreeing with the remarks that she had "cured" the children she worked with, Dr. Montessori wondered why children with neurotypical aptitudes were not reaching their full potential through education; reasonably, they ought to surpass her students who had such severe challenges to overcome. She wanted to try her materials and approach with more children.

Dr. Montessori was subsequently invited to work with fifty to sixty children living in subsidized housing that had been refashioned for low-income families in the San Lorenzo district of Rome. This group of children, roughly ages two to six years old, were too young to attend school and were left to run around the tenements during the day while their parents were at work. In 1907 Dr. Montessori created a learning environment in a ground-floor apartment in this neighborhood and began collaborating with an untrained teacher to present her learning materials to these children.[8]

The children that Dr. Montessori worked with—both her institutionalized patients and the San Lorenzo children—stunned the world with their responses and newfound abilities. Dr. Montessori pointed out that the children had taught *themselves* and that she was merely the one to unveil their heretofore hidden potentialities. She wrote about her discoveries, calling this the *child's method* rather than putting her name to it. Her reverence for the inborn powers of human development distinguished Dr. Montessori. She consistently directed her listeners to look not to her for the discoveries of children's abilities to learn and adapt but instead to the children themselves. She believed that children's behavior revealed how they learned best and that these discoveries could be applied as a scientific pedagogy of education. In fact, Dr. Montessori's first book describing her discoveries was titled *The Method of Scientific Pedagogy Applied to the Education of Young Children in the Children's House*. Because English translators believed this title too unwieldy, they simply reduced it to *The Montessori Method*, and the name stuck. Dr. Montessori spent the rest of her life asking audiences to think of this approach to children's education not as a "method" but rather as a discovery of truths about children.[9] (For this reason, I refer to Montessori as an *approach*.)

As Dr. Montessori began lecturing around the world and training teachers to implement her approach, she inspired countless others to begin looking at children in a new way. There are now roughly twenty thousand Montessori schools in the world, a reported forty-five hundred of which are in the United States. However, Montessori has still not taken hold in education departments of teaching colleges and graduate programs; today, most students majoring in education receive only a brief mention of Montessori's approach, if any, without much description of the structure or supporting evidence to the effectiveness of its application. In addition, parents and educators must look hard to find good examples of Montessori, even in schools that call themselves "Montessori." In the meantime, Dr. Montessori's work falls more readily into the studies of psychology or child development, where her educational approach—one that matches up to children instead of trying to make children match to it—is embraced as logical and practical. Until educators begin looking at human behavior to design schooling, as Dr. Montessori did, the two basic models of conventional and progressive education will dominate their landscape.

An Approach That Works

Whenever I hear people lamenting the state of education today, I want them to know that there is another option, one that I have seen firsthand in action for twenty-five years. After a passionate conversation about what schools should be like to truly help prepare children for the real world and agreeing on the traits that children need to develop, I share my own observations of Montessori education. My colleagues and I have witnessed the results of this approach for more than three decades at Forest Bluff School and at other quality Montessori schools around the country. My own experiences as a teacher and head of school and those of my mother, Paula Polk Lillard, and many colleagues demonstrate direct ways that the

Montessori approach benefits children. After witnessing amazing results time and again with children who reach potential far beyond what most would expect for them, we have collectively seen that Montessori really works. Montessori directly supports children to develop traits that enable them to succeed in today's world and workforce. But don't just take my word for it; listen to what some Montessori graduates have said when asked to explain what their educations did for them:

> What I love about Montessori is that it instills a passion for learning and a sort of entrepreneurial spirit. We were encouraged to follow our own interests.

> The key philosophy in Montessori is that at the end of the day, you're very responsible for your own learning and your own success. And part of that process is learning how to start your own activities and manage your own activities. Montessori teachers expect a certain amount of work to be accomplished every week or two weeks, and they're on top of that process, but as long as you are working, you're in charge of your own time.

> From Montessori, I developed an ability to focus that I notice many of my peers in medical school lack. In a chaotic hospital setting, where you have multiple patients, so much going on around you, and everything is urgent—the ability to just sit down and focus to get things done in the middle of all that is critical.

> In Montessori, no one ever told me, "you're not smart enough to learn that," or "you can't do that," so I learned that I can teach myself anything. If a professor was going too fast or there's something I need to learn for my job, I know that I can figure it out if I work hard enough or long enough. That's what we did in Montessori, where you're taught *how* to learn, not what to learn.

> When it wasn't too cool in high school to be doing your homework, I was still invested in my learning, I think because in Montessori, I was taught to love learning—and always have.

When asked, "How did your Montessori teachers teach you these things?" one thirty-year-old graduate answered with a smile and a twinkle in his eye, "With the Pink Tower." After laughing about this lighthearted remark with colleagues, I realized that our graduate had a serious point, one that I thought about long after hearing it. From years of experiencing the Montessori approach in action, I see that the full version of Montessori education is as simple, balanced, and sturdy as this iconic Montessori material of ten pink cubes, first introduced to children as early as two and a half years old to stack by size. Dr. Montessori not only saw that children learn by using their hands and exploring, interacting, and thinking simultaneously but also answered the dilemma of how to give children what they need to do this best.

In the materials themselves, such as the Pink Tower, children can experience keys that help them unveil how, why, and in what order things work. The gradual progression of each concept builds upon earlier foundations. Children make their own discoveries as their minds and bodies interact with the environment, learning materials, and people around them. These features make the curricular plan an imperative aspect of Montessori's effectiveness for children. The more closely you look at the approach, the more you'll see that Montessori prepares children to thrive in adulthood, just as these graduates attest.

Eight Character Traits Fostered by Montessori

To show just how the Montessori approach helps children develop their potential, I will point to eight character traits that I've consistently seen in Montessori graduates. There are, of course, many character traits that children in Montessori settings develop, but the following eight key attributes lead to important life skills of persisting, maintaining resilience, thinking creatively, working with others synergistically, and many other skills that children ought to learn through their schooling. These eight traits are:

engagement	**courage**
focus	**collaboration**
organization	**respect**
curiosity	**resourcefulness**

Through the first chapter, these traits will be bolded to help readers begin to recognize them; thereafter, they will blend into the regular text.

The emergence of these traits explains Montessori's desirable outcomes. Montessori graduates are **engaged**, in the sense of getting actively involved with productive work. They tend to be busy, always working on something, creating something, or thinking about something, because they have been doing this every day, all day, from the time they were little, *in school*.

Montessori graduates have a strong ability to sustain their **focus**, because they have practiced concentrating their attention at will while disregarding irrelevant distractions. They have been developing this skill since their earliest years in Montessori classrooms.

They understand spatial organization and can **organize** their knowledge, because their classroom environments offered visual order, logical sequences in activities, and a hierarchical curriculum displayed openly on the shelves. Information was presented for them to explore with clearly recognizable interrelationships and interconnections.

Montessori graduates are notably **curious**, with that sought-after love for learning most educators hope to impart to their students. Their curiosity drove their educations every step of the way and became a strong force in their personalities, instead of fading away with age.

Montessori graduates are full of **courage**, because in place of grades and competition, they could mature under their own personal pressure to improve, a tendency that all humans are born with. They have learned that mistakes are part of every learning process. They repeatedly experienced that, with practice, they could succeed when they put in effort, worked together with others, and honed their skills.

Montessori graduates tend to **collaborate** with ease, as they were encouraged to work with their friends and classmates during impressionable ages and to help one another, rather than compete for scores or prizes.

They appreciate people's unique contributions and demonstrate **respect** for adults, peers, strangers, belongings, and the environment. This respect was imparted in the stories of the earth's history and human progress and was modeled for the children in action. Both grace and courtesy played essential roles in their early school lives.

Finally, Montessori graduates are **resourceful** because they spent much of their time in classrooms finding their way around obstacles before—or instead of—resorting to asking adults for help. They found many different ways of doing things that could work, not just one tactic introduced or insisted upon by an adult or by a learning program.

These eight traits enable people to think creatively, to work well with others, and to understand and take an interest in the world. They lead to the very abilities that help us to adapt and to succeed happily at work and in life. Ultimately they empower young people to effectively innovate and to solve world problems such as societal conflict and the preservation of our planet.

The Potential Within

There is a catch with Montessori education, however, and we can only promote it with full awareness of this fact: due to wide misunderstandings and the many incomplete implementations of Dr. Montessori's approach, "Montessori" education is not working everywhere. A widespread lack of knowledge and poor practice has led to mixed results in many Montessori schools, and the full potential—for the approach and for the children in our schools—is not reached. Because of this inconsistency, most people have heard of Montessori education but cannot be sure of its results. I see the need to take a good look at this ongoing problem and to bring Montessori—authentic Montessori—into our national conversation. This is particularly relevant as we debate how education can and must help our children prepare for adult life.

In this book I will demonstrate how Montessori education helps children to become their unique selves and to become **courageous** contributors who are adapted to the realities of their times. I will show Montessori's potential by expanding on the positive results that students, my colleagues, fellow parents, and alumni experience first-hand.

I will also explain the confusion about Montessori and why such a wide variety of schools exist. Along with learning what makes Montessori work, you will come to understand why it falls short of expectation when incomplete. By reading this book, you will see how educators can create Montessori programs that really do help children to develop these eight traits in both private and public school settings.

The Montessori Potential will show you that the Montessori approach works because it precisely matches how children learn. It is a comprehensive educational plan that covers the scope of birth to adulthood as a continuum. Montessori is effective because the core principles of the approach are incorporated into every aspect of its full implementation. If our goal is to prepare today's youth to adapt and succeed in an unpredictable future, Montessori is the answer.

Some anecdotes in chapters 1, 2, 3, and 6 are composites to illustrate what I've witnessed. Those in the introduction, chapters 4 and 5, all journal notes, the epilogue, and wherever parents share their stories throughout the book are accurate to my notes taken at the time. Some facts and names have been omitted or changed to protect identities.

1

MONTESSORI IN ACTION

What Happens in Montessori Classrooms?

Walk into a Montessori classroom of young children, and you'll notice right away the difference from conventional education. The room feels like a workshop, where every individual is busy doing something with interest. A boy is painting pensively at an easel, while another pours water back and forth between two small glass pitchers. A girl traces a large cursive letter made of soft sandpaper on a pink board, then carefully draws that same shape on a chalkboard. Three children bend closely over a rug and count out loud in unison as they touch colorful glass beads, which are wired together in numerical sets. The teacher sits on the floor among the children, working with a few of them quietly, showing them how to do an activity that they subsequently repeat on their own. In essence this space is bustling with calm, industrious activity. But you might wonder, "How do the children know what to do? What is directing them to choose these activities? What makes them behave this way?" To answer, I will explain how Dr. Montessori's discoveries about children play out in these Montessori environments, which are modeled to closely match children's developmental stages.

Recognizing Four Planes of Development

When Dr. Montessori observed children in her travels to many countries across Eurasia and the Americas over a span of more than fifty years, she recognized four developmental stages of childhood.[1] According to her findings, these distinct stages are consistent across cultures, countries, decades, socioeconomic conditions, and races between birth and adulthood. All children in a given developmental stage have similar characteristics and needs; stage transitions are delineated by brief periods of dramatic changes around ages six, twelve, eighteen, and twenty-four. The characteristics and timing are somewhat predictable and common, although they of course vary slightly in manifestation and duration. Between the four transition points are six years of comparatively stable plateaus, when children seem focused on developing certain aspects of themselves. Dr. Montessori called these plateau-like stages the *four planes of development*. She spent her lifetime designing ways to support children through these four planes with continuity in their developmental journey from birth through adolescence.

The following anecdotes give examples of how the developmental phenomena Dr. Montessori discovered in the four planes manifest through children's activities in well-functioning Montessori classrooms. In most major Montessori schools today, you will probably see children of ages three to fifteen, or preschool through eighth grade, so I will describe a three-year-old, some children aged six through nine, and some twelve-to-fourteen-year-olds. Although there is much to say about Montessori programs for infants and children under age three and for high school–age adolescents, I have chosen to use one brief example from each plane of child development to demonstrate the most noticeable needs and characteristics of each plane and to keep this book concise.

More precisely, we will look at one example of a child in the first plane of development—birth to age six—directly **engaging** with his surroundings, forming his ability to **focus**, and creating an internal **organization**; a child in the second plane of development—ages six to twelve—developing **resourcefulness** by pursuing his **curiosity**, and building skills to **collaborate**; and an adolescent in the first half of the third plane of development—ages twelve to fifteen—gaining **courage** and self-**respect** by embracing her role as a valorized contributor to her community. To complete the explanation of how the four planes of development map the passage from childhood into adulthood, I will also briefly relay a young adult's story to represent the last plane. The full expression of each plane of development in a child's life builds the foundation for the next stage and, ultimately, for adulthood.

First Plane: Building the Foundation with Purposeful Work

We begin at the first plane, between birth and age six, when children are growing very rapidly, building a foundation for their childhood selves. In these early years, children learn to walk and talk. Seemingly on a constant quest for words, young children ask what everything is called. They take on the mannerisms, preferences, and language of the surrounding culture. At such young ages, children primarily acquire information about the world through their heightened senses of touch, smell, sound, sight, and taste. It is, by nature, a self-centered time, because little children have an immense task to focus on: building functioning bodies and emerging personalities. Dr. Montessori designed the learning environment to offer activities that appeal to children at these ages so that they can satisfy their needs to move, explore with their senses, and acquire language and culture.

Dr. Montessori proposed that we respect children's actions as being their purposeful work. She pointed out that every young child's ultimate task is to build a person. Every action, therefore, is part of a child's deeper work of forming his or her own unique self as a human being in the world. Conclusively, all cognitive and intentional actions, including children's play, have developmental purpose and are the children's "work." Dr. Montessori observed that children experience elevated sensations about working when deeply **engaged** and **focused**, which adults may be able to relate to; think of how you feel when you are fully immersed in something you love to do. It could be cooking, writing a poem or speech, solving a math equation, or helping a client. If you have work that absorbs you in such moments, then you understand that inspiring work feels good to children too. These feelings are even more intense for young children because they do not work for the same reason that adults do. Dr. Montessori realized that while adults work to change their environment, children work to perfect their own movements; they are motivated to repeat actions by themselves, not to achieve an end result. Their end result, unconsciously, is having mastered a new action. Therefore Dr. Montessori observed children expressing complete contentment, and often joy, during or immediately following concentrated work that they had chosen to do. When adults respect children's purposeful actions as being their important work, children absorb the message "What I do matters."

True work involves effort. You may observe that when a young child finds some piece of work that engages him or her fully, effort is like a friend that naturally cultivates perseverance. Montessori education is geared toward helping children find that personal match between challenge and interest to inspire deep concentration. With the Montessori approach, children experience challenges as part of every learning process, multiple times a day. The amount of effort required, however, is up to each child. A child unconsciously measures and responds to an activity and adjusts to any sensations of effort. The effort is completely unadulterated—that is, not manipulated or created by any outside forces. This response to one's *own* willingness to engage with effort differs completely from being given an assignment, as children tend to experience in other school settings. By learning to push themselves willingly first, at young ages, children later do so for others by choice, based on numerous earlier effortful experiences with self-determined activities. With such continual practice in a Montessori setting, children regularly engage in those deeper levels of focus, popularly referred to as *flow*.[2] With repeated practice, Montessori children develop hardworking personalities.

Here, read about how a young child **engages** with full effort in a Montessori activity, which helps him to **focus** and to independently **organize** his thoughts and actions.

Dustin Washes a Table

Three-year-old Dustin walks into his Primary classroom with twenty-six children between ages three and six and greets his teacher with their customary handshake. His teacher is sitting on the floor cross-legged, working with two children who are learning to read phonetically spelled words by matching labels written by their teacher to some tiny objects placed in a column on a small table.

"What would you like to do today, Dustin?" his teacher asks, smiling. Dustin pauses, looks around at the shelf behind him, and the teacher confirms for the child sitting next to him, "Yes, that is *pig*." The child places the label he just sounded out next to a tiny porcelain piglet.

He turns back to Dustin. "Yesterday I showed you the bell mallet and the sound damper; perhaps you'd like to work with the bells, or . . ." the teacher scans the room to jog his memory of Dustin's recent work. "Or you could take out the Pink Tower, or wash a table?"

Dustin smiles, nods, and says, "Wash a table," and then quickly walks away.

"OK!" the teacher says, and then returns to the children with the labels and objects. The second child sounds out a label written just for him, "ffff-rrrr-ahh-g . . . ffrrah-g. Frog!"

Dustin pulls a child-sized apron over his head and carries a rolled mat and a very small bucket of items to a low, child-sized table. He sets the bucket down and spreads out the mat on the floor. Dustin pulls the child-sized chair carefully out from the table and lifts it with one hand on the front of the seat and one hand on the back side. He carries it a few feet away and places it carefully alongside the wall, out of the way. He arranges the items from the bucket on the mat in the order they will be used: a tiny pitcher, a small bowl for water, a miniature sponge, a bar of soap in a dish, a scrub brush on a little dish, and a small washcloth for drying. Squatting down alongside his things, Dustin straightens the items in their row on the mat and then carries the small pitcher to the low sink. He fills it, returns, and pours the water carefully into the little bowl. Then he is ready to begin.

Dustin dampens the sponge in the basin, squeezes it out with both hands, and wipes the table with big strokes in rows from left to right, from the far edge of the table to the closer edge. He then puts the sponge down on the mat and wets the scrub brush in the basin. He swishes it around and then raises it, lets the water drip, and gives the brush a shake. He rubs it against the piece of soap until suds form and then starts to scrub the table's surface with little circular motions, starting in the left upper corner and moving gradually to the right.

Dustin washes the table with such gusto and flourish that he seems completely unaware of the other children walking past him and talking. He does not appear to hear the bells a child is playing on the far side of the room, the water splashing in the sink as another child fills and refills his own pail just five feet away, the classroom door opening and closing as a child enters, or the girl at a table three feet to his left tapping her feet while counting out loud with a Bead Frame. All this and more swirls around him while Dustin bends over, apron hanging down and wet with water, making big, round motions with his arm as he scrubs the surface of the wooden table. His curly bangs swing over his brow, and the shoelaces of one shoe lie untied across the floor. He rocks forward and up on the balls of his feet to reach the far side of the table, one hand flat on the table to support his weight.

Dustin pauses when he has made soapsuds cover every part of the table surface. He stands upright, takes a step back, and brushes his dark curls from his face with a wet forearm holding the little scrub brush. He glances up at the child sitting near him and then quickly bends over the floor mat to his left with all the table washing materials laid out on it. He rubs the scrub brush on the soap bar again, stops and looks at the bristles, rewets them in the bowl, and rubs them firmly on the soap again. When he notices suds building, he pauses again and looks at the underside of the brush, then returns to scrubbing the table surface. He scrubs and scrubs, moving his circular motions around to cover the entire surface again.

His concentrated repetition continues for a good ten minutes. Beads of sweat form on Dustin's forehead, and his hair starts to stick to it. He seems unaware and unfazed, completely absorbed in his whole-body movement. Then he puts the scrub brush on the floor mat, squats down to reach the sponge, stands, and starts wiping the table in long, smooth swipes from one side to the other, eventually removing most of the suds.[3]

As Dustin bends over and plunges the sponge into the water bowl, another boy comes over and says something to him. Dustin smiles up at him, then looks back down and squeezes the sponge out with both hands. The other boy walks away, and Dustin stands straight up, looks after the other boy for a moment and then watches the water dripping into the bowl from his sponge in long, slow drips. He looks thoughtful, watching. . . . Then he squeezes the sponge out with more force, examines it, and starts wiping the table again.

Dustin stops after several minutes and sighs. He stands upright again and notices a girl walking by with a tray of real flowers: a daisy, two carnations, and a cluster of purple asters. He dries the table with the washcloth by pushing it forward and back with both hands, using all his weight. When he deems the surface dry, he starts to clean up by pouring the water carefully from the bowl into the bucket and carrying the bucket of dirty water to pour into the child-level sink. He takes the scrub brush over to the sink and rinses it with a gushing stream of water—it drips from his hand the whole way back to his mat, but he does not notice.[4] He squats down at his mat and puts the items back into the little bucket in the reverse order: pitcher, scrub brush, dish with soap, and sponge. Then he stops, pulls the items all out again, and wipes the inside of the bucket with the washcloth. He carries the dampened cloth to the hamper across the room to discard it. He walks to the shelf and takes a fresh washcloth, walks back to his mat, and again puts each item into the bucket, placing the folded fresh washcloth neatly over the other items. He carries the bucket by the handle, swinging it slightly as he walks, and replaces it on the shelf.

Dustin returns to the table and rolls up his mat tightly, pauses, and straightens himself up. Slowly and ceremoniously he carries the mat towards the shelf with an upright posture, holding the rolled mat like a flagpole in a parade, observing his feet through his peripheral vision, with a dignified, somber expression. When he reaches the shelf, he places the rolled mat next to the other table-washing items. He removes his apron and rolls it up tightly, placing it on the shelf next to the tray. He walks away with a relaxed, refreshed expression on his face.

Episodes like this repeat throughout the day in Montessori Primary classrooms. Dustin was interested in caring for the materials and the environment because children this age have a craving for purposeful work—not for the work of washing a table per se, but for unconsciously building all the cognitive and coordinating aspects of their personalities. The activity of washing a table is a deliberate way to satisfy this developmental need. Dr. Montessori pointed out that children are drawn to such self-**organizing** activities with real purpose and connection to community life. They offer ways for children to build themselves by coordinating their minds with their movements. The ability to choose meaningful work activities aligns with these developmental needs, and notably, choice and interest are necessary for the full benefits to take hold. In this example, the teacher assisted Dustin in making his first work choice of the day by mentioning a few ideas. While some children need a little prompting from the adult as their independence in choosing develops, most will choose their own work right after greeting their teacher in Montessori classrooms. This practice in self-direction leads children to become increasingly independent and confident about making their own decisions.

Simple activities—washing, cleaning, arranging flowers, polishing, preparing foods, and other so-called practical life activities—lay the foundation for children to organize their thoughts as they experience logical sequences of actions and their outcomes in all their stages and orders. For instance, Dustin's teacher had previously demonstrated all the steps of washing a table: The dampening of the table, then soaping, rinsing, and drying. He presented these movements with left-to-right and top-to-bottom strokes of wiping the table to introduce useful patterns to Dustin. These patterns prepare each child to explore language, scientific processes, and mathematics. Even when a young child is unconscious of his process, Montessori's **organized** practical life activities deliberately and precisely set the stage for all the intellectual work to come. In this way, the Montessori approach uniquely employs such practical and purposeful activities as the building blocks for thinking in action.

Integrating these components is key: the description of Dustin's activity shows how a child integrates his will (decision making and self-control) both with his intellect (thought processing and understanding of sequences and order) and with his body's gross motor and small motor movements. Such deliberate activity promotes the natural integration of the psychological and physical aspects of one's personality, a necessary integration Dr. Montessori was very aware of as a student of medicine, psychology, and anthropology. This thought-directed movement, which is still somewhat subconscious in young children, deserves much opportunity to develop, as it is vital to success in life.

The reason that such a real-life activity appeals to children ages one to six can also be connected to phenomena that Dr. Montessori recognized as natural, internal forces that seem to drive children in their behavior. In the anecdote, three-year-old Dustin is exhibiting specific *human tendencies*, as Dr. Montessori called them, for exploring, orienting to the environment, seeking out and creating order, manipulating objects with his hands, abstracting ideas from his real experiences, and working actively. These tendencies are like urges, and they are present in every human being from birth. Three-year-old Dustin also experiences certain *sensitive periods*, during which he focuses even more intensely on, and acquires, a sense of order of objects and sequences. He is drawn to explore tactilely, to move with precision, and to repeat actions and behaviors in order to perfect his abilities. Dr. Montessori observed that distinct periods of being intensely sensitive to specific aspects of one's surroundings guide human beings to develop those abilities at certain ages.

Finally, these practical life activities are effective in laying a base for further learning because children under age six have what Dr. Montessori called *absorbent minds*. This term describes the incredible ability for acquiring vast amounts of information simply by exposure. Unlike children over the age of six, who must study something to remember it, younger children soak in how to talk, walk, and do other enormous feats almost effortlessly. Dustin absorbs the ideas of **organization** by experiencing the physical layout of the materials and the order of the actions in each sequenced exercise. Young children spontaneously repeat these exercises because the tasks feed an inner need in them, manifested by outward delight or satisfaction. Because of this ability to absorb so much about the world with seeming ease, the period before age six is a vital time to give children activities through which they can prepare themselves to learn everything they are exposed to in the subjects of language, biology, geography, sciences, geometry, mathematics, human history, art, and music. The Montessori classroom appropriately gives young children a wealth of information about their immediate world.

The natural phenomena that Dr. Montessori called the human tendencies, the sensitive periods, and the absorbent mind, are described and explained in much more detail in other books about Montessori, and I encourage those interested to read more about them and to look for them in live examples. These are the inner drives that guide children in their learning and that direct children to choose what is most urgent for them to learn. The human tendencies, sensitive periods, and the absorbent mind are recognizable qualities of early childhood—gifts, or strengths, of nature that when integrated into the entire educational approach, enable children to develop to their fullest potential and set the stage for further learning. In sync with such internal forces urging children to interact with their environment, Dr. Montessori's approach also provides *indirect preparation* by deliberately designing activities to lead from one action to the next in sequence. This progression eases the difficulty of acquiring such new skills as reading and writing. Indirect preparation makes sequential successes possible. Because the activities themselves are attractive, the children make discoveries and self-educate, driven by their interests to do the very things that will prepare them for what comes next.

Second Plane: Collaborating and Persevering with Intellectual and Social Exploration

Around age six, noticeable changes begin to occur in children. Their limbs become more elongated, their adult teeth begin to replace their baby ones, their hair often changes in texture or color, and they do not get sick as often. There are psychological changes as well. Children between ages six and twelve no longer experience sensitive periods as defined by Dr. Montessori, and they lose the ability to learn easily through their absorbing minds. Instead, their abilities to reason take center stage, so they want to find out *why* and *how* the earth goes around the sun, not just that it does. They can think more abstractly, so they begin to grasp abstract concepts such as clock and calendar time.[5] Elementary-aged children also imagine scenes that they have never witnessed; they can mentally travel through space and time. They can imagine early humans living in caves, or the dark, silent vastness of outer space. In such ways, children's absorbent minds become reasoning minds that can abstract and create something new. This makes fantasy books very appealing to them at these ages. This is the time to **engage** children's imaginations as powerful tools for learning.

Newfound physical stamina, coupled with a new ability to reason and imagine abstractly, makes the years between ages six and twelve an intellectually active period. Children at these ages become fascinated by gobs of information in sources such as Guinness World Records books, and they develop multiple interests. They seem to want to be everywhere at once, sometimes leaving messes behind them; the attention to detail and order that attracted them in prior years now morphs into a desire for efficiency and reason-based thinking. They delight in making inferences and connections between topics, people, and bits of information. This makes it an important time for children to consciously create their own organized mental structures of interrelated information. To match the characteristics of this plane of development, Dr. Montessori gave an expansive curriculum of interwoven relationships to explore and proposed an imaginative manner of delivery. She referred to her Elementary plan as *cosmic education*, meaning that the entire cosmos, with all the information in it, is the appropriate fit for children who now have the insatiable imagination to grasp it.

This second plane is also a stage of **focused** social development, which is driven by an impulse to be with others. Important aspects of social organization are established in the Elementary years, making it a prime time to cultivate feelings of **respect** for all peoples and the desire to **collaborate**. In their constant interactions, elementary children become practically obsessed with rules and social behaviors. They want to understand right from wrong and to see justice done—so they "tell on" each other, make up clubs, exclude or include peers, and worship their personal sports, historical, and action heroes. During all this, children at these ages evolve in their thinking about how to manage things as they experiment and mature. Through this experimenting in the social realm and reading others' responses to this experimentation, children solidify their individual moral compasses by experience. Dr. Montessori designed a learning environment that appeals to these social urges in intellectually rich ways and that assists children in developing their abilities to empathize and think morally. These are imperative qualities for true **collaboration**.

Our next anecdote shows a child developing his **resourcefulness** and abilities to **collaborate** with classmates as he explores a topic he is **curious** about.

Thomas and His Friends Make a History Chart

In a Lower Elementary classroom of twenty-four students between six and nine years old, the teacher vibrantly tells a fifteen-minute story about the need for early human beings to communicate with each other to survive. The story, "Communication in Signs," is one of Montessori's five Great Lessons that make up the backbone of the Elementary Montessori curriculum. Because "Communication in Signs" follows three previous Great Lesson stories, which introduce the origins of our universe, the evolution of life-forms on Earth, and the history of the first human beings, the stage has been set for the children. They have explored those topics enthusiastically, and they are now **curious** about what may have happened next in Earth's and humanity's histories. The context is clear, and interest is piqued.

This particular story inspires children to imagine and question how human beings started to speak and write—a distinguishing feature of our species. At the end of the story, the teacher says, "Perhaps we should say thank you to the Phoenicians, the Egyptians, and the Greeks!" all of whom the children now know contributed to creating, recording, and spreading the use of alphabetic symbols, like the ones we still use today. This repeated directive to think appreciatively about others throughout history inspires the children to **respect** what those who came before have done for us and to understand how all of today's accomplishments stand on the shoulders of others. This habit of awareness and gratitude also gives children the opportunity to think of themselves as potential contributors.[6]

The teacher concludes the story with a brief invitation for the children that generally follows every Montessori story or presentation: to study this topic further guided by their own **curiosity**. As the children pop up from their places on the floor, eight-year-old Thomas loudly proposes, "Let's make a chart; who wants to make a chart?"

Little six-year-old Emily answers, "Me!"

They take each other by the arm and approach other children, who are milling around and talking excitedly, forming groups and pairs to dive into their own original questions and to research their interests after hearing this story. After approaching several, Thomas and Emily find two seven-year-old boys planning to write a report about alphabets. These two seven-year-olds, Archie and John, eagerly join Thomas and Emily, who propose that they all make a big chart with information and illustrations. The four sit together on the floor and discuss ideas (the first step to **organizing** themselves and their project):

"I think we should make our own language and try to say things with it."

"Yeah!"

"Or we could learn sign language . . ."

"Or let's find out where English came from . . ."

"Yeah—let's do THAT!"

"Let's go get some books . . ."

"Maybe we can make reports *and* a chart."

"No, a chart, it has to be a chart."

"I just think I want to write a report . . ."

And so it goes for a few minutes, before they agree on making a chart about where the English language came from and decide to ask their teacher if they can go to the library to get some books for this research. (This is where the children exercise their **resourcefulness** in collecting information.) The children know that their teacher will ask for a more defined verbal plan for their topics, and they clearly want to make it a group activity. They pause their progress to debate whether it is OK to each do separate reports and just collaborate to draw illustrations on the chart, or if it needs to be the same topic with all writing and illustrations on one chart.

During this conversation Thomas stops to listen and now and then proposes solutions, but the two younger boys are very determined and keep changing their minds. They say at one point that the two of them might break off and just write a report together. Thomas and Emily become visibly perturbed and talk them into being a larger group of four again. Emily stands or sits somewhere among the others and timidly interjects ideas. Finally the group agrees to look for some books about early languages and the migration of early peoples, tracking the progression of the English language. The oldest three get permission from their teacher to walk to the public library in town.[7]

Thirty minutes later, the three boys return with several books, flushed from their brisk walk in the late-October air. They check in with their teacher and spread their twelve books over a table as they remove their coats, and then they dive into reading and looking at the illustrations in their books. Emily rejoins them, excited to see the three books they specifically found for her.

"Oh, cool! Look at this map!" Archie exclaims.

"Oh, wait," they look over an opened book. "Is that Asia?" John asks.

"Yeah," says Thomas. "See, people might have walked across to there . . ." His fingers follow a curving red line into Europe over the Mediterranean Sea.

"How did they get across the water, though?" Emily looks away from her book about early cave paintings written for children and leans over the book with the others.

"In boats. Remember from the story: the Phoenicians were sailors," Thomas tells them.

"Or they could have walked this way, maybe?" Archie points to a green line winding through what is now Israel and up into Turkey. "Whoa . . . is that a long way to walk?"

They examine the map, then John says, "OK, let's start writing. I'm going to get paper." He returns a moment later. "Are we getting small pages for a chart, or are we using normal pages for reports?"

"Well, we could do both if you want—" Thomas suggests.

"No, we decided on a chart, remember?" Archie insists.

"OK, OK!" John says.

The four children spend most of that day on this work, huddled at a low table on the floor together, with the teacher occasionally observing their progress. All the other children move around them, working in their own groups on similar and different projects stemming from the day's story or from previous work in all subject areas. For most days over the next three weeks, Thomas, Archie, John, and Emily work off and on for a couple hours on their particular project. During this time the children correct their spelling and sentence structure with each other's and the teacher's guidance. They draw on their chart paper, which is one meter high and extends across the length of the classroom. They glue the numerous five-inch squares of lined paper with their carefully written, researched reporting onto the chart paper, spaced every few inches. Such charts are a great way for children these ages to create visual and thematic **organization** in their work. The teacher stops by briefly to make a suggestion or to give a two-minute demonstration to help them now and then over the course of the project.

The children spend several sessions in the hallway practicing how they will present this chart to their class, reading their pages and taking turns, pointing to and explaining their illustrations. The chart is beautiful: Across the top the title that the students decide upon, after many discussions, HOW DID ENGLISH GET HERE? is stenciled in large, colorful block letters (with two letters backward and attempts to rewrite them apparent underneath the final lettering). The children's four names are written underneath, and many illustrations cover the blank spaces in between the squares of lined paper. These are the children's efforts at sketching realistic early humans trudging across mountain ranges and making cave drawings and writing language symbols. They painstakingly depict the famous drawings from Paleolithic times in Lascaux, France, as an example.

Thomas, as the oldest child in the group, writes several pages about the migration of peoples through Europe, showing what his library books suggest about the origins of the English language. This is not an easy topic for a child this age, because most available books about the migration of languages are written for adults. Thomas proposes several times to make up an alphabet of his own instead, but the other children want to make the chart more about migration and point out that as a group within the class, they specifically "want to find out about English." By getting a little help from his teacher as well as an eleven-year-old from the neighboring classroom to decipher the books' meanings, Thomas fills nine five-by-five-inch pages with his own wording to add to the chart. His interest deepens, and he uses purple paint to imitate the unique Tyrian purple dye that the Phoenicians created by crushing certain shellfish. Thomas uses the paint to draw some early writing symbols pictured in his books.

The children are very eager to present their chart to their classmates and agree on a time to do so. When the four children give their presentation, they are poised and professional: they arrange themselves to take practiced turns reading their pieces and explaining the illustrations; they stand straight, look into the eyes of their audience of classmates and the teacher, and field questions at the end of their presentation.[8]

This is a typical progression in a Montessori Elementary classroom: The children had ideas they were excited to execute. The teacher's delivery encouraged the students to **engage** right away, follow their **curiosities**, get **focused** and **organize** themselves and their work, be **resourceful** in finding information, and **collaborate** to bring the project to fruition. Each child envisioned how he or she wanted to do individual work, but the overwhelming desire to be in a group with others demanded that they work through differences in their opinions and open up to one another's ways of seeing things. The children could see that the result of their collective efforts, the chart itself, was something bigger than what each one might have accomplished alone.

Such experiences give children countless opportunities to develop communicative skills for collaboration. The students must work with a variety of personalities, so they build personal repertoires of how to propose an idea, convince others, concede, lead, follow, and ultimately, function as a team. This example shows the differences between Montessori's approach to group work and both the conventional and the progressive school models: Many conventional schools promote "group work," but the teacher makes the decisions for the children and arranges them and directs their work. Many progressive schools promote "project-based" learning, but children might be left on their own to go in any direction without much context for self-**organization**. The Montessori example here demonstrates a continual process of inspiring children with a true story that results in a clear purpose, mentored by examples from the eldest children and guided by the teacher only as needed. In the end students produce an original, real product as a small group and share their newfound information with the whole class. This exercise of **collaboration** repeats and repeats, across the variety of subjects, rendering new results every time. The youngest child in a group will someday be one of the eldest, so everyone gets to play every role in leadership and group dynamics. This all happens naturally, without much adult interference. The teacher gets involved when asked to or only when he or she sees a need to steer the group in a more productive direction. This setup is a solid training ground for grown-up life, where skills and experience may differ but a common intellectual goal and interest binds the group into a **collaborative** effort. In Montessori Elementary classrooms, children are allowed to exercise their budding abilities to interact socially. This is especially valuable in the years between ages six and twelve, when the stakes are still manageable and personal changes occur more readily.

Also in this example, we see the natural human tendencies in action. We see children constantly moving: walking the fifteen minutes outside to the library for research books; cutting a huge piece of chart paper that is almost as tall as the children themselves; spreading it across the length of the classroom floor; crossing the room to collect colored pencils, writing paper, and glue; and lying across the chart to illustrate it. We see human tendencies to abstract information as the children imagine the early times and try to draw their own pictures from those in factual books. The children ages six to twelve explore, orient, and create order as well, but instead of manifesting in physical ways as with younger children, these tendencies are expressed by elementary-aged children through their abstract mental activity.

By exploring ideas and orienting themselves to the migration of a language, these elementary-aged children determine the direction of their own learning. Because of their established knowledge of how the earth was formed, how vegetation and life-forms spread across it, and how human beings survived on it, the children have a framework into which they can attach the new information about the development and spread of spoken and written communication. They incorporate their knowledge of geography and human history to examine the migration of their native language and are actively forming their own **organization** of knowledge in their minds. The next step is for the teacher to play off these children's interests in the origins of English by telling them more tidbits to encourage further studies. Montessori's curriculum offers further stories and premade charts to spark study into the Proto-Indo-European roots of language, the evolution of spelling, the migrations of the Normans and other peoples, and many aspects of language, such as sentence structure, grammar, poetry, and composition. The Great Lesson story is a springboard for all the language work in the Elementary classroom. The children continue to learn from hearing one another's original reports on such topics, which show that the quest for knowledge never ends and that every bit of information connects to what came before and what will come afterward. This example gives context, value, and meaning to the study of grammar and spelling; having context, choice, and shared enthusiasm makes such topics fun and interesting.

The reason that the teacher's storytelling appeals to elementary children and inspires their intellectual **curiosity** and desire to collect information by researching is, again, connected to the developmental characteristics of these ages. Dr. Montessori recognized that six-to-twelve-year-olds are particularly drawn to stories. They love to use their very active imaginations, to exercise their new powers of reasoning, and to discover things for themselves rather than be told the answers. Elementary children can imagine the early humans and picture them hunting and needing to work together and communicate for survival.

This imagining differs from fantasizing because it springs from the reality they experienced in the first six years of their lives. On a firm foundation of reality, the elementary children abstract and create original ideas that are connected to things and images that they understand are realistic. For instance, these students are not confused by fantasizing that early humans might have flown through the air or used rays from their eyes to blow up animals! They know the difference between reality and fantasy and understand where each applies. In response to the constantly active imaginations and reasoning power of six-to-twelve-year-old children, Montessori employs this age-specific power and puts it to work. In this example the approach to the second-plane child builds upon the foundation of the child's development in the first plane.

Empirical research supports the efficacy of the two anecdotes presented. In short, children—and indeed, most adults—learn best when they can move and manipulate objects while trying to understand them;[9] when there is choice and perceived control; when the abilities to concentrate, to plan, to inhibit one's actions, to hold on to an idea, and to shift from one task to the next—all executive-function skills—are activated; when their focus is drawn in; when there is personal interest in the subject; when they are motivated by intrinsic rewards; when the environment is not cluttered or chaotic; when they can learn from peers with different ways of explaining or showing things; when there is meaningful context provided; and when the adult interaction style is kind and attentive. These points summarize what Angeline Lillard found when examining how empirical research in education and psychology relates to the Montessori educational approach.[10]

Montessori education not only touches on each of the listed ways to ease learning but also interweaves them seamlessly into the approach in every lesson and every activity. This makes Dr. Montessori's design for children in the first two planes of development brilliant. As you will see, she didn't think that such a customized education should end at age twelve. In fact holistic educational support may be more important than ever for this next stage of life.

Third Plane: Building Courage and Confidence Through Community Work

Dr. Montessori noted that dramatic changes occur in adolescents as they leave childhood behind, around age twelve. This is a sensitive time emotionally and physically. Adolescents are more vulnerable to illnesses than elementary-aged children typically are, and they feel abruptly and alternately energized or exhausted due to their rapid physical growth and hormonal fluctuations. Dr. Montessori called these emerging adults *social newborns*, who undergo a kind of rebirth as their capable, fully grown childhood selves morph into temporarily awkward, developing adult bodies and minds. Adolescents need adults to welcome and support them in order to understand and join adult society as valuable, contributing members. To best support adolescents in this stage of their development, Dr. Montessori proposed that educators provide a farm setting, where they can be responsible for raising animals and produce, living together as a small, interreliant civilization while they study the ways that academic knowledge relates to real-life situations. In such a setting students sell products they make and design small businesses to **engage** in economic cycles. This is a practical way to learn about how the world works on a fundamental level. To help young adults develop life skills, self-esteem and confidence, and the eight traits we have discussed previously, some Montessori adolescent programs are set on farms, have a minifarm adjacent to their property, or take regular visits to work on such properties. Adolescent programs may also include sporadic work trips or involve students in the adult world in other ways, such as internships in stores or learning crafts alongside experts.

Where a farm is not available, as in the following example, a Montessori adolescent program might provide multiweek trips, which allow students to complete unique projects that contribute to other communities in adultlike ways, mainly in natural settings away from home. In this particular case, a group of sixteen twelve-to-fourteen-year-olds are preparing to travel to Wisconsin to camp out on a YMCA's four-hundred-acre property and independently build some permanent wooden structures to be used by hundreds of community members and YMCA campers in future summers.

Here learn how a young adolescent girl gains **courage** and self-**respect** by contributing to her classmates and the larger community.

Maddie Heads Out to Do Adultlike Work

Thirteen-year-old Maddie distractedly pulls her shirt cuffs down over her wrists as she walks into her Montessori school's Secondary Level building, which solely houses a classroom of sixteen twelve-to-fourteen-year-olds. Maddie hangs up her coat and backpack, saying hello to her peers as they enter and leave the walk-in closet by the front door. Holding her shoulders tensely, she crosses the room to shake hands with each of her two teachers and say good morning.

Her classmate CJ walks up to Maddie and says, "Maddie, you and I need to have our student Safety Committee meeting. Can you do it now?"[11]

"Sure, let me get my stuff." Maddie hurriedly collects her notebook and pencil, and the two sit down to look through the first-aid bin and check a list of items they need to stock for the upcoming class trip.

The room smells pleasantly of the apples and zucchini in the drying machine, some of the food the students in the Food Committee are preparing for two weeks of camping and cooking their own meals. Measured food bags are stacked in boxes along one wall. Partly filled backpacks line the other wall, waiting to be weighed with a hanging scale tied to a ceiling rafter by the students on the Gear Committee. The Gear Committee will also be testing the camping stoves outside in front of the building—in between working on algebra, conducting science experiments, and writing papers. On another day, the students will weigh all the camping items and foods and distribute these to the individual backpacks along with the work tools, tents, tarps, pots, and pans. The two teachers will double-check the students' processes and results as they go along, providing suggestions and guidance where needed.

Maddie and CJ continue planning together. "OK, we need to collect everyone's permission forms and health forms that haven't come in yet," Maddie realizes aloud.

"And let's look up the common injuries in the *Wilderness First Responder* book."

"OK . . ." Maddie pauses and reads down through the list of to-dos they have started, then adds, "And then we need to get more supplies for the first-aid kit. I think there might be snakes in southern Wisconsin by the river, so maybe we should find out whether we could get snake bites and what to do."

"Really? Snakes . . ." CJ grimaces.

The two cross the room to look over the map on the wall that the student Transportation Committee has been marking up to get the exact location they'll be camping in and then walk over to the computer in the corner of the room to find some current information on snakes at this time of year in rural Wisconsin.

During the week, Maddie and CJ devote about thirty minutes a day to researching and putting together a one-page report that they will explain to the class.[12] The two arrange to bike to the pharmacy with an adult to replenish the first-aid kit, using funds that the student Finance Committee allots them. When the week is done, each committee of two or three students shares their findings, and everyone asks questions and discusses—with teachers present—what still needs to be addressed by their student committees of Safety, Gear, Food, Finance, and Transportation.

The preparation for the students extends into their homes: One evening Maddie lays out all of her camping gear and clothing on the floor of her room and checks it against the list that the Gear Committee gave her. She still doesn't have work gloves, so she asks her dad whether he will be able to take her to the hardware store to purchase some the following day.

Many days later, when the actual trip begins with a drive of several hours, the students hike out from their parked rental vans with their two teachers, with the students on the Transportation Committee referring to their map and pointing the way. After getting lost two times while their teachers silently follow behind them, the adolescents eventually reach the campsite they were aiming for and set down their heavy packs. Several students notice that it looks like it might start raining, and the two teachers encourage the students to hustle to set up the tents and the cooking tarp between the trees. Most students work together quickly, while some struggle to get their own rain gear on and prop up their backpacks that keep falling over and spilling. (Every adolescent is in a different stage of learning how to be **organized**, to be **resourceful** in meeting their own needs, and to **collaborate** to help one another.)

Tired as they are, the students dive into their respective cooking groups, set up their kitchen areas on the ground, light their stoves, collect water, and cook their first meal from scratch: pasta, tomato sauce, dried zucchini squares, and spices. After eating they clean out their dishes, with their teachers circulating and commenting where guidance is needed. The older students, now in their second year, noticeably take the lead by helping younger students and thinking ahead to what needs to happen next. Having been through these scenarios many times, they are more aware of problems that may arise if a pot isn't cleaned and rinsed thoroughly or if bits of food are left on the ground to attract animals at night. There is uncomfortable work to be done, but the students converse as they labor together. They gather around a campfire when everything is finally cleaned up and organized for the next day. Most of the adolescents stare into the fire, huddling to get warm, while four students distribute tin cups of steaming hot chocolate.

"OK, so let's start off with what went well today," their teacher, Mike, proposes.

"Well," Maddie begins, "even though we got lost a couple times," (some chuckle) "we made it here and got to our campsite before it started to get dark. I thought that was pretty good."

The others murmur in agreement, and then one boy says, "Our first meal was definitely great. I want to thank Dez and Mila in our cooking group for doing such a good job." This starts a round of thanks for several individual feats from the day. Because every person contributed to the group's success in some way, each one receives thanks for something by the time they finish.

The next day, while standing in a semicircle in a drizzling rain after having cooked, eaten, and cleaned up their breakfasts, the students hear about the project they will be undertaking for the YMCA camp. A building expert who works for the camp, affectionately known as Buffalo Bob, explains that he will offer support and supervise the collective tasks to clear a space for and then design, engineer, and build a lookout deck and steps leading down the hill to it.[13] They will need to remove some trees and brush, grade the slope of a hill, and create steps by securing horizontal wooden beams into the hillside.

With teachers' suggestions, the class splits up into groups to address each part of the work. The adults ask whether the students have questions and give input and suggestions on the project. The adults work alongside the adolescents to demonstrate proper use of tools and to give tips. At first the students ask their teachers and the building expert many questions and need specific verbal directions. But the adolescents are increasingly capable of working independently. For instance, Maddie and another girl dig a trench, measuring it to a foot depth, and then check it with an engineering level, lying on their stomachs on the ground and putting their heads down low to read the level properly. They find that they have to get back up and dig some more to flatten the grade. When they finish, the students alert a boy and a girl who have been preparing wooden beams. These two students carry a beam over and lower it carefully into the pit. Maddie and her partner fill in the spaces with gravel and dirt, then move on to another area to dig the next trench. The adolescents' system and teamwork get smoother and better.

The days are filled with hard work: hacking at buckthorn tree roots and lifting the stumps out by physical force with tools and ropes; digging trenches and holes for beams and posts; and using electric and manual saws, axes, hammers, and nails. At the start of each day, everyone dons hardhats, goggles, work boots, and gloves. Even though they are trying to be cautious, one fourteen-year-old girl hits her thumb with a hammer, and a twelve-year-old boy falls back when pulling on a small tree trunk and bumps his head on the tree behind him. The teachers assess these injuries, using their *Wilderness First Responder* skills, with Maddie and CJ as the Safety Committee in attendance with the first-aid kit. Thankfully, assessments show that the students do not need trips to the nearby hospital, and the girl and boy are both eager to get back to work alongside their companions.

Everyone has a job to do. All the work is challenging and demands concentration and effort. The group experiences low points when some students become exhausted from the daily physical demands and become irritable. They also have memorable high points where they joke around in silly voices, tell stories while they work, or play a card game or ultimate frisbee in their down time. At the end of the two weeks, the group stands back to admire the beautiful lookout deck and the winding staircase that they built up the bluff. The structures are large, impressive, and beautifully crafted. The students' pride and appreciation for what they have accomplished is palpable in their broad smiles as they pause to take photos on the last day.

When the vans pull up to the school after the two weeks away, the students pile out, a little dirty but standing taller and stronger. The group gets straight to work, airing out the tents in front of their building and checking that the camping stoves and cookware are clean and put away neatly. Having become accustomed to such work, everyone is now busy and pitching in. Maddie is particularly chatty in the car on the way home. She tells her father about the tornado warning they received one night and their hilarious final-campfire talent show. She says that it was freezing in the early mornings and that her right hand aches from so much hammering. But pride radiates from her voice. She seems unconcerned with her appearance as she describes everyone's physical accomplishments. Maddie expounds, "Our staircase was fifty steps! We cut every single board. And the deck fits sixty people. You should see it. It really is beautiful up there, especially when the sun sets over the river."

Doing real work, both physical, outdoor work and the necessary mental planning for such work prepares adolescents for adulthood. The young adults feel proud to take on such responsibilities; they feel **respected** by the adults they worked alongside. In such a project, adolescents practice skills of **organizing** and **collaborating, focusing** on their tasks, and being **resourceful** by gathering the information they need in preparation. They exercise **courage** to participate in the trip away from the comforts of their homes and families, to share their thoughts, and to make their own judgments. Pursuing information is often driven by personal **curiosity**, such as finding out whether local snakes are dangerous and what to do about them, how many calories a hiker needs, and where they might get gas on the six-hour drive. As two longtime Montessori Secondary Level teachers say, "This is the difference between being taken on a trip and going on a trip," and "It's an initiation into the adult world."

Measuring, using tools, building, estimating, collaborating, and working together to solve real problems—not those from textbooks—allows children to build confidence in their own abilities, to bond with each other, and to build their individual identities too. Combining skills and knowledge of engineering, physics, trigonometry, chemistry, verbal communication, and written directions with real-life work helps adolescents realize the value of the subjects they study back in the classroom and how their knowledge applies to past, present, and future human civilization.

In a practical sense, learning the realities of preparing for such endeavors, and then carrying out each necessary step ultimately helps young adults to understand how society functions. Every aspect of considering a group's needs for surviving and thriving comes to the surface. For instance, Maddie could see how tending to her own preparation contributed to the group and how taking the group's needs into account helped them all function as a team for the greater good. Dr. Montessori called this process *valorizing*, the building of courage that adolescents desperately need in order to have confidence for adulthood.[14] Dr. Montessori recognized that education must give young adults opportunities to deliberately build this part of themselves in supportive but challenging formats. She pointed out that "all work is noble,"[15] stressing the value of every worker. By contributing with both their hands and their heads, children come to **respect** and appreciate the different kinds of work that all human beings in a well-functioning society contribute.

The Montessori approach also considers that adolescents are highly sensitive and have a strong desire for their dignity and that of their peers to be acknowledged by adults. Because of this, twelve-to-eighteen-year-old students crave confidence-building experiences, and to be sincere and effective, these experiences must sometimes involve risk. When adolescents face and overcome concrete challenges, they build personal repertoires of strengths for adulthood. Montessori-trained adults can support adolescents as they navigate healthy risks—such as building things with real tools, learning to live with all kinds of weather, working with farm animals, or enduring other physical challenges—to find their strengths and prove to themselves that they are capable. Through such actions, young people ages twelve to eighteen *valorize* themselves. Wilderness settings provide the perfect environment for such challenges to be inherent in any activity, while giving adolescents the healing benefits of nature. As one graduate said of his Montessori school's trips, "Some of the most impactful times of my life are when nothing is going on. You look out and there are no boats, no smoke, no signs of human civilization. You can just think." This is the solace that the trips into the wilderness give adolescents for their growth in this vital stage of life.

In the work described, you may recognize the adolescents' traits of **engagement** by having real work to do; necessary **focus** because the stakes are higher where real risks are present; **organization** as they navigate the camping gear or plan and cook meals; **collaboration** since they need one another to accomplish tasks; **courage** as they each perform their contributions for the good of the group, despite their individual insecurities; **respect** for one another, the materials they are handling, and the challenges of weather and living in nature and self-**respect** from building a structure for others to use; and finally, the **resourcefulness** in finding their way after getting lost or by correcting their frequent mistakes.

This level of autonomy and foresight does not arise overnight; these young adults are capable of a high degree of responsibility only because they have previously built the foundations in childhood. To be a continuum on this path to adulthood, Montessori adolescent programs (spanning seventh, eighth, and sometimes ninth grades or even through high school) aim to meet the needs and characteristics of this age group in various ways. There are many examples of such adolescent Montessori programs around the United States, Mexico, Europe, and beyond. One graduate of a Montessori adolescent program reflected, "You're twelve, but someone's treating you like you're an adult. You have to pack all the food for the group. Everyone's counting on you. No one is coming to get you. Nowhere else do I see people give twelve-year-olds this responsibility." He also advises others, "For the best success, go all the way through [the adolescent years in] Montessori. This is where everything you've learned comes together."

Fourth Plane: Embarking on a Career

At approximately age eighteen, another period of developmental consolidation occurs. Between ages eighteen and twenty-four, young adults become more confident, mirroring a social characteristic of their elementary years, as they now branch out and become more outwardly oriented. This time, however, they are not entering a miniature society of classroom peers but society at large, with the knowledge and experience of a young adult. Eighteen-to-twenty-four-year-olds mature both physically and emotionally, and this is a time of consolidation in brain development as well. It is also a time for intense study in universities and for responsible work in the adult world. In short, these young adults are ready to embark on their personal contributions to the world, perhaps even finding life partners and starting their own families. By now the traits of **engagement, focus, organization, curiosity, courage, collaboration, respect**, and **resourcefulness** are apparent in a graduate's choices and behavior.

In the following descriptions, recognize how the eight traits manifest in the early stages of adult life, in this final plane of child development.

Ashley Becomes a Sportscaster

One of our Forest Bluff graduates, a twenty-nine-year-old named Ashley, tells me that her college professors warned her and other communications majors against trying to become broadcasters, mainly because so few people actually make it in the industry.

"I remember thinking, *Well, why not try?*" She explains, "I think from Montessori, it was never implied that we wouldn't be good enough to do something, so I didn't let the idea of failing scare me. I thought, *There'll be something else to try if I don't make it.* I thought, *Why can't I be that one person who makes it?*"

And then Ashley did. At age twenty-four she was on camera with Fox Sports for the first time, and a year later she was traveling with professional sports teams as a sideline reporter. Ashley has a dynamic presence, a big smile, and eyes that sparkle with enthusiasm. Even as a five-year-old in the Primary classroom, her intense **curiosity** to get to know others and to tell their stories was easy to spot. And now, what Ashley says she loves most about her job is connecting with the athletes themselves, who have interesting life stories and are out there pushing hard every day.

Ashley tells me the most challenging aspect of her career is being live in front of cameras and in front of thousands of people in stadiums, with every mistake being captured by the public. Because any little mess-up will be played back, this could cause crippling social-media anxiety. But Ashley's inner confidence helps her to walk out onto the fields with grace. And instead of being hardened from criticisms and competition, she admits, "Although it never stops bothering me when people are rude or say unkind things, I've gotten better at handling it. You just have to stay **focused** on the positive and be yourself."

Ashley's **courage**, desire to **engage** with others, and **curiosity** to learn others' stories are visible in her work. Every one of the traits we discuss was also necessary in certain places along her journey to succeed. For instance, she has to **focus** on her goals and **organize** herself and her work—to guide the interviews with the players, to design her line of questioning, to show up where she needs to be, and to be ready to go on camera. Ashley actively developed these traits in her childhood in Montessori, and she continues to develop them in her twenties.

Very often we hear that our Forest Bluff graduates successfully launched a business at a young age or earned recognition or a high level of responsibility in their job. A US senator chose a Forest Bluff graduate to be his press secretary when she was only twenty-five because of her composure and clear communication under pressure. Another graduate was named senior vice president in a leading financial institution's international banking department at age thirty-four. One graduate founded a medical-device company as a college student, designing and commercializing continuous vital-sign sensors that are used by laypeople and doctors around the globe. The list goes on. From such a small school, this is a noteworthy trend for Montessori.

Most Montessori-educated alumni seem to have a "go for it" attitude, balanced with good sense and people skills, that makes them good candidates for such positions. The precise skills of thinking for themselves, solving problems, working with others, and having the **courage** to take initiative seem to be ingrained among the Montessori graduates I know. Their success stems from the constant support within the Montessori approach to develop important traits such as **curiosity** for life, **engaging** with what and who is around them, and **organizing** their ideas to present them effectively. A result of having these traits may be best expressed by one twenty-three-year-old Montessori graduate who became a mechanical engineer. He says, "I love what I do. I can't wait to get up in the morning."[16]

Dr. Montessori suggested that in a person's midtwenties, his or her massive job of building a mature young adult comes to a conclusion. Notably, though Dr. Montessori based her conclusions on careful and consistent observations, she had no modern science to show the changes occurring in the brain. As Montessori education was gaining popularity in the 1970s and 1980s, technology demonstrated scientific findings which support Dr. Montessori's observations. Indeed, the first three years of life have great importance with massive brain development, and around the ages of six, twelve, eighteen, and twenty-four, spurts of rapid brain change occur.[17] By the time each person reaches his or her midtwenties, the architectural foundation of the frontal lobes is finally consolidated.[18] Although, of course, our brains continue to forge new pathways and to prune others, brain science gives credence to Dr. Montessori's four recognizable planes of development. Because children have different characteristics and learning needs at their different stages of development, the educational environments must differ to match. The whole journey, and education's supportive role, is completed as children's brains mature at their midtwenties, correlating with Dr. Montessori's proposed timing of childhood's conclusion and the beginning of adulthood.

Matching Education to Children's Development: A Recipe for Success

In response to her observations and discoveries of the four planes of development, the human tendencies, the sensitive periods, the absorbent minds of young children, the psychological characteristics and reasoning minds of elementary-aged children, and the social newborn in adolescents, you can see how Dr. Montessori designed environments that meet children's needs as they evolve.[19] You may notice that there is a correlating expansion of freedoms and responsibilities in the learning environments described here. For instance, a youngest child's routines might occur within an hour, an elementary-aged child's projects may last several weeks, and an adolescent's endeavors have their beginning, middle, and completion over longer periods and on a grander scale.[20]

While children progress from one plane of development to the next, the physical and mental scope of their explorations—leaving the classroom, the school property, and moving farther and farther out into the world—progress as well. In this way, Montessori is an education deliberately designed to mirror life's stages. At the same time, each stage builds on the previous one so that there is continuity and a gradual adaptation to adult responsibilities and freedoms. In this careful plan, children are not asked to face realities of the larger world and its problems before they are developmentally ready or able to solve such problems effectively. Knowledge, experience, and skills for success develop through deliberate stages, very gradually. For example, elementary-aged children need to study earth science, botany, chemistry, and physics first before feeling pressure to solve mysteries such as global warming or even talk about such topics coherently. Adolescents, on the other hand, may be ready to discuss such issues effectively and even to propose possible solutions based on knowledge. In their twenties (in the fourth plane of development), Montessori graduates are then eager to experiment and participate so that they can add experience to their proposed solutions.

For education to support human development, specially designed learning environments, such as those designed by Dr. Montessori, must consider what she gleaned. In Montessori's approach children's natural characteristics propel them into action. The sensitive periods and human tendencies are guides to recognize and support. When teachers have faith in the natural processes that unfold and support them, children thrive. Children love to learn while gaining experience with managing their work time and organizing their work. Children learn that effort is a healthy and often necessary part of working. They learn to concentrate, to persevere intellectually, to dive into **collaborative** endeavors, and then to enter adulthood with **courage** and **resourcefulness**. Because Montessori students find themselves in environments so aligned to match their needs, we see them at ease and fully **engaged** in learning by interacting with what is around them. Above all, their learning experiences are authentic, interest-driven, and personal. This is Montessori in action.

In the next chapter, I will explain Montessori's overall framework. It is this framework that allows the eight traits to develop in the children, every day. The framework that Maria Montessori designed and presented is what makes her approach not only possible but also highly effective.

2

THE FRAMEWORK THAT MAKES MONTESSORI WORK

Montessori in a Nutshell

Now that you can picture what happens in well-functioning Montessori classrooms, you next need to understand the inherent structure behind this approach. Clearly Montessori differs from *conventional* schooling by how it looks in action and by the ways it matches child development. But Montessori is also unlike *progressive* models, because it involves more than a few disjointed components like "hands-on learning," "multiage classrooms," and "following the child's interests." In fact, the Montessori approach is designed with a coherent structural framework that supports children in very specific ways, with a deliberate balance in its every aspect.

Montessori, in a nutshell, could be described as an education that recognizes all children as active learners who build themselves through experiences with three components: the surrounding environment; an adult who models behavior, prepares the learning environment, and actively links the child to it; and freedom and boundaries that foster responsibility and further independence. These three components—the

environment, the adult, and the balance of freedom with responsibility—
act as pillars that scaffold a framework. Strengthening this framework
and forming all the connecting beams is Montessori's curricular plan.
This chapter is an expanded explanation of this nutshell description,
which offers a way to understand Montessori and a way to explain it
to others.

Montessori's New Paradigm: The Child Forms Himself

Dr. Montessori's perspective is that all children—of all ages and from all
backgrounds—actively build their own brains and their bodies, psychologically and physically. She called this phenomenon *self-formation*. This
phenomenon points educators towards *how* children learn: they interact
with their material surroundings to learn about the world and build their
unique perspectives, intellects, and knowledge.

This process is easy to see once you look carefully at how children
behave naturally. Think of the seven-month-old baby boy who crawls
across the floor by his own efforts, exploring everything that interests
him. He investigates and manipulates anything he can touch with his
fingers, his brain and body constantly communicating. Considering this,
you can imagine the futility of strapping an infant into a chair and giving him a visual presentation to teach him how to move his body and
interact with the world.

Children create their views of the world with intellectual information
as well. When this same boy is ten years old, he reads about a historical
figure doing a daring act, and he imagines a scene. He asks his parents
and his teachers questions. Perhaps he looks for more information in
books and starts to write his own report about this, or begins to create
a play with his friend depicting their version of the story. His curiosity
drives his thinking. And just as when he was a physically exploring baby,
this boy's thoughts are those of a self-directed learner, not one who sits
and waits to be given ideas. This is in direct contrast to conventional
schooling, which would expect ten-year-olds to sit still and listen to a
topic chosen by the teacher.

In other words, children's intellects grow from self-directed interaction with their immediate surroundings—with things and people—and this is how each creates a unique view of the world. The baby *has to* be moving around and touching his environment in order to learn, the ten-year-old boy *has to* be asking questions and gathering information from different parts of his environment in order to think about and foster his interests, and an adolescent *has to* be talking and interacting in order to learn about social life. This may seem obvious, yet the methods for teaching children in conventional schools tend toward passivity. No matter the varying teaching methods or fads in education, children *must* be active, doing the learning by their own efforts. Montessori speaks directly to this.

Dr. Montessori saw that children's natural drive for exploration directs their learning. She also recognized that all aspects of children's personalities—physical, psychological, social, and intellectual—develop in sync. Education, therefore, must aid this process deliberately by considering the whole child. This perspective offers a clear way of seeing the purpose of childhood and the potential for the role of education.

A Montessori educator's goal is to help each child's individual process of learning and developing. Although we cannot see inside them to understand these processes exactly, children clearly strengthen their personality traits of engagement, focus, organization, curiosity, collaboration, courage, respect, and resourcefulness when the learning environment and approach specifically foster them. By being aware that this self-formation is occurring in children all the time, adults can very carefully supply the best conditions.

Because this Montessori approach to education is entirely based on the fundamental fact that human beings build themselves, three pillars are paramount:

- the prepared environment
- the prepared adult
- freedom with responsibility

Together, these pillars constitute the framework of the Montessori approach and support the expressions of children's self-formation. With this basis, the following is how I have come to understand

Dr. Montessori's directives through my own teaching experiences, Montessori training, and study in this field.

Pillar One: The Prepared Environment

Because children form themselves by interacting with their immediate surroundings, their environment takes on great importance. In the first years of life, children use all their senses—touch, sight, taste, smell, and hearing—to absorb information. Older children form themselves further by interacting with their physical and abstract surroundings with an accentuated social orientation: they talk about what they are thinking, ask lots of questions, and use objects they find around them to make things they can share with others. Because building oneself as an individual is also a creative process, every child becomes a unique being. No two will be alike, even when having interacted with the same environments.

This Is the Place to Start—Everything Stems from Here

Since the setting makes such a central contribution, Dr. Montessori urged adults to put great attention toward the classroom itself. Educators must prepare an environment that provides the best of their culture with the richness of reality. The prepared environment should represent the *keys to the world*: all that children can explore to learn the beginnings of every subject of study. The Montessori educator's every action stems from first preparing the learning environment with purpose.

The learning environment must be prepared in two ways: mechanically and spiritually. The room must be mechanically accessible, meaning that it is easy to move about in and everything in the environment matches the age group's developmental needs. For example, shelves and furniture should be low at the children's level. The environment must also be spiritually appealing. It should be made beautiful by the adult's careful attention because Dr. Montessori observed that children are attracted to beauty. And it should be simple. Such points are important, Dr. Montessori explained, because children have a developmental need to create internal order in their minds. As they orient themselves to their surroundings, the attractiveness, external order, and exactness of the environment help children to internalize organization. Every learning material has a place on the shelf and is returned there after use. The language materials are displayed in one area of the room and math in another, and areas of music, geography, and botany are all neatly arranged in groups. Materials relating to artistic expression might be in various areas of the room, and most everything is interrelated in its use. The classroom's appearance is orderly, fresh and clean, colorful and inviting.

The learning materials are exposed on the shelves, and the children are invited to work with them as soon as they enter the classroom. This is in direct response to Dr. Montessori's observation that from early ages, children need to be active so that they can gain balance, hand-eye coordination, and control of their fingers and hands and can collect sensory information about the world. Ultimately, thought-directed activities allow children to strengthen meaningful pathways in their minds, to learn to focus their attention at will, and to concentrate.

In the spiritual sense, children learn to respect the objects in the environment and also one another with small, deliberate acts of grace and courtesy that the teacher demonstrates and repeats. Because children are also developing socially, they are encouraged to speak and interact with one another respectfully in spontaneous and self-directed ways throughout the day. The teacher greets each child as he or she enters the room and makes sure each one connects with some enjoyable work or activity.

When children leave the Primary years and reach the Elementary years, the Montessori classroom environment evolves to match their emerging characteristics and needs, though some essential elements remain. The materials continue to be physically organized on the shelves to represent the curricular order of ideas, areas of study, and concepts, as they were for younger children. Materials are also still neatly arranged on open shelves so that children can see and access them easily. But now, this arrangement encourages Elementary children to make more advanced, abstract connections between the subject areas and notice the interrelationships of concepts.

Between ages six and twelve, children especially want to explore their ideas verbally and collaborate with others in their work, further building their *internal* order of ideas and abstract information. In response, the environment differs from that for the younger children in some ways. Now, these older students must exercise their recently developed powers of reasoning and internal organization by gathering what they need from different areas of the room—and perhaps even from outside the classroom walls—to execute their self-determined work plans. Deliberately then, the Elementary classroom no longer offers prearranged trays of every item needed to do a particular exercise, as was physically done in the Primary classroom. Instead, the Elementary children must become resourceful by using their reasoning minds to determine what they might need to carry out an idea. For instance, paper, art supplies, and construction supplies are available in various cabinets around the room; children retrieve what they desire for manifesting their abstract ideas. To encourage the children to work together and to help one another, the Elementary classrooms have larger tables and ample floor space, where children can sit together in groups and spread out large, collective projects. This encourages the children to pursue big, collaborative work.[1]

The spiritual and mechanical aspects of the Montessori classroom are interconnected, and all aspects of the environment relate. In this way, the children in a prepared classroom are like a metaphorical *organism* whose health depends on the inherent balances of mental and physical freedoms and responsibilities.

The Mechanics of the Prepared Environment

There are four defining characteristics of a Montessori classroom that must be present to classify it as "Montessori":

1. A **prepared space** that is functional, age accessible, simple, realistic, and orderly, with every fundamental subject area made available to study
2. A **three-year age span** for the children, specific to developmental stages, with roughly twenty to thirty students, one Montessori-trained teacher, and depending on the circumstances and state regulations, one assistant[2]

3. A three-hour **uninterrupted work period** each morning for concentrated work and teacher presentations to small groups and individuals, during which children choose their occupations
4. The developmentally specific **learning materials** that Dr. Montessori curated for each age group

Each one of these must be addressed in Montessori schools to ensure successful outcomes.

The Prepared Classroom: Walls, Shelves, Floors, and Furniture

In order to support the developing traits of concentration, focus, and organization, the walls of a Montessori classroom are simple and practically empty of visual distractions, with just a few carefully selected, framed pieces of artwork for the children to see at their eye level. The shelves, which are at a height where children can reach them independently, display the learning materials, set out in a sequential order and with spaces between them. The teacher is careful to arrange the room so that nothing loudly detracts from the beauty, color, and placement of the Montessori materials themselves.

The classroom floors are clear of obstacles and provide sufficient space for the children to work and still be able to pass by without disturbing one another. The child-sized furniture is proportioned specifically to the dimensions of children's bodies, varying for the size range of the children in the class, so that they can sit comfortably in the chairs and bring their hands to the table surfaces with ease and upright postures. Attention to these details affects the children's ability to develop healthy posture habits and to move around into comfortable positions. Because of this, they focus fully and engage in their work.

All this preparation of the environment demonstrates true respect for the children and their learning. When a small child walks into a Montessori classroom for their first visit, the adults often witness her unabashed delight at feeling that this place was designed just for her, all down at her level, with everything she needs sized and accessible to her. The little visitor's obvious joy is often expressed by not wanting to leave to go home!

A Three-Year Age Span, One Teacher, One Assistant, Twenty to Thirty Children

It is important to group children using the three-year age span in a Montessori classroom. The oldest children in a Primary classroom will be ages five and six, and if they have been in the Primary Montessori classroom since at least the age of three, they will be leaders and helpers to the younger children. Because younger children look to older ones for guidance, there typically only needs to be one teacher and one assistant in the room with as many as twenty to thirty children, or more. The children learn a great deal by seeing each other working, and at any given moment, the variety of work they see expands their own choices and raises their interests.

Children who have been shown how to use the materials properly enjoy presenting their knowledge to younger children, often in the exact way that the teacher taught. This child-to-child teaching does not replace the teacher but rather facilitates more independent learning and fosters peer relationships. By choosing to take on this role of responsibility, the older children benefit by deepening their knowledge as they impart it to others. In sum, there is a little society that evolves in the classroom where children live and work together for three years, going through the cycle of youngest to middle to eldest. This cycle repeats with each subsequent level through adolescence. I have often heard that, as adults, Montessori graduates attribute their interest and compassion for other people to this practice of working with children of different ages, abilities, and personalities during their earlier years in Montessori classrooms. After growing up this way, they sometimes find it odd that people would want to group themselves, especially to the exclusion of others. This natural development of empathy—in its true meaning of relating to others openly and recognizing their worth—is paramount in our world today. In Montessori it happens not from lectures on morality or social skills workshops but by practical, spontaneous, unforced interaction. Once again, Dr. Montessori recognized something natural in children and created opportunities for it to flourish. These children reach their human potential through experience.

The age groupings cannot be random, however. As you will recall from the description of the four planes of development, distinct changes occur around ages six and twelve. Children in each of the four stages share characteristics and needs, making them best suited as classmates and necessitating the classroom environments that serve differ accordingly. It makes no sense to put children ages two, three, and four in a classroom, for example, thinking that this meets the three-year age span for Montessori, or to separate them from five- and six-year-olds. When they first come into the class, three- and four-year-olds look to the five- and six-year-old students as role models to help them. Five- and six-year-olds benefit from this opportunity to counsel and guide younger children, as older students had done for them when they first arrived.

Here's an example. One day, five-year-old Eliza notices that three-year-old Freddy struggles to zip his coat on its hanger. She places her Metal Inset work down on a table and walks over to him.

"Do you want help with your zipper, Freddy?" she asks, looking at his face, which is turning red while tears of frustration well in his eyes.

He nods slightly, and she puts her hands on the zipper parts and starts to fit one part into another.

"Here, I'll hold this down and you pull up on the zipper," she tells him, standing to the side but still holding the parts in place.

He grabs the zipper handle and tugs. When it doesn't budge, Eliza shows him to reposition how he pulls it. Freddy succeeds in zipping it all the way to the top. With an expression of relief and satisfaction, he lifts his coat up by the hanger and walks off to hang it in the closet.

You can see here how younger children's engagement and focus are supported by interacting with slightly older children who are still interested in the same kinds of actions and who are interested in being helpers. The mutual respect and collaborative attitude are demonstrated repeatedly by the teacher's ways of helping children to do things for themselves, and the children become eager to imitate this. Children build their courage to try things because they can find the right amount of support—not too much, not too little—from others. Everyone can find a job to do at any given time, and it is clear to each child what she or he can do to step in and help, to receive help, or to be resourceful by solving some of their problems without adults. In an established Montessori classroom, such scenes occur spontaneously, naturally, and constantly.

The Scheduled Three-Hour Uninterrupted Work Period

To develop the deeper kind of concentration that Dr. Montessori observed was possible—and in fact necessary—for real learning to occur, the day's schedule includes a three-hour uninterrupted work period. *Uninterrupted* means that the children are choosing their work and are working at will, the teacher is presenting materials to individuals and small groups, and no one is being interrupted by announcements or having to leave the room for specials or events. In short, the children know that they can get deeply involved in their work and that they will not be arbitrarily asked to stop what they are doing until the three hours are over. This guarantee means that everyone present can respond to their desire to engage in work, can build their focus, get into the habit of concentrating every day, and can enjoy the results and feelings that come with productive work.

The children come to expect this morning routine.[3] They adjust to the significant stretch of time without distractions. The length of three hours is one Dr. Montessori discovered by repeatedly testing it. A three-hour time span appears to be just right to allow a complete working cycle to occur. This cycle involves a period of concentration, then a short period of restlessness, followed by an even deeper concentration and engagement—perhaps not unlike the distinct cycles that occur when we are sleeping. Montessori teachers are taught to recognize the stages of these cycles and to work with children to support a learning community committed to an atmosphere of concentration and work.

Surprisingly, young children get so involved in their work that they often do not want to stop after three uninterrupted hours. I remember that more than once, when I announced to my Primary class that it was "time to put away our work, straighten the room, and come sit down for dismissal," one very small four-year-old girl would say under her breath, "Oh, *darn it!*"

The Learning Materials

A full set of Montessori materials is designed to meet the needs of all the children of certain ages in a classroom. They present the richness and fullness that forms a foundation for understanding our world. While there are multiple purposes to each material, and though some are meant to be used in more than one way, there is *only one* of each material to demonstrate one single point so that nothing in the classroom is superfluous. Each Montessori material is a physical representation of abstract ideas to be explored.

When you walk into a Montessori classroom, you will immediately notice that the curriculum is literally on the shelves. Children can see distinct areas of knowledge at a glance. The materials are grouped by subject on open shelves, progressing in the order in which they will be presented to each child. It is easy to understand the connections between subject areas because the children recognize them through their daily experiences. For example, botany materials are in one area of the room, and language materials are in another, but because there are language cards labeling the botany leaf shapes, language obviously relates to botany. Botany and language materials also closely relate by the Latin word parts that make up botanical names and are also explored in the study of words. Children make such connections constantly and delight in the creativity of doing so.

Because each material has a space on a shelf and is returned after use to that exact place, children have a framework for their studies and an assurance that they will be able to locate each material every day. The materials are almost identical in every Montessori classroom for a certain age range so that children can recognize them in any country around the world. They form the backbone of the curricular plan, making every topic accessible to the students and teacher throughout every day. Through the presence and placement of the materials on the shelves, the curricular structure is a steady presence.

Dr. Montessori and her colleagues designed her specific learning materials over several years by experimenting and adjusting them to find what was most effective in imparting a certain point, what was most inviting to touch and explore, and what best addressed more than one aspect of learning. Dr. Montessori arrived at each material specifically after she and her colleagues carefully observed children's reactions to each. There are reasons behind the chosen sizes, the materials (such as wood or cloth), and even the paint colors. These are all based on seeing what made each material most attractive to and most effective for children at different ages and developmental stages.

For example, the original Red Rods—as Dr. Montessori designed them—are sized to be long in proportion to a three- or four-year-old's arm span (the longest rod is exactly a meter long[4]) but thin enough to fit easily in their small hands. The children are taught to carry each rod while appreciating its full length, reaching with their arms to experience what makes each different. Exploring the lengths not only provides the children an opportunity to develop their physical and spatial awareness but also requires that children focus their attention on their body control, engaging them in a challenge which most young children enjoy. Specifically it is not easy for children of ages three and four to carry each one of the longest Red Rods without knocking it against something or someone as they pass. The original sizes Dr. Montessori designed are therefore deliberate. To make them even more attractive, the Red Rods are painted a brilliant, glossy red.

Each Montessori material has a primary purpose, but most also have multiple educational uses. The Red Rods, designed to vary by one decimeter each, demonstrate the differences in gradations of length, and they subtly introduce the concept of ten, as there are ten of them differing successively by length. Because length is the *only* difference between each rod, children learn to recognize these differentiations of length. So the primary purpose of the Red Rods is to demonstrate gradation of length. But with this material, there are many other purposes that fuse together children's developing body control, their spatial awareness, and their intellectual preparation for understanding math. Another purpose is to name the qualities of length so that children learn to verbalize their discoveries: "This one is long, this one is long*er*, and this one is the long*est*; this one is short, this one is short*er*, and this one is the short*est*." Doing this helps young children create organized relational structure in their speech and self-expression. It helps them to discuss length as a physical description and prepares them to name the abstract concept of length comparisons for other situations they will encounter. As a further extension, older children will write labels for these qualities when they begin to write and to study suffixes, matching "longer," "longest," and the like to the Red Rods. Then they label other objects they notice around them with these qualities of length. The Montessori materials, by their repeated uses and familiarity, give children a solid base in many such ways for their explorations of the world, inside and outside the classroom.

While each material has a specific purpose and often multiple purposes, one also leads to another in a larger sequence of interrelationships. For instance, the Number Rods that help children ages four and five learn to differentiate between the amounts one through ten are the exact sizes and dimensions of the Red Rods. These are introduced to children after they have considerable experience with the Red Rods. The Number Rods, painted red and blue alternately in decimeters, show amounts as *entities* whose lengths can be compared. Developing on these experiences, children are introduced to the written number symbols that match the entities one through ten. At another point, the teacher introduces the natural wood-colored Spindle Boxes, which present number amounts in a different way—as *groupings of units*. Each spindle represents a unit, so that two of them together are called "two," three of them together are called "three," and so on. With both the rods and the spindles, the children count out loud and move their hands to touch or pick up each object as they speak the name of the amount.

This progression from the Red Rods to the Number Rods to the Spindle Boxes demonstrates the clear way that the Montessori materials help children develop their fundamental understandings of numbers. They lead systematically to many other math materials that show the fundamentals of the decimal system; the operations of addition, subtraction, multiplication, and division; fractions; and so on. Each child receives this full progression of materials gradually, as they are ready for each one, in the three years they are in a Primary classroom. As extensions of the original presentations, the teachers show the children several games, which encourages repeated use and thereby helps each child to solidify their understandings over time. Repetition through a variety of purposeful games is key to solidifying and deepening the children's understandings and memory.

The materials actually progress up through the classroom levels as well, having multiple purposes that meet development and intellectual needs at subsequent ages. For example, a child learns how to build the Binomial Cube in the Primary level classroom between the ages of three and six and works with it many times during those years as a three-dimensional puzzle. When she reaches the Elementary classroom of six-to-nine-year-olds, she is given a presentation on how to build an equation with it, using letters a, b, and c to represent the lengths of each puzzle cube and prism. Then, sometime between ages nine and twelve in the Upper Elementary classroom, she learns to supplant the letters with numerals and uses the Binomial Cube's formula to create and solve equations. By that time, the child has worked with this material so much that she can most likely extract its pattern from memory and solidly understand the logic of the algebraic formula and all its components. There are many extensions of this progression, leading into cubing numbers, finding the cube roots of large numbers, doing equations with differing powers of numbers, and many kinds of advanced math stemming from physical cube combinations that relate to abstract equations. The child and teacher progress at the rate that best matches the student's development, which may vary slightly from child to child. This example with the Binomial Cube in the Primary, then Lower Elementary, to Upper Elementary is an example of a sequence that extends over stages of children's development, offering continuity and familiarity that supports their learning.

The materials also have a unique feature that is either physically built into the material or expressed through its presented use. This feature is what Dr. Montessori called *the control of error*, a crucial characteristic that differentiates authentic Montessori materials from other learning materials. This is a sort of clue built into the material or the exercise that points the child toward the correct use—but only as a natural byproduct, not as an oversimplification that detracts from the material's inherent challenge. The control of error supports the child in a way that makes him or her less reliant on the teacher's minute-by-minute guidance, thereby fostering independence in children's learning. This feature might be noticeable, as with the Solid Cylinders for children aged two and three: if a child places a cylinder in an incorrect space and does not notice the misfit, he or she will find a cylinder left over that will not fit into a remaining space, prompting the child to look for, discover, and remedy the mistake, all on his or her own. The control of error makes recognizing and remedying one's mistakes a largely private affair. This helps children focus on the internal process of correcting oneself with curiosity, rather than on possible feelings of shame, embarrassment, or any public reaction to their mistakes.

A Montessori material's control of error may also be in the expression of the exercise, involving the child's own emerging awareness over time. For example very young children begin to notice that the Pink Tower's three-dimensional structure of ten cubes just doesn't look or feel quite "right" to them when it is built unevenly, out of sequence. When children place each piece in its proper place, they begin to sense that it is best this way; not only is the tower better balanced physically but also children seem to notice, or feel, that the tower is most *visually* balanced as well. This works because a sense of visual and spatial balance is a developing feature in human beings, one that Dr. Montessori noticed small children are drawn to practice repeatedly. The concept of a control of error, enabling children to learn in a unique and somewhat independent manner, is central to Montessori's success.

The Spirit of the Prepared Environment

The aforementioned mechanics of a Montessori classroom are sometimes listed to determine what identifies a Montessori classroom, but there is an important element missing from the previous description, what I'll call the *spirit* of the Montessori environment. A teacher can be Montessori trained to present all the materials and may have set up the physical environment but have a classroom that doesn't "feel like" a Montessori environment. This happens because the true approach of Montessori education involves more than the mechanics of implementation; the spiritual life of the children must be considered.

By *spiritual* Montessori educators mean the psychological, intellectual, social, and emotional aspects of the environment. Dr. Montessori recognized that natural beauty attracts children's interest; they seek it out and delight in it. She proposed that teachers take this into account when preparing classroom environments. Children can sense and respond to the care and attention their teacher gives to the details of the room. They recognize that each item is thoughtfully chosen for them.

This spiritual attention goes beyond the physical aspects of the classroom; children also pick up on the emotional atmosphere of an environment, which the teacher sets and maintains by his or her example. This atmosphere should be intellectually inspiring and engaging, welcoming and safe, courteous and graceful. Soft instrumental music might be playing, and beautiful artwork from the community's cultures may be thoughtfully displayed. The adult is attentive, keen, pleasant, enthusiastic, gentle, and kind. In these ways the Montessori classroom is not sterile and stagnant but inviting.

Dr. Montessori also observed that when children are encouraged to interact with the environment and the adults in it, they want to work. In response, Montessori teachers prepare atmospheres that invite children to be active. Dr. Montessori realized, perhaps by chance, that an activity is especially satisfying when it has purpose. The first Montessori school was called Casa dei Bambini (or the Children's House)[5] because Dr. Montessori was working with children in a neighborhood zoned for housing, not for a school. The room where she watched children and developed her approach was in a ground-floor apartment designed to be a home. As with so many of her discoveries, Dr. Montessori observed what the children did when given freedom, and she used what the available environment had to offer: the rhythms of family life in a home and garden. Dr. Montessori saw that her charges delighted in carrying out the actions they had seen adults do in their own homes. The youngest children wanted to clean, prepare food, garden, and sweep the courtyard. They wanted to carry large buckets of water, arrange the garden tools, and hang clothes on the line. The children did these things with a concentration and effort that seemed to meet some inner drive. Dr. Montessori realized not only that these actions were spontaneous expressions of the children's love for family life and community, but also that they were perfectly suitable for a learning environment for children under age six. In fact, they enhanced learning, because the activities prepared the young children for academic efforts by fostering a foundation of concentration and self-control.

This spiritually prepared Montessori classroom can also be described as peaceful and uplifting, even when no one is in it. More specifically, when you walk into a Montessori classroom before the children arrive in the morning, you will notice that the teacher and children cleaned and prepared the room with attention to every detail the day before. This happens because the children themselves gradually become active agents in this daily preparation. During and at the end of each day, the teacher and children clean the room and set everything just right for the next morning. This becomes part of their normal routine. The members of this community care about each other and all the objects in their classroom. They share a sense of ownership and responsibility for the space. The courtesy and respect for others, oneself, and the environment and all its belongings manifests in the placement and condition of every item. This resets a Montessori classroom every morning to be a calm but active place for reflection, joy, contentment, excitement, curiosity, and intellectual exploration. Such a range of qualities are simultaneously present because there are many children in the room who are each doing something differently. You see a society rich with variation and individuality, which forms the spiritual environment. Montessori teachers are called on to prepare and care for this spiritual environment.

In these mechanical and spiritual ways, the environment itself has a crucial role in supporting the children's development of engagement, focus, organization, curiosity, courage, collaboration, respect, and resourcefulness. The next balancing component, or pillar, is the adult teacher.

Pillar Two: The Prepared Adult

Dr. Montessori considered it deeply important that adults prepare themselves to be of service to children's processes of self-formation. Because a paradigm shift is needed—where adults stop thinking of children as products to be molded or empty vessels to be filled with academic information—Montessori teachers must go through a transformation in their own approach to education. They must come to understand and embrace the idea that children are forming themselves. As the entire educational structure reflects this paradigm, the teachers' actions should also reflect this revolutionary orientation in their behaviors and their roles. A thorough training course is needed to give teachers information and sufficient practice in how to approach children in this different, more helpful way in the classrooms. Complete and sustained immersion in this educational approach is most effective for teacher trainees.

The Training Is Transformative

The two most established, long-standing Montessori teacher-training organizations are the Association Montessori Internationale (AMI), based in Amsterdam, and the American Montessori Society (AMS), based in New York City. Both organizations have training centers around the United States and the world that offer courses leading to Montessori teacher certification. Here are the most common courses that train teachers.

- To guide children from birth to three years old: Assistants to Infancy or Nido and Toddler Level / Young Children's Community
- To guide children ages three to six years old: Primary Level or the Children's House
- To guide children ages six to nine and nine to twelve: Elementary Level or Level I and II
- To guide children ages twelve to eighteen: Adolescent Orientation or Secondary Level and High School

In a training course teachers receive lectures in the theory of the Montessori approach. Trainees learn how to present the materials to children effectively and how to determine children's readiness for each material and each presentation. They are taught to keep careful teaching records of presentations and to plan for each day, week, and month. Teachers also learn to look for each child's signals of their developmental needs. Montessori trainers give teachers advice on how to work with children in private or public school settings and with children who exhibit different learning or behavioral styles. A good Montessori trainer also demonstrates how to model grace and courtesy for the children of the relevant age range and how to treat children with sincere respect for their development.

Many Montessori teachers report that through the training process, they experienced a personal transformation on some level. From her earliest courses, Dr. Montessori conveyed the importance of acknowledging how profound children's natural development is. When adults embrace the new dynamic that they are not the controllers of the children's learning process—which happens quite independently from adult direction—then their responsibility becomes that of respectful supporter. As teachers begin to focus on understanding and working with each child's self-direction, a change, whether conscious or unconscious, occurs in their approach to children. This prepares teachers for the work before them.

In her first course Dr. Montessori explained to her trainees, "If I should say that it is enough for you to follow me, to listen to me, studying, I might as well say that work, a form of diligence, all the material conditions, were enough for you. . . . But it is not so. It is not in this way that you can learn what I wish to teach you. You must realize . . . that the inner disposition is just as important."[6] She said that teachers must develop a certain capacity, a "sensitiveness which allows you to learn the intimate facts which the children reveal . . . to [recognize] which is an important thing . . . worthy of claiming attention."[7] She emphasized the importance of learning to observe the children objectively and sensitively, because by doing this herself, she had been able to make discoveries about how children learn. Adults can be quick to judge a child's actions or make assumptions, but it is only through patient, objective observation that we can see what children's behavior reveals and discern how best to help them.

An imperative part of this transformation is becoming more self-aware of one's own biases and prejudices and how these may influence one's thoughts about students and treatment of them. With heightened national awareness of the need for justice and action against racism in the United States, Montessori teacher training programs now attend to this aspect of self-preparation even more thoroughly. As Dr. Montessori clearly proposed the importance of seeing and accepting children as they truly are, not as one thinks they ought to be or expects them to be, covering this self-awareness in training courses is consistent with Montessori's approach.

In this way, teachers set out to teach in a Montessori school, oriented in their thinking to sensitively and fully support each student's development.

The Teacher Prepares and Maintains the Environment

When they begin, teachers first prepare the environment, creating the consistent learning space described in the prior section. Teachers maintain this environment and also expose children to variety by rotating pieces of artwork, objects, and language cards every week or so. They might bring in botanical specimens or insects and other real, interesting objects from the outside world for the children to see, touch, and learn about, before returning those items to the outside world.

Next, teachers have an important, constant task of connecting the children to the learning environment so that they engage with it to serve their needs. Observing children to see what may interest them is an important step in this process. Teachers also serve as models for good language and behavior, speaking clearly and treating everyone with respect, grace, and courtesy. The children pick up on manners and intentions, so it is imperative that teachers be confident, kind, and positive.

How Montessori Teachers Present the Materials

Montessori teachers link children to the learning materials with precise presentations. Dr. Montessori explained, "There is a direct interchange between the child and his environment while the teacher with his offerings of motives of interest and his initiations constitutes primarily a link, a *trait d'union*, between them."[8] Teacher presentations become an interplay of watching, taking turns, and discussing. A lesson or presentation may be as brief as two minutes or as long as fifteen minutes, depending on the content and the children involved.

To begin, the teacher invites children to touch and move the materials as early on in the presentation as possible. With children under the age of six, in the first plane of development, the Montessori-trained teacher begins by inviting each child to his or her presentation of a material. The teacher speaks slowly and clearly, emphasizing his or her graceful, deliberate motions to entice children this age to imitate such self-control, and gives opportunity for the child to repeat the exercise many times during and after the presentation. The child's innate desire to focus, to mimic, and to internalize organized sequences and exaggerated movements drives the lesson. A teacher working with children in the second plane of development, by contrast, must appeal to the very different characteristics that motivate children at ages six through twelve. The Elementary-trained Montessori teacher, therefore, might speak and move more rapidly. He or she asks questions to get the children thinking, wondering, and making connections to previous knowledge. The children's curiosity drives the lesson.

A Primary Presentation

In a Primary classroom, the teacher walks over to three-year-old Dominique, who is coasting along the shelves, looking restless.

"Dominique," the teacher says, bending down to face him. "I'd like to show you something new. Would you come with me, please?"

Dominique nods and follows her over to a shelf. She again bends down and faces him, touching the edge of a tray on the shelf gently with one hand.

"This is the Flower Arranging."

Dominique smiles widely at her and nods.

"This is how we carry it."

The teacher squares herself to the shelf, reaches forward with both hands, and carefully wraps her fingers around the two outer edges of the tray. She then slowly lifts it, takes a step back with each foot, and stands up straight, holding the small tray in front of her waist. She looks at Dominique, who looks like he's about to hop up and down, he is so excited. She replaces the tray carefully, straightens up, and says, "Your turn."

Dominique squares off to the shelf, lifts the tray level to his waist, turns, and smiles up at her, holding the tray. His teacher smiles, too, and then walks slowly to a floor table and motions to it. Dominique follows her, carrying the tray with a hand on either side. He sets the tray down carefully on the table.

"We need something else; come with me."

The teacher walks back over to a large vase of flowers on the shelf, close to where the Flower Arranging tray was. She turns to Dominique standing next to her. "Would you like to pick out a flower?"

He points to one, and his teacher shows him how to lift it out, holding the others back with her other hand. She invites him to choose another one. Dominique imitates his teacher's manner of carefully lifting each flower until they have three, which he carries back to the table.

Next the teacher shows him how to carry a tiny pitcher from the tray of Flower Arranging materials. Dominique picks up the pitcher with two hands, as she has shown him to, and follows her to the child-level sink in the corner of the room to collect water. They return to the table.

Dominique's teacher shows him, step by step, how to cut the flower stems, remove the extra leaves and stem parts, and put these into a small bowl that he can later empty into the garbage. She shows him how to fill the vase with just enough water and how to carry the tiny vase of flowers and a cotton doily from the tray to a child's table. In every step the teacher allows Dominique to carry out the actions after she demonstrates them.

At the end the teacher asks, "Would you like to make another arrangement?" Dominique nods, and she tells him, "OK! You can take out the Flower Arranging whenever you'd like to. I can show you how we put it away when you are finished with it."

She smiles and walks away to work with another child. Dominique walks to the large vase of flowers to choose three more flowers on his own.

In a subsequent presentation, the teacher would introduce Dominique to the names of each flower—day lily, common daisy, carnation, and so on—and on another day, she may teach him the names of the parts of the flowers—pistil, corolla, stamens, etc. In such ways, the teacher introduces an organizing physical activity on one day and a classifying language on another. The difficulty is broken down into parts, and there is always more to learn, following the child's interest that has first been piqued by the invitation to be active.

Every presentation is different, but some steps will always be the same: The teacher invites the child to the presentation and shows him where the material is on the shelf so that he can find it next time and knows where to put it back. The teacher gives the child the name of the exercise and shows him how to lift and carry the material. She demonstrates how to put it back on the shelf, then invites him to carry the material to a table, rug, or floor table. She shows him how to do the exercise. She tells the child that he can choose this material any time in the future (or she might give him a limit, such as "Please come tell me when you'd like to do this," if applicable). In other words the teacher orients the child to what they are about to do, gives the steps to the exercise, and suggests it as a future choice for work. It is a respectful way to interact with children and to teach them new things. While every teacher, child, and exercise differ, Primary teachers move slowly and deliberately and are concise with their words—gentle and inviting, positive and clear. They appeal to the child's desire to move, to touch and engage in the activity, and to focus his or her attention on details. Teachers remain calm but charismatic when presenting activities.

An Elementary Presentation

In a Lower Elementary classroom, a teacher gathers three seven-year-olds for a lesson and invites them to bring a shallow, purple box of compartments to a table. He asks each child to bring two other components that will be needed for this lesson: the box of grammar symbols, which they are familiar with from previous lessons, and a purple box of cards that match the purple box of compartments. The two girls and one boy sit down facing their teacher, and he begins.

"Remember when we worked with the Verb Grammar Box? Well, today we're going to talk about another part of speech. I'm going to ask you to do a few things," their teacher says with a sly smile. "Would you please sit *underneath* the table?"

The children look at each other and then push out their chairs and move under the table to sit there, giggling. The teacher smiles down at them and nods.

"Great. Come on back to your chairs."

The children do so.

"Now, how did you know where to go?"

The children point out that he said the word *underneath*.

"So, this word, *underneath*, told you where to be in relation to the table?" They concur. He asks them to do a few more amusing things:

"Tommy, would you go stand *behind* Debbie's chair, please?" Tommy looks confused but stands and positions himself. "Ah, I see you're standing *behind* Debbie's chair. How did you know where to go?"

"Well . . . you said to stand behind her chair."

The teacher nods, looking down and scratching his head. "I see. Debbie, would you please walk *out* the door?" The children giggle and look at each other. Debbie stands up and leaves the classroom; then he returns.

"Thank you, Debbie. Sheryl, would you please put the tissue box *on top of* the supply cabinet?" As Sheryl does this, the other children watch, amused.

Sheryl comes back, and the teacher asks, "Now, I'm curious, how did you know what to do?"

"Because you told us!" Tommy says, laughing.

"But what words told you?"

They discuss this for a few minutes. Then the teacher turns his attention to the purple box of compartments and says, "I am going to show you how you can explore these words further. Let's begin by setting these cards into the corresponding compartments here, and then we can read the first one together."

After placing the cards neatly into the compartments of the box, Tommy, Debbie, and Sheryl put their heads together and read the first card, sounding the words out loud: "Set one chair opposite another chair." They do this action, discussing what *opposite* might mean.

Then their teacher says, "OK, let's put the grammar symbols over the words, as we have before in past lessons for the article, noun, and verb." They arrange the colorful grammar symbols.

Next, the teacher holds up a small, green bridge-like symbol and tells the children, "Here is the symbol for these words that tells us where something is in relation to something else." The teacher places the small symbol above the card that reads OPPOSITE."

"Can you uncover the name for these words there, in the Grammar Box?" The children slide back a card, revealing the word PREPOSITION, and read it aloud. The teacher confirms, "We call these words or phrases the *preposition*."

The three children read and act out the next card while their teacher watches them: "Arrange two chairs along the wall. Arrange two chairs against the wall." The children sift through the many one-word cards in the compartments of the box, searching for the ones that make up these two sentences. The cards from each part of speech have their own color-coded compartment. The children place the corresponding symbols above each word in the sentences they have constructed, adding the new symbol they just learned above *along* and *against*.

The teacher leaves the children to continue. They delight in reading and acting out each command, sometimes laughing, and generally having a great time. They love to discuss and consider the subtle differences in the meanings of the words, such as *along* versus *against*, so that they can act out the commands most accurately. For the next thirty minutes, they work through commands and then rush back to the table to symbolize each sentence.

Notice that Elementary Montessori teachers ask many questions. In lessons involving physics, chemistry, math, or geography, they might ask, "Why do you think it's like that?" "What might that tell us?" or "If we choose this amount, then what might happen?" Montessori teachers are not trying to trick the children, to test them, or to search for a certain answer; they are, however, quietly checking children's comprehension and ability to express their thoughts. Teachers help their students to practice expressing what they understand so far and to wonder aloud what they will find next—to hypothesize. Asking questions during Elementary presentations also invites everyone present to figure things out together. This actively engages children in their own discovery processes.

What Happens Next

Every time a teacher gives a presentation, he or she orients children to another work choice in the room, expanding children's choices over time and covering all subject areas during a child's three years in a classroom. The real learning happens when children repeat their use of the materials and choose to take them out again without the teacher, working independently or, in the case of Elementary children, sometimes with peers. Children often create some original, physical representation of their understandings, which in the Elementary years is expected and formally called *follow-up work*. During follow-up work, children might simply work through the exercises and replace the materials on the shelf, or they might produce pages of writing and illustrations. They might produce research reports or any number of artistic, linguistic, or mathematical extensions of their work when appropriate. They might conduct a scientific experiment, collect specimens, write a theatrical script, compose a song, or make other various expressions of their expanding knowledge. In this way, a child's growing body of knowledge may be represented by an original portfolio of sorts. The Elementary teacher will suggest ideas for follow-up work and will guide children to improve the quality of their work as they progress.

The Teacher's Role, the Materials' Role

The Montessori teacher is responsible for keeping track of what he or she has shown each child, noting the child's comprehension and progression in detailed, personalized records. The teacher plans what to present to each child and makes adjustments in the lesson plans where help is needed. It is the teacher's responsibility to make sure each student is interacting with every subject area and progressing through his or her curriculum. As teachers guide children with their own enthusiasm and introduce them to presentations in every subject area regularly, most children develop an appetite for all subjects. If a child tends to shy away from a certain subject area, it is the teacher who helps to make the closer connection. It surprises many parents to learn that this is not a common issue in Montessori classrooms, where everything is available and made enjoyable; most aversions are acquired from outside influences, not from within the children themselves. But if a child has a certain difficulty, say, in engaging with language materials, the teacher is made quickly aware through his or her observations and record keeping of the children's activities and responses to lessons. The teacher may need to repeatedly engage a child by making it a daily habit to work with that material together and to track any changes. In some cases, a child's aversion is how a learning difficulty is spotted very early on, long before it may have been noticed in a conventional setting, where children do not learn to read, write, or do math equations before kindergarten or first grade. While giving presentations and making notes on each child's progress in all subject areas, teachers allow children to make work choices as independently as is reasonable and possible.

While it may seem as though Montessori teachers do very little when they leave children to work on their own for parts of the day, the Montessori teacher has the task of observing carefully and stepping in to guide children back to productive activity when necessary. By giving these short and frequent presentations to many children, the Montessori teacher is interacting and modeling industrious activity all day long. With this teaching format, the Montessori teacher can cover the wide range of subjects necessary, accounting for the varying abilities, learning styles, and interests that children have. He or she thus meets individual needs in a classroom community in a natural and seamless manner.

When it comes to the Montessori materials, they are not to be used didactically for the teacher to *teach with*, but rather as materials for the children to *learn by using*. "The magic does not lie in [the materials]," Dr. Montessori pointed out, "but in the psychology of the child."[9] She explained further, "The work of education is divided between the teacher and the environment. . . . The profound difference that exists between our method and the so-called 'objective lessons' of the older systems [such as with Fröbel's teaching materials] is that the objects are not a help to the teacher. The objects in our system are, instead, a help to the child. . . . It is the child who uses the objects; it is the child who is active."[10] In the previous anecdotes, you can see how the teachers invite children to take part in the presentations and to touch the materials and use them early on in the lesson. The children then continue with the materials, long after the teacher has stepped away.

Because the children work independently with the materials, the teacher must know precisely how to present the use of each material so that the children can work with it on their own in a way that is truly useful and effective. A Montessori teacher presents the materials in a definite sequence, progressing in difficulty, each step building on the earlier ones. Children make discoveries with the materials only when they are interested in that material and their minds are ready to comprehend, two conditions that a trained teacher learns to recognize and respond to. If a child works with a material repeatedly during a time of readiness, he or she may see something revealed in the materials, a truth the child discovers independently. Though teachers have an important guiding role, they point the way rather than act as the center of the child's learning experience.

Teachers give as many presentations on how to use the materials as possible, every day, to as many children as they see are ready for new presentations, or in some cases, re-presentations. They must find the balance between presenting to or helping students and leaving them alone to concentrate on their work. Although training courses cover both the presentations themselves and how to determine when a child needs a certain presentation, teachers must develop for themselves an awareness and sensitivity when observing children and making these determinations. Having many children in the room with only one teaching adult protects the children from having an adult interfere too much; it means that the children must develop some independence in their learning and figure out how to learn by watching other children working. The children also help one another, so their own skills and knowledge deepen through peer-to-peer teaching. In these ways, the children develop resourcefulness through their work.

Veteran teachers like my mother, Paula Polk Lillard, have shared stories from their more than forty years of teaching wherein they sat down to show a child something for the first time, only to find that he or she understood the material so readily that a presentation was hardly necessary. In such situations a child had watched other children working with the material and been intrigued with it. Dr. Montessori called this *indirect preparation*, which eases the difficulty of learning a new task. In such cases, a child may have also observed a teacher like Mrs. Lillard present the material to others and retained much of what he had witnessed. Delighted that the material was now in his possession, the child might want to repeat what he'd seen others do, or he might be ready for his teacher to go straight to a subsequent presentation with the material, which the teacher is free to do.

Having the flexibility to respond to the children they teach means that Montessori educators can guide each child to the material and its use most effectively. The timing, manner, and language that teachers use will be customized for each child they are working with. By pointing the way, Montessori educators allow children to teach themselves through the materials. Graduates often say that in Montessori they learned exactly this: "How to teach myself." The ability to learn independently was fostered in this deliberate way—and endures in their spirits.

The Teacher's Leadership

The primary role of the adult present is to be a leader. As leader, he or she prepares the environment, models behaviors, and actively *links* the children to the environment. Adult leadership becomes more noticeable during times of the year and situations when this linking needs to be more active and instructive. Then, as the teacher succeeds, there will be times when he or she can allow children increasing freedoms, as when witnessing their abilities to conduct themselves responsibly and productively. But Montessori teachers learn that it takes a long time before they will look around their classrooms and see the children all guiding themselves in positive behaviors. They must remember that Dr. Montessori (and many, many Montessori teachers since her time) discovered that this is absolutely possible in a classroom of twenty or more children, but it takes time and diligent attention. A cohesive harmony and a high level of self-composure is a point of *arrival*, which can take a few years of working with the same classroom community to reach. And because children are always changing, successes ebb and flow.

Each child benefits tremendously from being an individual in a community with a leader that supports the child's increasing independence. The ultimate test occurs when the teacher has become so involved in an activity that when glancing up, he or she sees that the children are all working harmoniously and independently. It should be as if the teacher could leave the children for a few moments and return to find the class working as if he or she had never moved. The children in such a case have become their own masters, in full control of themselves, expressing their desire for productive, positive activity as their norm. Montessori children take great pride in reaching such a state of independence as a community. The feeling is palpable to them, and they seek to recreate it once they have experienced it. With this goal in mind, the Montessori teacher cannot hesitate to stop destructive or disrespectful behaviors so that the path to a productive and peaceful community can be forged.

The reason that just one teacher (and typically one adult assistant) can have twenty to thirty children in one room of three-to-six-year-olds is that the three-year-olds someday become the six-year-olds. Children who start in the room as three-year-olds adopt the respect, organization, and composure that the older children model for them. The teacher becomes a leader with many independent helpers in the oldest children, making her less prominent over time. The children experience leadership firsthand and gain confidence from it. The continuity of having the same community in a classroom that builds over the years means that this process gets smoother and easier with time. A new class can take up to three or four years before reaching its societal potential, but from then on, a teacher can maintain this high standard indefinitely. The cycle need never repeat itself completely from scratch, if maintained conscientiously.

When it comes to guiding children's behaviors, Montessori works so well because the approach is centered on *learning with interest*. By interesting children in something they can actively engage in, Montessori teachers continually lead children back to cooperative behavior. The Montessori teacher is the dependable leader, who redirects any disrespectful or destructive behavior and immediately engages a disrupting child in some positive activity if able to. Doing so, again and again, shows children what to do with themselves and each other when misbehavior occurs.

I have been impressed by the ways that Montessori children internalize this manner of redirecting others when necessary. For instance, I have watched older Montessori children work with much younger ones and seen them react, swiftly and quite naturally, when little children present difficult behaviors. Without skipping a beat, an older child responds by firmly and confidently redirecting a little one's attention to something positive with a comment such as, "Oh, let's go look at the fish in that fishbowl!" and taking the little one by the hand. Or "My, we'll clean up this spill with a mop; let's go find one in the closet!" in a cheerful tone. The little ones often forget what they were protesting about and get immediately involved in the new activity. This learned technique, modeled by their Montessori teachers, is a great example of being resourceful, appealing to a younger child's curiosity and desire to become engaged in something that draws on their innate desire to focus.

There is a settling of a child's personality that occurs, as Dr. Montessori witnessed, when teachers give that child something productive to work with. When a teacher connects children to some activity that fascinates and engages them, their own self-discipline begins to come to life. To explain this, Dr. Montessori pointed out, "The first glimmerings of discipline have their origin in work. At a certain moment a child becomes intensely interested in some task. This is shown by the expression on his face, his intense concentration, and his constancy in carrying out the same exercise. Such a child shows that he is on the way to becoming disciplined [from within]."[11] However, the teacher must choose something to show a child that specifically interests him or her. "Work cannot be presented in an arbitrary manner," continues Dr. Montessori, "and this is what lies behind our method. It must be the kind of work that man inwardly desires and for which he has a natural inclination, or which he can accomplish bit by bit. This is the kind of work that gives order to a person's life and opens up to it infinite possibilities of growth."[12]

This is where the teacher, as a leader, must observe and determine what work may be most interesting and challenging for a particular child at a particular moment. The trained teacher leads by offering work that has purpose for each child in order to engage his or her whole personality and thus lead that child to develop self-discipline from their earliest years of life. This is how the natural traits of engagement, focus, and organization of oneself were recognized by Dr. Montessori and why this approach, with a prepared environment and a trained adult, directly helps children to develop such traits even further.

Pillar Three: Freedom with Responsibility

Understanding the Concept

The final pillar that is fundamental to the Montessori approach is the concept of freedom with responsibility. This manifests in a delicate balance of choices and boundaries that helps children develop inner freedom and active responsibility.

Dr. Montessori realized that the idea of freedom in education has widely appealed to educators and theorists. She acknowledged, "That freedom should be the basis of pedagogy is certainly not new. . . . The principle has existed but has never been put into practice."[13] But no good examples were available for educators to turn to and learn from. Dr. Montessori concluded, "Something substantial in educational ideas based on freedom is missing because practice is lacking."[14] In practice, we do not have other educational models that show exactly how freedom can be supported effectively.

This was, and continues to be, a challenge. The reason that children are not given much freedom in schools is that it requires a deep understanding of the concept of freedom and the creativity to manifest an approach to responsibility in everything that the child is given in the educational environment. Freedom and responsibility, in a balance, must be infused into everything. In order for this to be a living experience that benefits the children in their development, the adults must have a real grasp of this balance and Dr. Montessori's ways of incorporating it.

Dr. Montessori compared the balance of freedom and responsibility to the balances in nature. For example, the planets move but must follow certain natural laws of physics. As a result they stay in their orbits rather than crash into each other, and thus harmony is maintained. Dr. Montessori made many analogies to strengthen this point that nature has balances, and that is what makes our world function. Likewise, children, who are always developing, respond to natural, internal balancing forces.

When explaining this idea of a balance between freedom and responsibility, I like to use the metaphor of a river. A river current is like a young child's life energy: strong, fast, and determined to move forward. Gravity brings water down the mountains and pulls it into the bends of crevices, and this is how the environment and the river coordinate to make a unique form. But without the banks, the water would not be a river. It would not travel and would just spill out like a flood and dissipate. The banks are necessary to keep the water flowing forward. The boundaries that environments naturally entail, and the guidance from adults, provide the metaphorical banks for the children's energy.

However, it is unwise for adults to try to stop the energy of the river from flowing. Big obstacles in the way of a current, like boulders in the middle of a river, causes the water to surge around the obstacles with even more force and fight against them. If adults put too many obstacles in a child's path, they inadvertently create a dam and a flood. In a Montessori view, this energy is a positive force, driving the child to grow and learn. Montessori-trained teachers support children by setting boundaries clearly and lovingly, allowing the force of the river to move. Adults cannot dictate the strength or speed of the rushing water, but they can keep the banks sturdy and appreciate and respect the river's energy. They can work with, and not against, the child's behavior and desires. They do this by giving each child something appealing and productive to do.

Montessori reminds us that adults are also responsible for drawing boundaries where they belong: to stop destructive behaviors. This successfully brings about positive results when the child's need to do something constructive is simultaneously recognized and redirected through suggested alternatives. There must be appropriate freedoms in place, in other words. This act of adult respect gives children courage and resourcefulness for their lives.

The Prepared Environment Offers Choices and Boundaries

The prepared environment itself provides choices and boundaries. When using real materials, for instance, children get much-needed feedback about their actions directly from the environment, without adults orchestrating the process. When a child drops a real glass and it breaks, he or she can see the real result; with the adult's calm response and demonstration for how to clean it up with help, children realize the value in using two hands to carry such items and learn to move more slowly the next time. Wooden chairs on a wood floor (or metal ones on a linoleum floor) make a loud sound if banged down, and this can be pointed out to them in an older child's demonstration of how to lower a chair softly. A real mop made of cloth rope (or sponge) will distribute too much water on the floor if not squeezed out sufficiently, and so on. In such ways, the classroom environment provides natural limits on what is or isn't possible in the real world. It gives the children information about their physical movements, allowing them to make adjustments and improve their mastery of their bodies.

While a prepared classroom offers choices—to move around, to carry the furniture, to approach a sink and use it, to select materials and place them on a rug or table to work with them—boundaries balance these freedoms so that the classroom is never a free-for-all. With only one of each material, children must wait to take a turn after someone else is finished (respect their classmates), handle it carefully (respect the object and its use), and only take out a material they have been shown how to use (respect the limits of choices). Children have the choice to speak with one another, but they have the boundary of not interrupting someone who is busy working. This is the balance. The environment's natural limits and the teacher's guidance flow together, showing how integral each pillar of this approach is to the others. This interrelation of each pillar supports the structure as a whole and makes the approach stable and effective.

Building Internal Structures with Montessori's Curricular Plan

Amazingly, even some teachers and administrators working in Montessori schools are not aware that Dr. Montessori created an extensive curricular plan. But she vocally insisted on a plan that would endure and help children to prepare themselves for any day and age. She said, "Education . . . must be . . . oriented towards a clear understanding of our civilization. . . . There is need of a syllabus. . . . What purpose would education serve in our day unless it helped man to a knowledge of the environment to which he has to adapt himself!"[15]

Dr. Montessori's very definite and thorough plan—further fleshed out by her son, Mario Montessori, their close collaborators, and later, the Association Montessori Internationale's Pedagogical Committee—makes this approach stand out from other progressive alternatives. Dr. Montessori tackled the question of what to teach, which has often sparked debate (especially today, as information changes so rapidly with new discoveries made constantly), by proposing that teachers simply begin with the *whole* and then proceed to examine its *parts* in logical steps. This liberates the potential for children to learn about *everything*, because they do so in layers and logical sequences by subjects and sublevels of subjects. This is made possible only by beginning with a foundational structure, following logical sequences, and allowing children to dive more deeply into any topic of interest in purposeful pursuits of knowledge.

The ambition of Dr. Montessori's plan to touch on a vast range of information reflects her personality. Dr. Montessori was an exceptionally intellectual person; one has only to look at her own educational career to see this. She was constantly excited by human discoveries, the latest inventions, and the history of past peoples. She found mathematics, science, and the natural world to be fascinating, and she saw that children often do too. Her public lectures frequently shot off into seemingly tangential discussions, such as the role of carbon in the earth's makeup, to make an interesting point or to show how everything is interconnected and has relevant purposes. Dr. Montessori relentlessly cited the work and discoveries of others throughout her discussions on any topic, orienting adult listeners just as she would orient children to knowledge from the past.[16]

Giving Children an Orienting Foundation and an Expansive Curriculum

The curricular plan in Montessori is not stagnant nor does it dwell on the past, but it uses the past as a firm foundation to build off of. Dr. Montessori felt strongly that a curriculum must orient, then expand and never limit, the children's interests in the world around them and beyond. She developed an extensive curriculum of presentations for children from ages three to twelve, touching on all subjects of knowledge. When you enter a Montessori classroom, look to see how many topics the children are exploring simultaneously, as this reflects the richness of the curriculum.[17]

Such an atmosphere makes it natural for children to recognize the connections between ideas and disciplines. On any particular day, variety will be visible: in a Primary classroom of three-to-six-year-olds, for example, you might see a child working with a map of Africa and learning the names of the countries Malawi, Uganda, and Mozambique; another just two feet away washing a table; a child working through an addition problem of 1,457 plus 2,368 with a friend, using the Golden Bead material; another skip-counting with a long chain of colorful beads grouped in multiples of four; a child tracing wooden geometric shapes (specifically, an octagon, a nonagon, and a decagon) with her forefingers and identifying them out loud; one child tracing a Metal Inset of geometric shapes, such as a pentagon and an ellipse, with colored pencils; another arranging flowers; two others practicing identification of nouns, articles, adjectives, adverbs, and prepositions as parts of speech with the Farm of realistic-looking animal figurines and reading labels; another child matching the botanical leaf shapes cordate, hastate, and obovate to cards; one learning the names of plants with photographs on language cards with the teacher; another painting at an easel; and yet another composing an original piece of music on the perfectly pitched Bells of the C scale.

A Montessori classroom has a workshop-like atmosphere of activity, where everyone is choosing what he or she wants to do and pursuing it without interruption. There is one of each material to ensure this variety and to facilitate the concepts of taking turns and making choices. AMI teacher trainers have told me that this variety of work choices is one of the first things they look for to determine how well a Montessori classroom is functioning and the teacher's success in sowing as many seeds of interest as possible.

When a teacher does this effectively through his or her weekly planned presentations and spontaneous responses to the children, the students naturally follow their curiosity in all subject areas. Not only do children learn more than they could possibly absorb when fed information in set lessons (whether interested or not), but also—through osmosis and exposure—their interests in various subjects are piqued and their ability to make connections across disciplines is fed. In a well-functioning Montessori classroom, children build an elaborate structure of information in their own minds, a structure that facilitates the organizing of incoming information for the rest of their lives.

Montessori Elementary teachers provide the curricular structure by introducing each subject area with a Great Lesson story, which gives the framework of basic ideas in an animated fashion. In short the first Great Lesson is about the creation of the universe and our earth, the second about the emergence and evolution of life on earth, the third about the appearance of human beings on the earth and what made us unique, the fourth about the emergence of spoken and written communication among humans, and the last about humanity's creation of a number system. All topics spring from one or more of these headings.

In the days after a Great Lesson, the teacher gives multiple offshoot lessons that elaborate on important sections of each subject area and get progressively more detailed in further lessons that follow the children's interests. As children build a logical structure of sequentially introduced information, starting from the *whole* to progressively more detailed *parts*, they eagerly respond to new information. Children develop their own ways of inserting new information into their uniquely formed structures of knowledge. They get especially excited about information that they themselves discover from different sources or materials. The connectivity they find not only is validating but also rewards children's natural, insatiable curiosity. In this way, one might say that children drive their own education from within. They are bold enough to keep exploring because they are forming an internal structure that helps them make sense of each new discovery.

Serving Buffet Style

One way to explain how the curriculum is presented to the children is to use the analogy of a buffet table. I think of Montessori's curricular approach as being like a buffet, as opposed to set meals. Consider that the delivery of conventional school curricula is akin to sitting at a table and having a preset menu brought to you, with a serving of each important part of a healthy diet determined by someone else. You might enjoy the food and get a balanced meal, though some will prefer more mashed potatoes or eat very little of their peas.

In contrast the delivery of the Montessori curriculum is more like a well-organized buffet. When you walk up to a buffet, you see many colors, shapes, and varieties of foods. It's enticing—so much to choose from! You can see the entirety of the choices and food groups at once, getting an orientation for the whole with many parts. You get to make choices and pile these onto your plate. You learn by experience when you've taken more than you can eat. When the meals are not balanced with protein, grains, and vegetables, you can also learn, with guidance, to make better choices. And what happens when you eat from a buffet? Most people tend to eat more, with more enthusiasm, and go back for seconds—maybe even thirds!

This is exactly what happens with the Montessori curriculum. Dr. Montessori proposed that we offer a wide variety of topics to children and support where their interests lead them. This approach teaches them to be choosers, to be active agents in their learning, and to balance their plates; and the teacher introduces all kinds of interesting topics from this buffet for them to pursue. Crucially, there is a structural *whole*, a framework, that the child sees *first*—akin to having the entire buffet laid out before their eyes—and this accounts for their success in building logical structures of information in their minds as they explore.

Children can cover an incredible amount of information when they are free to follow their interests and when a classroom culture of working has been established by the teacher and peers. Children's interests are inspired by their teachers' constant supply of presentations; by the accessible, interactive environments of their Montessori classrooms; by the uninterrupted stretches of time when they can dig deeply into what they are exploring; and by the exposure to what their classmates of different ages are pursuing all around them. Montessori classrooms are much like the interactive spaces where artists, mathematicians, social thinkers, and scientists collaborate, innovate, or pursue their own studies in the company of others. In the case of a Montessori classroom, these topics are all being pursued simultaneously.

It is important to note that the established curriculum is not to be followed like a checklist. Teachers must understand the spirit of the approach and use the curriculum as a guide. In a good Montessori training course, teachers learn never to take the Montessori curriculum and treat it like a conventional one, with a conventional schooling mind-set. Rather, Montessori teachers *sow seeds of interest* by presenting many different lessons every day to different children. These presentations are short, and a child may receive as many as two a day or as few as two a week, depending on their activities and the teacher's observations. Most of the students' time is spent on working with materials and following up with explorations that spring off from the teacher's presentations. The presentations that the teacher gives follow logical sequences and progress for each child, from very concrete, foundational ideas to more abstract, complex ones as the teacher sees each child's responses. What unfolds are individual paths in the curriculum, where every child's journey, driven by his or her own interests and understandings, will be slightly different from any other. The teacher keeps track of all these individual journeys and aims to provide the next step on each of them.

Many of the children's paths will intersect in presentations that the teacher gives to groups or to several children around the same times.

Nevertheless each child's record of where he or she is in the curriculum and how that student progresses will be unique to that learner. Because no two paths are the same, the classroom is rich in variety, and everyone learns from exposure to everyone else's interests. This is why I call it an *expansive* curriculum; while Montessori presents a foundation of core curricula, the possibilities of what students can pursue and learn are endless, just as in real life. In the Elementary years, the foundation is repeatedly reintroduced by the retelling of each Great Lesson story in cycles during a child's three years in a classroom so that he or she gets multiple opportunities to take different paths in each subject area every time.

As children experience this again and again, they hone their skills each time. With mathematics, for example, one exercise eventually becomes too easy for some students, and they then advance to the next challenging math process. Children in a Montessori classroom learn to seek the levels of challenge that feel best to them, and this becomes a way of life. They are fully engaged in their learning process, developing patterns of organization that help them to find correct answers, including a process of elimination and resourcefulness to try different methods. The entire experience helps children build courage to keep trying, even after inevitable failures.

Watching Elementary children collaborate and learn through demanding math problems, for instance, is incredible; the amount of teamwork, social interaction, struggle, humor, frustration, and fun that can accompany this depth of learning through a long division problem is amazing. Montessori integrates all aspects of a child's development as a person and as a mathematician. At times, a child may take hours to do just one problem, if one accounts for the self-correcting they may need to do, and this means that the learning that occurs is immeasurable. The more children work with these processes, the more efficiently they achieve success each time, which fuels their desire to tackle more challenges in other areas. The children hone their skills and become more efficient and thorough in their practices. Such experiences repeat in other subject areas in one way or another, from math to music, history to geography, biology to chemistry, and language to the arts.

This is just one example of how Montessori fuels the development of children's resilience and perseverance in a real, direct way. And because an Elementary Montessori classroom is a vibrant community where all the children work simultaneously on what interests them and see what others are doing, the attitude of pushing oneself until achieving success is contagious. Children will stop and help each other, discuss and share a conundrum, and sometimes get intrigued with each other's experiences of learning. The learning is therefore—in economic terms—a *positive externality*, meaning that the network of students spreads newfound information via witnessing and sharing experiences. Such experiences happen naturally in a Montessori Elementary classroom because of children's gregarious social behavior at these ages. Dr. Montessori designed an approach that integrates, rather than fights against, the developmental characteristics of children in this stage of life, when they are very social and want to find out what others in their age range are doing around them.

The Montessori approach to all subjects makes clear that the children don't just value the exactness of a true answer; they love that perfection exists to be found. The search is fun. They see precise answers as individual parts that connect to a greater whole, creating a universal balance to which each component contributes. The children have fun, often unaware that learning could be otherwise. Finding answers is like a game, sometimes eventful and always intrinsically rewarding.

The most important aspect of rigor in the children's work in Montessori's authentic approach is not just the impressive effort or how much children learn and retain; the *ultimate* goal is the development of character. Dr. Montessori observed,

> In fact one of its most indirect consequences is the formation of "character." The children not only make progress in a marvelous acquisition of culture but they acquire more mastery of their actions, more assuredness in their behavior. . . . Joy in life together with discipline seems to be more the result of their activities guided from within than from any outer circumstances. . . . They are more balanced and capable of orienting and valuing themselves, they are characteristically calm and serene, and for that reason they also easily adapt themselves to other people.[18]

Such empathy and character in hardworking, self-aware individuals is what our world needs more of!

The Framework and Curriculum Completes Montessori's Culture

The framework of Montessori, bolstered by the paradigm of the child as the active learner and the three pillars—the prepared environment, the prepared adult, and freedom with responsibility—creates a very different learning culture than those found in either conventional or progressive schools. The Montessori culture is guided by these tenets. It sets the school community up to succeed.

The curriculum and the way it is presented to the children form an active interplay that makes the framework come alive. Without Montessori's curriculum, the prepared environment, prepared adult, and the balance of freedom with responsibility could remain ineffective. This is why it is so critical that teachers have accurate information about how the curriculum works, what to present, and when the moment to present is optimal. In this way, we give children everything they deserve from their educations. When teacher trainers come to visit classrooms to consult, they often recommend that the teacher present *more* of the lessons, *more* often, and with *more* gusto. This constant sowing of seeds of interest inspires and feeds the children's activity. It cultivates a culture of work and intellectual enthusiasm that makes Montessori such an outstanding approach.

This culture, when it is comprehensive and clear, infuses the actions of the teachers, parents, and children in a Montessori school community. It palpably manifests in children who are joyful and hardworking, and who share an infectious enthusiasm for learning along with others. Children who grow up with this authentic Montessori approach have a depth of awareness and a respect for themselves, for their environment, and for others. They exhibit traits we have established as building blocks for success: engagement, focus, organization, curiosity, courage, collaboration, respect, and resourcefulness. The next chapter will describe a Montessori school that brings this framework to life through the children, the teachers, and the parents.

3

AN EFFECTIVE MODEL: A MONTESSORI SCHOOL

Be Humble and Whole

Montessori classrooms definitely look different from those in other schools, with Montessori's hours of uninterrupted work time and the freedom to choose work, develop interests, and collaborate with friends. But next I'll explain that a school may also look unique when it reflects the principles of the Montessori approach as a whole. In fact the physical arrangement; the child, teacher, and parent culture; and how such a school is run demonstrate that it is—specifically—a Montessori school.

The Montessori school format depends on adults to consciously prepare a place that supports children in every way. The first step in the Montessori approach is to observe and to recognize children's needs and characteristics as they truly are, at each age and stage of development. This task requires a bit of humility as adults endeavor to embrace an approach that is truly driven by children's needs rather than adults' needs. In any school adults may be tempted to make decisions in response to teacher desires or parent requests. Quickly, the agenda becomes an ever-so-common adult-driven agenda. This happens even when educators care deeply about children but only see children's needs and characteristics as they think they *ought* to be, rather than as they actually *are*.

Dr. Montessori gave guidance for how adults can avoid this trend. In *Maria Montessori Speaks to Parents*, Dr. Montessori wrote, "On every teacher and every parent, I urge not great instruction, but humility and simplicity in dealing with small children."[1] Dr. Montessori's call for simplicity is a warning not to overcomplicate things; she observed that children's needs are simple at the core. Taking Dr. Montessori's approach to heart means that administrators, teachers, and parents must align every aspect of their school with children's straightforward developmental needs for each age's characteristics. This orientation makes decisions simple and clear.

To judge whether a school is succeeding in matching children's needs and characteristics, a visitor might look for children's engagement, focus, organization, curiosity, courage, collaboration, respect, and resourcefulness. When these are abundant, you have evidence that a Montessori school, as a whole school, is functioning successfully. Let's see what that looks like.

Welcome to Forest Bluff, a Montessori School

Walk up to the front door of Forest Bluff School at ten o'clock on a weekday, and you pass flowering prairie grasses, trees, and winding walkways where four elementary children are running, shouting to each other, and playing with glee. One stands on top of a rock boulder and tells the others, "OK, come over here, and let's start over! Sophie's turn to be the king!"

Two ten-year-olds quietly walk along the paths with clipboards, sketching and collecting botanical specimens for a study they are conducting. Two thirteen-year-olds, a boy and a girl, are stepping out of the building. Both stop and hold the double doors open for you, smiling as you enter. One says, "Have a nice day!" as you walk through.

Once inside, your eyes go to the high ceiling, which draws upward with exposed wooden beams, metal rods, and pipes. Somehow the raw, unfinished look is beautiful. In the center of the hallway is an open office space, roughly twenty meters in front of you. Low white walls that come to waist height surround and define the office space. The only interruption of the smooth white walls on either side of the hallway are wooden doors leading to classrooms, a light switch at a child's height, and a fire-alarm box. The appearance is clean and simple, almost Shaker-like. You see four adults working in the office under a warm glow.

What you notice next is the quiet, though there are several children sitting on the wood floor along the sides of the wide hallway. To your left two eight-year-old girls are drawing and writing on a paper chart that extends down the length of the hallway. Colored pencils, an eraser, a measuring yardstick, tape, and several large history books lie here and there across the chart paper. The two children talk in hushed voices and look up at you briefly as you pass before resuming their work. A nine-year-old sits at a floor table with a pile of nonfiction library books about airplanes and a neat stack of ruled paper, writing intensely with his head bent. His neighbor is a five-year-old girl with a colorful Bead Frame and a math paper before her on a low floor table; she stops working and watches you as you walk past.

What looks like a study group is actually children of different ages who are here independently by choice. Each has asked a teacher whether he or she may work out in the hall where it is almost silent and where the presence of the busy office staff is the only semblance of supervision. You can tell right away that this is a high-trust community, where children know how to handle freedoms responsibly, at rather young ages. There is an atmosphere of calm focus; everyone is deeply engaged in what they are working on, some working collaboratively and others alone.

Before you reach the office you are walking toward, you notice that the two girls with the long chart are joined by a boy who in a very animated fashion implores, "You *guys*, we have to do the part about Vikings *first*; you're putting the wrong order on the chart!"

"It doesn't matter, Frederick!" one hisses.

"Yes, it does!"

This discussion instantly becomes heated and animated, but Frederick begins glancing sideways at the head of school, who is now looking up from her desk. Other children in the hall are looking over now too.

The head of school motions Frederick over and asks, "Would you please continue your conversation in your classroom? It's distracting us from our own work in the office. Thank you." She smiles warmly at him.

Frederick says, "Oh, yes, sorry," and he waves the girls with a frustrated flourish through their classroom door.

The children reemerge a moment later, having fetched their teacher for help. She walks with her hands clasped behind her back and calmly looks over the chart, listens to the children, then asks a question and makes a suggestion. In the following moments, the children resolve their issue, take up positions on the chart, and resume working, looking relieved. The teacher returns to the classroom, closing the door silently behind her.

You stand at the office desk in the center of the hallway, where the professionally dressed office manager stands up, smiles, and asks how she can help. The admissions director walks up to join her in greeting you. She begins your scheduled tour by introducing you to the other office staff: the business manager, the head of school, and a Montessori-trained support director standing at a low central island, organizing a pile of freshly laminated cards she just made for a classroom. Each pauses to smile and say hello, then resumes his or her work. You notice that they appear content and focused on working.

Visitors often whisper, "It feels so *peaceful* here." Sometimes people are surprised to see that when everyone is clear about meeting children's needs, there is a palpable atmosphere of respect, joy, and concentration that feels serene. The quiet that visitors witness is not a controlled quiet, but rather, a sense of relief; the children feel respected, they are learning how to be respectful toward others, and they can be their true selves. Of course, if you stayed for several days, you would see that not every child or adult is always happy or feeling peaceful at every moment of every day—that would be unnatural! (Remember the children arguing heatedly just moments ago.) But the simple conditions for feeling peaceful are present: the environment is thoughtfully prepared, the adults are linking the children to it and modeling courtesy, and the balance of freedoms and boundaries support all levels of the children's developing independence, inside and outside the classrooms. All three pillars of the Montessori approach are therefore in place, forming a steady, dynamic framework.

As you tour the classrooms, patios, and narrow strips of grass and gardens around the school, you see a lot of movement. Everywhere you look, there are children crossing the rooms, walking in and out of doors to fetch things from other classrooms, and playing games. They are carrying their work to other locations, collecting items from cabinets and shelves, getting up from and down onto the floor, moving into and out of chairs, and talking to each other. But you also see pockets of stillness and concentration. In fact the ebb and flow of movement is punctuated by profound moments of stillness. You hear noise levels rise slightly as many converse with each other or sing, or as a child strikes the musical bells or tone bars with a mallet; and then you notice waves of an almost library-like silence, where all seem deep in thought or concentration on their own tasks. In this setting children are building their abilities to tune out distractions and to focus as well as finding a relaxed state of awareness for what is going on around them.

Where Children's Needs Guide Decisions

The scene just described developed very gradually, starting more than forty years earlier when Paula Polk Lillard, Lynn Lillard Jessen, and Jane Sheehy Linari founded Forest Bluff School in 1982. They began modestly, as many Montessori schools do, with fifteen three- and four-year-olds in a rented classroom of an almost-empty public school building in Lake Bluff, Illinois. After having taught kindergarten and first grade in conventional schools using some Montessori principles and a few of Montessori's materials, the three educators wondered, "If a little Montessori produces the positive results we're seeing, what would happen if we were free to follow the Montessori approach completely?" This inspired Paula and Jane to get the AMI teacher training as Lynn had previously done, and to start their own school to serve the Lake Forest and Lake Bluff families they knew.[2] To be thoroughly Montessori, they aimed to provide a full set of materials to children of a three-year age span and to offer three-hour uninterrupted work cycles every school day. Over the years, the school expanded little by little, and by being fiscally conservative and remaining true to the mission of authentic Montessori, Forest Bluff School flourishes today, with programs for infants through fourteen-year-olds and roughly 150 students.

As teachers themselves, Lynn, Paula, and Jane knew they wanted to set very clear parameters to avoid being pressured by parents or board members who might not have the Montessori-trained perspective of what serves children best. Being AMI-trained, they formed the governing board themselves and decided to make all decisions for the school with their teaching team. They created a school run by current or former teachers who had all taken at least one level of AMI training, which ensured the school directors were focused on Montessori principles as unifying goals.

This inceptive orientation guides the employees of this small school to find solutions by incorporating Montessori principles in all that they collectively do. The approach guarantees that the needs of each child are met first, over the needs of adults. When a parent becomes upset or a child's behavior is causing problems for the community, the situation can appear complex at first glance. But as soon as the teachers and school leaders shift their thinking away from the agendas of ourselves to "What is best for the children?" the answers become clear. The success of a school completely rests on this mantra, which gives a constant, unchanging compass, aligned with Dr. Montessori's principles and practices. In this way, a Montessori school becomes an environment where children can develop their engagement, focus, organization, curiosity, courage, collaborative skills, powers of resourcefulness, and respect for themselves, others, and the environment.

I will explain what results when a school attends to children's simple needs by first looking at the children, then the teachers, and then the parents—in this prioritized order.

Children: Learning and Growing

The students at Forest Bluff School behave like children anywhere: some struggle to understand what is happening around them, while others are astute; some are surprisingly capable, and some develop self-control more gradually than others; and some have nervous tics or learning challenges, some are gifted, and most fall somewhere in between. But with the Montessori approach, all children are supported to build their abilities—gradually, by their own powers, and over time. Individual self-formation is respected and aided by the environment, the adults, and the balance of freedom and responsibility.

The ways that children figure things out, make connections, and develop the described eight traits are visible in what they say and do. Visitors can catch a glimpse, but Montessori teachers are in the rooms day after entire day, teaching all subjects and involved in almost every aspect of living with the children. This gives Montessori teachers a special window into each child's development. They watch the same children eating meals, exploring the outdoors, learning to tie their shoelaces and button their coats, and taking care of themselves. They witness the children learning to control their bodies and focus their minds. A Montessori teacher watches children strengthening their independence and perseverance through every task. They see children become innovative in solving problems and learning to think for themselves. Because a teacher works with each child for three years, he or she is able to be patient and convey respect, confidence, and faith in each child's ability to change and grow. The pace matches the child. Teachers see that one develops those eight traits in his or her own time. By teaching each child for a full three years and watching each grow up at the school in the years before and after those years, teachers witness gradual progress that inspires respect for the the individuals and their developmental process, and a certain faith in each child's journey.

A Journal of Sweet Moments

When I was teaching at Forest Bluff School, I kept a little notebook to write down the joyful and amazing things my students said and did. I made a habit of recording the moments that stuck out for me. By doing so I cultivated my love and appreciation for the wonders that the children realized. This practice fostered a positive attitude and approach in me that, in turn, affected my students. The Montessori approach makes this practice readily available. Rather than judge with grades or rank children against one another, and rather than point out when and where they err, the Montessori teacher observes and supports. Dr. Montessori wrote and spoke frequently of the profound love for children that makes teachers persist to best aid them. This positive outlook is at the core of the Montessori approach to education. I share these snippets here to give readers a feel for life in the classroom and to demonstrate the traits that are fostered.

Ages Three to Six

From 1995 to 2000 I was a Primary teacher for roughly twenty-five three-to six-year-olds with the help of an assistant. These are excerpts from my journal of these years:

For about ten minutes today, almost the entire class is walking on the line, all together, I have no idea why. I look up, because it is suddenly so quiet in the room that you can hear a pin drop, and there they are, each child concentrating on their feet, walking so slowly. I have shown them how to do this individually and in small groups, but I've never seen this before . . . It is magical.

The line in this case is blue tape on the floor that makes an ellipse about five meters across at its widest point. The children were spontaneously collaborating, focused and engaged in creating harmony as a group.

Clayton (age three) is on his third day in the classroom. When he closes the classroom door upon entering, the handle latch makes a loud sound. Linus (also three) rushes over, waving his arms and saying, "No, no, no, Clayton!" He very seriously and slowly pushes the large door handle down and says to him quietly, "You must push all the way down, like this!" He then motions for Clayton to try it, and he does. This cracks me up, because Linus struggled to remember this when he started in the classroom just three weeks before, and he would regularly slam the door.

Here Linus was expressing and establishing respect for others and for the classroom environment.

I overhear six-year-old Patty quizzing her friend Catherine (six) on all the multiplication equations on cards from a small box. When Catherine hesitates over four times three, Patty tells her, "Well, it's six plus six, Catherine, because you take two and two away from one of the fours and give it to the other ones; that's six and six. So, the answer is twelve." It took me a moment to figure out her reasoning . . . Wow, amazing!

Patty was organizing mathematically and creating resourceful thinking.

I ask Linus (three) when tracing the sandpaper letter a, *"Do you know the word* apple*?" He smiles at me and says, "Yes, I do know it." "Apple begins with the sound 'aaaa.'" "Yes, it does," he affirms, beaming up at me.*

He was fully engaged in learning, taking pleasure in it.

Fritz (three) comes over by me and sits with his legs crossed next to me on the floor where I am working with other children. In a pleasant voice he tells me, "I was disturbing somebody, so I need to come sit next to you."

Fritz was self-regulating, practicing self-organization, making steps toward developing focus, and collaborating with his teacher by placing himself near me (using my help).

When I present the sandpaper letter v to Stacy (three) today, I realize her babysitter's name begins with v, so I say, "Vvvv, as in Vivian!"... When Vivian comes to pick her up, Stacy runs out to her and shouts, "Vivian! You're on a sandpaper letter!!!"

Stacy was expressing joy in making her own connections with her budding resourcefulness.

Gwen (four) writes with the Moveable Alphabet, "my favrit dol is mree I named her from a grl in scool." Ty, Marie, and Sarah (five and six) notice and come over to discuss the spelling with her. They all fix the doll's name together to read "Marie."

These children were collaborating to find the correct spelling as well as demonstrating a desire to organize the sounds and symbols to make sense to others. They were completely engaged in figuring it out. They also showed resourcefulness by doing this with peers, instead of coming straight to the adult.

I watch Lars (three) set out the items for table washing near the end of the year. Meticulously he places each item in order on his mat. I think, "Wow, did I teach him how to do that? How did that happen?" It hits me that it all sinks in eventually if I just patiently keep re-presenting.

Lars was organizing his things and the sequence within his process, fully engaged and focused on the process and on the steps themselves, without needing adult prodding.

Ages Six to Nine

The following anecdotes are from when I taught Lower Elementary Montessori classrooms at Forest Bluff, starting in 2000 and then off and on for a total of eight school years over a fifteen-year stretch. Along with the insights and beliefs children exhibit, notice the developing traits in these six-, seven-, eight-, and nine-year-olds:

"Mrs. Preschlack!" two seven-year-old girls yell as they rush over to me, both looking very concerned. "We don't know why Javier is crying." A small crowd is gathering around Javier, (six) who is sitting in a chair and holding his head down on the table, hiding his face with both arms. I approach, and the other gathered children start to tell me what they think is wrong: "Javier says we don't like him," a boy says. A girl says, "It's because people won't go outside with him." "Well, we were making a group, and he wasn't in it!" a boy explains. [After lunch in this school, children form groups of two boys and two girls for twenty minutes of unsupervised play, then return to the classroom to resume working.] *"You cut him out, Gerald," another boy accuses. "No, I didn't. He was never in it!" Javier lifts his tear-stained face long enough to interject, "Yes I was! I started the group, and then you guys got more people without me!" His distress is so palpable, I almost want to cry myself. I can barely get a word in edgewise as the children debate the sequence of events. Finally, it's clear that there was a misunderstanding: Javier had first asked two girls to be in a group to play outside, but when another boy approached the girls to ask if they wanted to be in a group and they said yes, he had already "gotten" another boy, so now there were two boys joining two girls . . . who were supposed to be committed to Javier, who was off look- ing for a second boy to form a group of four.*

As this was revealed, the children started to think of solutions: "Maybe this time we could go out five people?" one of the girls asks me. I am just about to say this sounds fine when Javier's muffled voice rises up, "I don't want to go with you guys!" "Javier, we didn't mean it," one of the boys starts trying to talk to him, bending down. "Gerald didn't know you already asked them!" he implores.

I am momentarily pulled away from the discussion to answer some other children's questions, and when I return my attention, one of the boys is suggesting they start all over by looking for more people to go outside with so there will be two groups, four in each. The children seem to like this idea—they suddenly dash around the room, asking people if they want to go outside. Finally, they return, having found one more girl. Now there are six children. . . . They ask if they can look in the classroom of older students to get more play partners, and Javier is starting to lift his head and wipe his face. One of the girls says, "C'mon, Javier, come with us!"

A few moments later, while I am now giving a math presentation to some other children, the recently expanded group comes to me and stands by my table, waiting for my attention. They are buzzing with happiness. When I look up at them from my low chair, Gerald explains, "OK, we are going to go in two groups, if that's OK: a group of four—me, Javier, Sally, and Sharon," (OK, this is the original group. Do they realize this?) "and another group of Fred, Patrick, and Marcia." They look triumphant but also worried that I might say no. I ask if they looked for another girl for the second group. [The guidelines are to get two boys and two girls, if possible, to even out the social groupings and mix things up regularly]. *"Yes, we did, but no one else in any of the classes wants to go out," Gerald says. "OK, then your plan sounds good to me," I say, smiling and almost laughing. They rush off in a herd for the calendar book to record their departure and return times and their names: "OK, let's go write it down! Get your watches!"*

These children were resourceful to come up with their own ideas about how to solve the problem with care for everyone involved. They had to collaborate to resolve every issue. They were engaged, and they all got involved and stayed with it until the end. Javier showed courage to trust the others again, and the children were courageous in trying to reach an understanding, even after Javier's feelings were hurt. They respected their classmates, and they organized themselves into new groups.

Two little girls (both seven) spend the entire morning finding Factors for numbers on the peg board. They had chosen the number 102. After almost three hours, I am actually going to make them move on to something else, because it seems like "busy work" by its apparent futility, when I eat humble pie: they come up to me with reams of paper to show me with awed expressions, "Mrs. Preschlack! Can you believe that the ONLY factors for 102 are 1, 2, 3, and 6, and then 17, 34, and 51!?"

The students had literally repositioned the pegs on the board until they had exhausted every possible combination of 102 to find these factors. They showed focus, engagement, determination, and patience to continue with a lengthy process, and curiosity to find those factors.

Poor Sam and Phil (both eight): Over many weeks, they had made a chart about the ancient Sumerians,[3] and Phil took the chart home to show it to his parents. He was supposed to bring it back so that he and Sam could present it to the class. For several days he shows up without the chart, looking worried. He says he can't find it. Finally, after a week, Phil comes in and tells us that a house cleaner had thrown it away. I can't believe it. Both boys are very sad. Then, after about twenty minutes, they come up to me and Sam says, "Mrs. Preschlack, we decided we are going to make another one." They are going to start all over!

(Phil's parents told me later that before the chart was tossed, Phil had gathered the family and made them sit in the living room, his sister had helped him hold the chart up, and he had given them a formal presentation on it. So Phil had already had the satisfaction of the complete chart; the reason he decided to remake it was so that his coworker could experience this satisfaction as well.) What perseverance, resilience, and engagement Sam and Phil demonstrated when they chose to begin again, making a whole new chart!

Sally's (eight) research with Patrick (seven) on ice is incredible. When they told me they wanted to do research on ice, I thought, "Well, this will be a short one . . ." But how wrong I was! Their chart covers such things as how ice hockey rinks are maintained, how ice expands and splits rocks to make geographic formations, temperature extremes, ice ages and when they occurred and what parts of the planet ice covered in each, what melts ice . . . It just goes on and on. They worked on their chart off and on for six weeks, and it extends all the way across the room, covered with writing and drawings.

Sally and Patrick were resourceful finding all that information related to ice in different books, showed great collaboration to produce the work together, and sustained their focus over several weeks to follow their curiosity. How many people are that interested in *ice*? They brought this enthusiasm to the whole class. We all watched their progress and learned new things from listening to their report.

At our individual weekly meeting today, I take gobs of work out of Martin's (seven) drawer and say, "Let's just put this pile to the side for now. How about you finish the six things we will leave in your drawer, and then tackle this other work one piece at a time?" He likes this idea. He starts way too much work and cannot finish anything; he gets overwhelmed. His drawer is overflowing every week with unfinished work. We'll try this technique for now.

We meet every few days to organize his drawer again and catalog what is in there. I suggest, "When you come in each morning, first choose two things to finish that day, and start one of them right away." It's a plan for now, and Martin appears relieved and engaged.

This shows how a teacher supports a child to organize his work and manage his time. She respects him and collaborates with him to try some techniques to gain independence and success through another strategy. By doing so, she demonstrates how to be resourceful. Supporting him to develop ultimate independence in this area, whenever that may occur, is her constant goal.

Edward (six) is determined to write a research report his first week in the class, which he sees older classmates doing. I help him to sound out the lines in a book about the sun, and he writes about two lines per page in his own words and draws a picture for each. After working on it for a while each day for three days, his report is four pages (eight sentences) long. "The sun is not a planet. It is a star. It is made of fire," etc. We edit it together, and I help him to staple the pages to make a booklet, and he draws a cover. Then he finds that he cannot read it. I review it with him again and again, and he asks any available child in the class to do this, too, for a few minutes every hour or so. He then stands out in the hallway and practices presenting to an imaginary audience by himself. At the end of the week, he stands in front of the class, just as he has seen others do. His short legs spread in a wide stance, shoelaces strewn over the floor and shirt untucked. He holds his report up high in front of his face and proceeds to give it to us so smoothly that I realize that he is not reading—he has memorized his words!

Notice how resourceful, courageous, engaged, and focused Edward was. The entire exercise fueled his desire to labor through learning to read—a gradual process with many differing approaches that he would master because this ultimate goal was tightly aligned to his efforts.

I often ask a child in his or her weekly meeting, "So what's your goal with this?" referring to a piece of unfinished work that's been in his or her drawer for a few weeks. When I meet with Daryl (nine), she pulls out each piece of work and begins, "So my goal with this is to finish it by next week, and I just have to do the illustrations now . . . And my goal with this one is to just edit it with a friend, and then check it with you, then it should be done . . . And my goal with this is . . ."

Daryl organized herself and her work, showing her resourcefulness by using a technique I'd shown her and adopting it as her own. She was also very engaged in this process, having thought it through before our meeting and being familiar with every piece of work she was showing me.

Tara (six) often says "It's too loud in here" when it's pretty quiet. I don't think the external surroundings are distracting her actually; I think her own mind is so active that it distracts her. She comes over to me every two minutes to tell me something: "I can't find my pencil," then, "I found my pencil." "I'm not sure what I want to work on," and later, "I think I'm going to compose some music." "Do you know what three times three is?" then, "I'm looking for someone to do the Checkerboard with," then, "I found Gabe to do the Checkerboard with me." It is driving me crazy, these constant interruptions! I keep talking to her about this, but finally I have to limit her to asking or telling me something just four times in a morning . . . until she's out of times and has to wait until afternoon. This is hard for her, but giving the definite rule seems to help. "You can decide" and "Hmm" and "What do you think you could do?" and all my other responses just haven't been doing the trick. I think she just enjoys the comforting contact with an adult, but I need to wean her away from this constant attention.

Later in the year:

Tara comes up to me for the third time in an hour. When I say to her, "Tara, you are very smart. I bet you can solve that problem," she says, "I have a solution," and holds up her finger. She comes back a few minutes later: "I'd like to move my table to the hallway to work alone." I say that would be fine. A few minutes later she comes back to me, "I'm wondering where the names for the provinces came from" (of Canada, which she is writing a report about).

Over her three years in my classroom, Tara gradually became more independent, and in her last year in the class, as a nine-year-old, she starts to love helping younger children learn things.

Recorded two years later:

The very last day of school, the children and I "super-clean" the entire room. It is a particularly hectic super-clean, and I finally leave the room to use the bathroom, near the end of the three hours. When I reappear a moment later, I find that everything has been put away and all the work is done—Tara (now nine) is standing on a chair next to the stand of the US flag (on a chair, oh no!), and she's holding the flag out for all to see. The class is gathered on the floor in front of her, and she is leading them in a roaring "Oh-ohh say, can you see, by the dawn's early light, what so proudly we hailed . . ."[4] I catch my breath. Tara has become a leader. How did that happen?!

I realized that, over a long period, Tara became more self-organizing and even enjoyed organizing others into an activity. By working with younger children and helping them with their work, she mimicked my organizing behaviors with students and became like a teacher to others. This helped her teach herself how to sort through her own thoughts. She also kept repeating again and again the process of finishing projects and presenting them to others. This child's weakness—her overactive awareness of what was happening around her—gradually over three years came more under her control, so that it became a strength. She was able to see the other children's needs and to organize them into an activity. She used her dramatic flair to engage others' attention. She had gradually learned how to focus her energies to be productive.

I see transformations like this one—from struggling with executive functions to developing strong skills—happen all the time in Montessori education. Perhaps such dramatic growth happens because it is supported by having one teacher with a child for three years, sequentially and in all subjects. Such continuity allows for real progress to happen. Children correct their own weakness by steady, repeated work and from a desire within them, ignited and encouraged by the teacher and the community. Because of the way the classroom functions, this happens with dignity intact. Despite having challenges, a child such as Tara was able to respect herself, to increase her focusing abilities, to learn to collaborate, and to become more resourceful and less dependent on the adult in the room.

Teachers: Being a Team

After the children, the next priority is the teachers, because they are on the front lines, directly interacting with the children in the classrooms. At Forest Bluff School the teachers make everything run smoothly and effectively for the children. The following descriptions come from my years as the head of Forest Bluff School, when I was at times simultaneously teaching a Lower Elementary classroom. I refer to myself as both a fellow teacher and a head of school.

Working Together

Everyone works together as a team at Forest Bluff. All the teachers have AMI Montessori training so that they share a common vision of the approach and have the same preparation for how to implement it in the classrooms. This clarity of vision and commitment to Dr. Montessori's principles is what attracts most teachers to this school. Applicants often say that they are looking for a position where they won't be at odds with an administration when teaching in the ways they were trained. They can see that in this school, where the head is also a Montessori-trained teacher, employees are supported to align their decisions and actions with their AMI training.

The organized routines and physical spaces make this a school where teachers can focus on their work with children without being distracted by extraneous events or duties during the day. Teachers are not called away from the children during class time for meetings or to respond to parent phone calls or emails. As a Montessori school, the uninterrupted time *with* the children is the clear priority.

Teachers also say that they appreciate the Montessori style of collaborating with colleagues to find the best ways to tackle challenges. They feel respected in a school where their input is encouraged and valued. Outside class time, Montessori teachers can help to brainstorm administrative ideas, communicate policies and guidelines to parents, and make important decisions collectively. Every team member is responsible for maintaining the school culture, which consists of three things: the vision of the Montessori approach as the guide; respect, or "grace and courtesy," in all adult and adult-child interactions; and teamwork.

This Montessori culture is palpable in day-to-day interactions, inside the school and outwardly in the community.

Leadership

Every group needs a leader. The leadership style at Forest Bluff School is very collaborative, meaning that the teaching directors make decisions for the school *with* the head of school and the assistant head of school. (Teachers are also called directors at Forest Bluff; the two titles are interchangeable to signal that they are—secondary but very important—decision makers on school policies too.) As the head of a Montessori school, it helps to prepare oneself daily by reading a paragraph or section from one of Dr. Montessori's books and considering how it relates to the children in the school. This exercise is centering, and it helps the thought leader to encourage the teachers to look for certain things in their classrooms. It also enables a head of school to explain more clearly, for teachers and for parents, what is happening in those spaces. Without this rootedness in Montessori principles, coupled with an awareness of contemporary topics in other fields, any Montessori administrator or teacher can get pulled off track by adult agendas or external pressures. All schools, of course, can stray from a shared mission when their leader isn't conscientious about bringing everyone in the community back to the school's founding principles and practices. Such a key responsibility requires daily attention. Our advantage as a Montessori school is that we have clear, timeless principles to work with.

To lead the team of teaching directors, Forest Bluff School uses two formal formats: the Mission Meeting the week before school begins and the Directors' Meetings, which happen every Thursday afternoon during the school year.

Kickoff: The Mission Meeting

Forest Bluff teachers and school leaders begin each year by coming together for a week at the end of August, preparing the classroom environments and ourselves for the school year ahead. This Directors' Week begins with a Mission Meeting, where each teacher and school leader shares his or her goals. As head of school, I start by giving the team some thoughts about the Montessori approach and a theme for the year ahead. Despite our many years in this educational approach, we all need to return to the orienting paradigm and the three pillars that form the Montessori framework. This orientation reminds us that adults' role is to support children in this process by preparing the environments (pillar one); maintaining environments, actively linking the children to them, and modeling behavior for the children (pillar two); and providing the balance of freedoms and boundaries to facilitate independence and responsibility (pillar three). This format gives me an opportunity to inspire everyone to think more about Montessori themes and to actively appreciate what each teaching director contributes to the collective conversation.

After making a brief introduction, the teachers take about twenty minutes to find quiet spots outside in a natural setting that lends itself to self-reflection. They and I sit silently to write and think, creating our own goals for the year ahead. Afterward we gather and each share three goals: one goal as a teacher, one larger professional goal in the Montessori community, and a personal goal. These shared and individual missions set the stage for our year. The rest of the week we prepare classrooms, review safety procedures, organize our paperwork, and prepare for conversations with the parents.

Sealing the Bond: Weekly Directors' Meetings

The teachers and I continue to connect throughout the year in important weekly team meetings every Thursday afternoon from 4:00 to 6:00 PM. These Directors' Meetings occur in the mezzanine of a room with a high ceiling, big windows, and a large wooden table that we gather around. It is our prepared environment for adults! To this simple and beautiful space teachers bring their current aspirations, challenges, and contributions. The format for our meetings follows the same pattern from the school's first years, with the head of school sitting at the head of the table to lead and steer the conversation as needed. Each week a different teaching director leads us through an agenda; this rotation gives everyone experience leading the group conversation a few times each year.

The first hour of the meeting covers the agenda of items we need to be alert to, discuss, and make decisions about. I only put items on the agenda that involve the whole group, and never more than five. The last agenda item is called Students and Celebrations, to guide us to end this first hour by sharing positive stories about the children from that week.

The second hour of the weekly Directors' Meetings is dedicated to discussing a book we are reading together. This book discussion is also guided by that week's leading director, who prepares a few questions before the meeting to generate conversation. Getting every person to speak is a goal, so the leading director sometimes asks teachers of the youngest children to answer a question, or teachers of the oldest and so forth. The point is to get to know each other better and to think collectively. Most often we end up talking about the needs of students and brainstorming about our classrooms. We get ideas from hearing about one another's successes or offer advice to a teacher who is struggling.

These meetings revive us. Because people feel respected and safe sharing—and eventually this happens for even the most reserved personalities—we learn about one another's childhoods, the life experiences that have shaped each person, and how we each see the world. What is shared at the table stays confidential among the group. At times, the conversation may turn to a difficult parent interaction or a struggle with a student, and a teacher might end up asking the group for their input or suggestions. This openness with each other creates a very supportive atmosphere and proves to be most productive for group problem-solving. This sharing experience is essential to the group leader and to all of us working together. I honestly cannot imagine keeping a teaching team in sync without this weekly practice. The meetings one afternoon a week are our times to be together as the whole team, with a format that guides the conversation in positive directions. We appreciate our Thursday Directors' Meetings because they reset us on a constructive path for our work with children.

I know I am not alone in feeling that our work using this educational approach betters us as teachers and as people. Maria Montessori wanted teachers to look within for wisdom, to observe with humility, and to strive to reach children through deeper understanding. This practiced respect for each individual and the freedom to develop oneself protects Montessori from being a cult—which some have mistakenly taken it for! To become a Montessori teacher requires learning to be open-minded, self-aware, and supportive to others.

A former Forest Bluff teacher says that these meetings helped her invest in her own journey as a teacher and as a person. Because of this format, she reflects, "We were always growing."

Solving Problems by Collaborating

The architecture and physical layout of Forest Bluff invites teacher collaboration and movement; the classroom doors in the building connect the rooms to the hallway, to one another, and to the outdoor patios. These connections encourage teachers to communicate with each other, particularly in the mornings before school and directly afterward. Teachers constantly look to one another for tips and advice, and to brainstorm to solve problems. As head of school, I circulate before and after school to listen in on these conversations and to join in if needed. Communication among all the adults is continuously ongoing.

In addition the teachers meet more formally with the head of school every four weeks or so to discuss the needs of a particular age level: Young Children's Community, Primary, Elementary, or Secondary. Sometimes we combine two adjoining levels so teachers can plan and discuss when students will transition from one level to the next during the year. These meetings take place in the morning before a school day and are kept under an hour; the agenda is compiled of anything the teachers or the head need to bring to the table. This is a chance for the head to find which students might be struggling, any issues to attend to, or any inconsistent practices between the classrooms. Teachers often need support to keep their standards high, advice to ease a difficulty, or aid to find some new strategy to address a classroom issue.

Whenever we have a problem to solve—whether it be stopping parents from gossiping about a student, what to do about street salt from the children's boots ruining the wood floors, or how to keep voices respectfully low in the hallway so the office staff can concentrate—we find that putting our heads together helps us come up with the best solutions, in a faster time frame, and with Montessori principles in mind. We remind ourselves that the children's needs must come first. We cooperatively discuss ideas, then propose and decide on a plan of action together. This collaborative and respectful Montessori approach feeds the whole community.

Parents: A Partnership

From Forest Bluff's first years, the founders discovered that one of the most important aspects of teaching with a Montessori approach is communicating with students' parents. It is necessary to keep up a continual dialogue to help parents understand what happens in the classrooms and why. In conventional schools parents can feel reassured by the familiarity of schooling techniques that they themselves probably experienced. Most parents of children in a Montessori school, however, did not go to Montessori schools themselves, and they don't have Montessori backgrounds. This means that parents may feel uneasy or conflicted at times. They may not understand why the teacher is doing—or not doing—certain things with their child. When particularly stressed, parents may doubt their choice of Montessori education altogether, especially when their friends are raving about the latest new program offered at a neighboring school. Some may miss the comfort of being with the majority of American families who choose conventional schooling. Others may find it challenging to explain the Montessori approach while their friends describe their children's conventional schooling very easily.

Looking at this on a deeper level, Montessori teachers have to consider that most parents *already* feel a certain level of anxiety about their crucial roles as parents; not understanding or being able to explain how the schooling approach they've chosen benefits their children only adds to their uncertainty. Even when it may be obvious to the educators that Montessori is helping a child, it is understandable that a parent may simply feel anxious. An anxious parent might hassle the school with questions and request concrete facts—such as test results—for reassurance. Because Montessori schools do not typically measure students with the standard metrics of grades or test results, Montessori educators have to speak to the power of the learning process itself and explain clearly how Montessori-taught children demonstrate their cognition and abilities in more meaningful ways. When Montessori educators respond to parental anxiety in a proactive fashion by connecting them continually to the Montessori approach, they bring the parents along with their children's progress. Therefore, the Montessori educator's job extends to helping parents understand the Montessori approach.

Teachers can do a better job when they ask parents to describe what happens at home as well. When parents explain how their child behaves outside school and what strengths or struggles they witness, it gives teachers valuable clues for how to best help that child in their full development. The parent-teacher relationship is therefore a dynamic one, which ultimately benefits the child when everyone communicates clearly and collaborates.

Sometimes Montessori educators need to gradually bring a parent around to seeing a situation through a Montessori lens. The following story demonstrates one such case.

Marissa's parents are very concerned about what they think of as her academic success. They often ask to speak with her Lower Elementary teacher, Beatrice. They want Beatrice to "push" Marissa (age seven), because they think their daughter "wastes time" when she's allowed to choose what to work on in class. When they quiz Marissa at home on what she is learning in school, Marissa slumps in her chair and can't answer what one-fourth plus one-half is or correctly spell the word *question* in her letter to her grandmother. The parents ask that I, as head of school, have the teacher drill Marissa on fractions—which they think she should know by now, since she started working with fractions in her Primary class when she was five years old and seemed to understand them better last year. They also ask that our school start giving spelling tests to make sure their child improves her spelling in a more systematic way.

Marissa's parents describe their concerns to me over the phone. I ask to have a few days to investigate the situation, and I invite them to meet with me and Beatrice at a specific time the following week. I observe Marissa a few times while she works in her classroom during the day and I ask to speak with Beatrice afterward. First, I listen.

"This child doubts herself a lot," Beatrice tells me. "She wants me to choose her work for her, but when I do that, she doesn't engage in it with any sincere interest."

The obstacle (besides her parents' possibly overbearing approach), her teacher surmises, is that Marissa is deeply engrossed in figuring out her social interactions with peers. As you may recall, obsessive focus on social development is often an observable characteristic in children in this second plane of development, ages six to twelve. Until Marissa works through whatever she is learning in that area, Beatrice laments, Marissa's academic prowess may be secondary in her instinctive priorities.

Beatrice and I both know that Montessori teachers can guide elementary-aged children to work together to combine their interests, making intellectual growth occur in tandem with social development. It works both ways. Dr. Montessori also wrote that engaging in intellectual work settles children and has many benefits to their character development and social interactions. As a result, children emerge from years of working in effective Montessori classrooms having not only covered more academic material through their peer interactions than they might have on their own but also gained crucial collaborative skills. While brainstorming together, Beatrice and I agree that we consistently witness this in our own students. We think about Marissa's issues some more, and Beatrice brings the story to the other directors in our weekly meeting that Thursday afternoon. She explains that she regularly tries to get Marissa engaged in working with other children but Marissa frequently argues with her peers, which too often results in breaking off to work alone.

The other teachers listen, then Farley pipes in. Farley taught Marissa in Primary class when she was younger, and Farley remembers observing that Marissa loved the opportunity to help children who were younger than she was.

"It could be a confidence boost," another teacher suggests, "for Marissa to review those math and spelling skills by helping younger children to learn them."

Another experienced teacher offers, "I have a boy who is new to my class, Nicholas, and he needs some help with spelling. Maybe ask Marissa if she would visit our class for a few minutes each day?"

The teachers agree to this plan, and they discuss how to arrange it so that Marissa can be invited to spend some time being helpful to someone younger. Perhaps the opportunity to boost her confidence through other relationships will make Marissa feel steadier with her peers. Then she might be more willing to challenge herself academically. We decide to try this and see what happens next.

The other issue, of course, is how to help Marissa's parents understand our goals and our Montessori approach to helping their daughter. If we abruptly tell concerned parents that their child's lack of confidence needs some attention *before* her intellectual abilities can progress, we dismiss the parents' own priorities. They are not wrong to care about their daughter's academic progress, but our challenge is in how to help Marissa's parents see the whole picture. We aim to address their academic concerns while showing how a child's social development and intellectual progress are intertwined.

Farley recalls a conversation she had with a different parent recently, where she felt that the parent came around to understanding the need to sometimes attend to one skill before another can be addressed head-on. The teachers listen and we conclude with a plan of how to phrase our approach to Marissa's parents in a way that will be helpful to them and, ultimately, helpful to Marissa.

I review for the group that any parent meeting has three goals:

1. Tell parents what is helpful (or necessary) for them to know.
2. Explain what the teacher and school are doing to help the child.
3. Suggest something productive parents can do from home to support their child.

When we discuss any problem with parents, this last component, making them a part of the team with a plan for action, often relieves their anxiety.

In this case Beatrice calls Marissa's parents, acknowledging their concern and explaining her goals for Marissa and what she is doing in the classroom. But Beatrice also suggests that the parents ask Marissa to help at home a little more with cooking, where the fractions in the measuring cup and measuring spoons will give her practical experience. This will make fractions a natural part of their discussions at home, rather than an abstract quiz. It will also give Marissa the opportunity to be helpful in the kitchen and thereby build her self-esteem as a contributing family member.

Beatrice also recommends that they encourage Marissa to write for pleasure more often at home and, instead of pointing out her mistakes, ask her whether she would like them to find two words that she might have misspelled, almost like a game. This way, her parents can share the correct spelling with Marissa, and she can fix the words on her own if she chooses to. Better yet, they could help her look up words in a paper dictionary at home, fostering her growing independence. Another idea is to encourage Marissa to write the family's grocery lists and other notes now and then, to give her more practical opportunities to write. Beatrice explains how it will pay off for her parents to be patient and relaxed about spelling errors while they encourage her to write more often. She tells them, "Just try to ignore the mistakes and respect Marissa's efforts. She is hard enough on herself already, so she *will* learn to perfect her spelling over time. As she sees that her writing is useful to others around her, she'll feel braver and more ready to correct any mistakes."

Beatrice and I also discuss in private that she'll spend time in the following weeks involving Marissa in a review lesson on adding fractions and learning where she can find how words are spelled.[5] Beatrice assures Marissa's parents by explaining how she is addressing these topics in class.

"Let's give this some time, and then we can meet," she tells them.

As these efforts combine in the following week, Beatrice notices that Marissa starts a report on dolphins with two girls her age. Beatrice makes sure to show all three how to help one another with their spelling and check their own, and each other's, work. The latter techniques support the children in collaborating with respect and becoming even more resourceful in their writing and editing. By the time Marissa's parents come in for the planned meeting, Beatrice has positive results to share with them.

This is an example of addressing parental needs without losing the focus on children's needs. One can easily lose this orientation by trying to appease parents with non-Montessori solutions, which in my experience are never as effective as the Montessori approach. Solving problems by brainstorming, using the compass of Montessori principles and resources, communicating clearly, and assuring parents at the same time builds relationships of trust between teachers and parents. Again, the children benefit most from these efforts. And the teaching team upholds the integrity of their Montessori school and deepens their own abilities to comprehend and communicate the strengths of their approach.

Prioritize Face-to-Face

To support children who—from a Montessori perspective—are forming *themselves*, adults must work together closely, but with the least amount of interference to the children's development. This means verbally communicating and collaborating without obstructing or distracting the children. Practicing grace, courtesy, and respect along with clear communication optimizes adults' abilities to coordinate their efforts.

With this in mind, Forest Bluff teachers and parents communicate directly and frequently when outside of class. With parents, the teachers and I prefer to communicate in face-to-face meetings or over the phone. Meetings and phone calls typically occur right before or after school when teachers are free. By making sure that Forest Bluff teachers are never interrupted in their classrooms to address parents, the school prioritizes the children's needs. Parents do not enter the classrooms to try to talk to teachers because they understand and value that the teachers' attention is on the children.

To keep in close communication, teachers leave brief voice-mail messages for the parents of each child every six weeks or so. In some cases, they might do so more often, throughout the school year if needed. When parents would like to contact a teacher, they call the school office to ask for a call back or they leave a note at the front desk. We keep paper and pencils available at the front desk for this purpose. Teachers respond with a phone call or schedule a face-to-face meeting before or after school. For a variety of reasons, teachers do not write notes, emails, or text responses to parents. It takes time to write a well-thought-out note—time that teachers need to prioritize for the children and for daily classroom preparations. In addition emails, texts, and notes can give false impressions or lead to misunderstandings, so Forest Bluff teachers avoid these means of correspondence.[6] By communicating through the school office phone or in face-to-face meetings at the school, teachers ensure that all necessary parties are aware of every conversation. This way, everyone at the school is better able to support one another and maintain a professional and courteous tone that benefits all.

Parents find these guidelines of correspondence to be very clear and sensible. As with all our decisions, these policies have been made in light of what helps the children most. In this spirit we explain to parents that the students need their teachers to be well rested and prepared in order to give students their best attention during the school day. Therefore teachers spend their evenings and weekends planning lessons, preparing for parent meetings, reviewing their notes, and renewing their energy to give their all in the classrooms. This means that teachers cannot always be available to parents outside of school hours. An hour before or after school every day is set aside to respond to parents, but time is not regularly reserved outside these times. Parents eagerly comply when they see how this boundary ultimately benefits the children, their own included.

Communicating Montessori to Parents

Because Montessori is a true paradigm shift in approach, we must help parents to understand it alongside us, in deliberate ways. To do this, Forest Bluff directors formally reach out to parents with a variety of scheduled presentations and events.[7] In addition to parent-teacher conferences twice a year to discuss a child's progress, we invite grandparents and parents to visit their children inside the classrooms three times a year,[8] we lead book discussion groups for parents who want to get together, and we host three social events and several important educational events. These educational events are called the Continuing Education Evenings, Coffee Discussions, Montessori from the Start lectures, and Secondary Level Evenings. Such educational events for adults are essential in a Montessori school because explaining our approach and exploring together how children learn best reveals philosophy and practices specific to Montessori. The better our parents understand what we are trying to accomplish and how we go about it, the smoother things go with the children in the classrooms.

Continuing Education Evenings

There are roughly four formal evening presentations a year, called Continuing Education Evenings. The purpose of these events is to communicate what Montessori education is, how it works, and why it is so effective. Parents come to Forest Bluff School's Continuing Education events wanting to learn something new each time. Someone in the crowd may have been coming to our talks for fifteen years, now on their fourth child, while another may have just walked in the door to see if they want to bring their eighteen-month-old to us; we must use language that both these audience extremes can understand and get something out of. We avoid using Montessori jargon and instead attempt to translate the Montessori approach in ways that people can relate to easily. We use simple, direct language with memorable anecdotes and live demonstrations of the materials. A speaker always has to consider the personalities and experiences of the whole audience—both those who crave more detailed content and those who prefer more introductory information. Combining these audiences is a challenge, but it can be done, and getting everyone together in the same room builds valuable connections in the community.

Every meeting with parents is an opportunity to communicate basic ideas about Montessori and to introduce something new about child development through a Montessori lens. The teachers and I try to make our presentations clear, inspiring, and informative, and we reserve time at the end for connecting the audience members with each other through discussion in question-and-answer sessions. One thing we have discovered is that a school representative must step up as the leader in these settings, to give structure and consideration to the entire audience. It doesn't work well if one or two parents dominate the room with ongoing questions or lecture fellow parents. But we also try to be sensitive and respectful when redirecting the more talkative parents, the same way we are with children in our classrooms, so that everyone feels safe asking their questions and expressing their opinions. The same skills Montessori teachers work on with children can be extended as courtesies to adults as well. Most often parents have insightful, helpful comments to share with us and with one another.

My colleagues and I choose Montessori topics we think parents are interested in each year and brainstorm catchy titles to entice them, such as "Mindfulness and Montessori in the Classroom and at Home," "Interconnected: How the Montessori Curriculum Works," or "The Emerging Moral Compass: Our Children on a Social Quest."

In most events teachers lead parents through a series of material presentations in their classrooms and explain their purposes, telling anecdotes about the children to make certain points, and then they open up the session for questions. Parents appreciate this chance to get to know their children's teachers and to understand better what their children are getting from their Montessori classrooms. Above all, the teachers and I find joy and excitement in showing people how incredible Montessori is and telling them about the amazing things children do in these settings. The ways children grow and learn and improve in Montessori environments often exceed our highest hopes, and we are eager to share our experiences of how this happens.

With any talk at Forest Bluff, we want parents to feel a partnership with their school and that their attendance is a real contribution to their children's experiences in the classroom. Our close relationships are helpful, but it is also important that parents and educators support one another's roles. As it relates to school, the parents' job is to prepare their children from home to get the most out of the school day. Parents do their best to help their children with sleep and nutrition so that they are ready to work with effort and engage with their classmates and teacher. This requires a lot of time, attention, and energy from parents. To indicate that we educators respect parents' efforts in these important tasks, the school does not require parents to volunteer their time to numerous other school activities. Instead, we steer parents to support their children by setting up their homes to respect their children's needs for becoming self-reliant and appropriately independent. This way, children can contribute to their families and reap the benefits that such activity provides.[9] Through discussions of how to balance freedoms and responsibilities, we find that parents are usually eager to collaborate with the school.

Finally, we make certain that every one of our presentations begins and ends on time so parents will know that we respect and value their time. We know that parents have children, relatives, and babysitters to get home to, and that teachers need to be rested for the next day of teaching. Accomplishing these dual needs means that the longest presentations last only thirty to forty minutes. This allows us to fit questions and a discussion period into a one-hour event. At Forest Bluff the teachers and I are strict with ourselves about this timing schedule; we rehearse our talks to make sure we can deliver on this promise. Teachers who arrive at Forest Bluff feeling unsure of their abilities as public speakers find that with the right support and practice, they quickly develop such skills. When Montessori educators focus on expressing what makes Montessori special and why they are passionate about it, giving talks becomes an enjoyable part of their work.

Coffee Discussions

A more casual way to discuss the Montessori approach is to meet with smaller groups of parents in what we call Coffee Discussions. Paula Lillard wisely started this tradition in the school's early years. Each season, we ask three or four families if they would be willing to provide beverages and host a parent discussion in their home, and we divide the parent body into groups so that everyone is invited to one of these discussions.

The teaching directors and I choose a topic we sense parents might be eager to discuss. The topics might address a common question parents have or a strategy for helping children at home. Often current events or publications raise a topic of interest to address. One year, for example, Paula presented "Helping our Children Learn Resilience, Optimism, and Joy," and in another, I spoke about "Helping Children Develop the Independence to Face Challenges."

After introducing the topic as it relates to the contemporary culture, the speaker quickly dives into how we address the issue through the Montessori lens in our classrooms. Next, we suggest concrete ways parents can support their children's development at each stage of their self-formation: young childhood, elementary years, and adolescence. We follow with a group discussion, where everyone is encouraged to share his or her thoughts and questions. These gatherings are truly enjoyable and uplifting. They are one of the most important ways parents forge friendships, and they help the head of school and parents get to know each other in a relaxed setting. Hosting them in homes also helps parents to get to know one another and to appreciate what different families bring to the community.

Montessori from the Start Mornings and the Secondary Level Evenings

At Forest Bluff we meet more regularly with two specific groups of parents, whose children are at the two most vulnerable periods of self-formation. These are the parents of infants to children age three and the parents of twelve-to-fourteen-year-old adolescents.

Parenting infants and very young children is a challenging—and sometimes lonely—experience. To support parents during their early years, we offer the Montessori from the Start program, with several morning lectures and alternate practical sessions. This program's goal is to bring mothers and fathers together for information, ideas, and inspiration and provide the opportunity to make friends with other parents and develop trusting relationships with the school. These sessions allow educators to explain how young children develop and to show parents concrete ways, using demonstrations and props, to support their young children in their homes. When parents align with the school and with Montessori principles from the very beginning, they develop confidence and give their children the best possible foundation.

The second initiative involves the Secondary Level, which is equivalent to seventh and eighth grades. We let parents know when they enter this program designed for adolescents that we will need their commitment to attend monthly meetings as a group. This is because their twelve-to-fourteen-year-old children will be in a stage of life that requires as much adult attention—albeit of a different style—as their earliest years of life. Dr. Montessori points out that adolescence is a tender and volatile time of development. When children turn twelve and enter their teen years, they undergo dramatic changes and exhibit increased needs. For this reason, we invite each set of parents to a personal meeting with the head of school to discuss the Secondary Level program and Montessori's approach for adolescents before their child enters it. At this meeting the head of school establishes that the family is on the same page with the school before they begin this more vulnerable and challenging journey with an adolescent. Because the program is well established and parents can see its effects, most families are very excited to enter the program. But it has to be a good match for the student and the family. By committing fully to attend every monthly Secondary Level Evening and the three annual Secondary Level Teas, these parents optimize our close communication with them.

We explain that Dr. Montessori recognized that twelve-year-olds stand on the brink between childhood and adulthood; adults must welcome budding adolescents into the adult world with new responsibilities and new freedoms. Educators and parents can consider the three pillars—preparing the environment, providing mentoring adults, and balancing freedoms and boundaries—as a guiding structure: we must seek to understand our adolescents, set up environments that meet their specific needs, model responsible, healthy adult behavior by providing mentors for them, and allow them appropriate freedoms and responsibilities to build their new selves. Adolescence is not always treated with the respect and focus it deserves, but this powerful time in life necessitates intense personal fortitude, a strong community of peers, and mentors who can inspire and guide.

At the monthly Secondary Level Evenings, our two Secondary Level directors give a brief presentation, where they share what the students are currently studying in the classroom, give information about upcoming events (such as wilderness trips), and ask the parents to consider some aspect of adolescent development with a Montessori perspective. These meetings also provide parents with the opportunity to share their own experiences and ideas on how to best support adolescents, both in school and at home. We draw from many excellent books, articles, lectures, and resources that offer ways to guide adolescents. When connecting parents with such resources, we convey their relevance to Dr. Montessori's unique perspective on the adolescent's self-formation. Parents of adolescents enjoy this source of support and camaraderie in the final years before graduation.

Results with Parents

The goal of all our parent interactions is to develop relationships based on positive communication for the children's benefit. When their parents are attending events and communicating closely with their teachers, children sense that the adults are on the same team. Children witness these healthy working relationships being modeled for them, helping them to develop confidence and security that frees them to attend more fully to their own learning experiences.

The parents appreciate these gatherings as well. According to one parent, "Forest Bluff is a community dedicated to supporting both students *and* parents. The events are educational, fun, and full of nuggets of wisdom. As parents, we walk out feeling more comfortable and informed."

Such remarks are rewarding for our directors and staff to hear. A father of an alumna recently told an audience of current Forest Bluff parents, "The school helps you learn and grow as a parent. Because parenting has been the most important role in my life, I was grateful for the conversations and guidance. I encourage new parents to take advantage of it. . . . You may not realize it at the time, but looking back, I now see how unusual the guidance we received was. It profoundly helped me and my wife be the best parents we could be." He teared up as he finished his last sentence. As I recalled some very difficult conversations between us over the years and the positive results that followed, I teared up too.

My colleagues and I want parents to leave every Forest Bluff event feeling inspired, relieved, and excited that their children are specifically in a *Montessori* school. We want them armed with a better understanding of what Montessori education is and how it works. The sign outside our school reads FOREST BLUFF SCHOOL: DISCOVERING THE NATURE OF LEARNING. The phrase reminds us that educators and parents are on a journey of discovery together, one that never ends in a Montessori setting.

Evolving Simply

Not all Montessori schools are just like Forest Bluff, nor should they be. Each Montessori school evolves to meet the needs and characteristics of the community it resides in. But what can be universal, and what I hope is helpful in reading about this specific school, is the respect and simplicity it represents—the focus on the children and the clear and efficient practices that reflect the Montessori approach. Every school has the capacity to work in this direction. The physical layout, the customs, and the way a school is run do not need to be expensive or fancy. In fact, when it comes to a Montessori school, less is more. Less playground equipment means more opportunity for creativity and resourcefulness with items that children can find and climb on and games that they can make up. The absence of an indoor gym means children get to go outside to be active. The absence of an auditorium means that children get to reorganize spaces in hallways or classrooms and to move furniture to create sets when they want to present dramatic plays or address audiences. And fewer implemented programs mean that children have more time to invent their own activities and extend their developing concentration. (As a side note, keeping things simple also means that we can keep tuitions lower and resist the desire to borrow funds).

The motto "keep it simple" can guide educators to accommodate children's needs within any environment, and its limits. As an example, where some Montessori schools have ample land for farming as an extension of their classroom activities, our Forest Bluff School property does not give us much space. My colleagues and I do what we can with what we have, squeezing a vegetable garden into a spot of sunlight and designing paths for children to run through our very small patch of prairie grass. Without the kind of playground some schools have, our children play games in our blocked-off parking lot or walk to nearby parks as a group. But every seeming drawback offers a chance to make an adjustment. Another example is that our building has almost no storage space, because it was designed and built on a limited budget, but this has made us disciplined about not acquiring anything extra. We only have room for the truly necessary supplies, and we are forced to keep them neat and tidy. Every Montessori school, in such ways, forms its own personality.

Giving attention to children who are developing with an authentic Montessori approach is imperative. For this, schools need a prepared environment, trained adults, and the balance of freedoms and respon sibilities where children can develop their engagement, focus, organization, curiosity, courage, collaboration, respect, and resourcefulness. These traits lead children toward persistent, resilient, and creative problem-solving and cooperative learning—preparing them for the real world.

In learning about this model, you may imagine that without the sufficient preparation of teacher training and a clear understanding of Dr. Montessori's work, too many Montessori schools may not reach the full potential of the educational approach. In the next chapter I will explain the variety of effectiveness and misrepresentation that you may find in Montessori education. Being informed of this dynamic will help you to see how this sound answer to today's problems of education has not been publicly realized, and what we can do to remedy the problem.

4

AUTHENTICITY: THE QUEST AND THE CHALLENGE

If It's So Great, Why Isn't Everybody Doing It?

Having learned how effective Montessori education is, you may agree that many parents would choose Montessori if they knew about it. But you also may wonder, why *don't* more parents know about Montessori education? Why hasn't Montessori spread further into American education? There are three reasons that I will explore in this chapter: The first two are the confusion over the brand name Montessori and what it means and the inconsistency in how the approach is implemented—accentuated by differences between Montessori organizations. Thirdly, a high level of dedicated study, continued learning, mentoring, and support is required to reach the outstanding results in educating children Dr. Montessori proposes, as in the serious endeavors of law, science, medicine, business, and the arts.

To begin with, authentic Montessori education has a branding issue. What exactly—in the public's mind—constitutes "Montessori education"? Unlike other approaches, such as Waldorf schools,[1] there is no formal trademark for the name Montessori, nor is there any measurable definition for the public to rely on. Any school can label itself "Montessori" yet not resemble the approach at all.[2] This leads to widespread misunderstanding and misrepresentation of Montessori education. And unfortunately, the less accurate examples confuse Montessori's outcomes.

With all the positives that this educational approach offers children and their families, this can be disconcerting. It is not uncommon to hear someone say that they've seen a "Montessori" school that didn't make a good impression. In my experience such results are usually linked to incomplete teacher training. Specifically, because Montessori training is not clearly defined, and because the differences between teacher training courses are not made clear to the public, the more thorough and authentic training courses are not consistently recognized as being so. Without full training, teachers are left to invent ways to implement the approach, while they search for information from a wide variety of sources to find what Montessori education should be. Understandably, this leads to mixed results.

If you want to find examples of Montessori schools, you won't have to search very far. Look around in almost any area and you'll find Montessori or "Montessori-inspired" schools. Many educators and schools claim the name as a whole or in part. Even in very traditional Country Day schools, preschool educators sometimes say, "I basically do Montessori in my classroom."

I have also met disgruntled parents who say that their brief experiences in some Montessori schools have left them uninspired. They'll tell me that Montessori education is "only good for preschool, and the children don't learn much after that." Similarly, others have told me that Montessori was wonderful for their younger children, who washed doll babies in bathtubs, cut pretend wooden fruit with pretend knives, and sang "Old MacDonald Had a Farm"—none of which, as you now know, truly reflects Dr. Montessori's principles or curricular plan. Then there are the families who enroll in a Montessori school, expecting to experience just what they received in their previous one, only to be disappointed by how very different it is.

We can solve this branding problem by first understanding that such a range exists. By appreciating the differences between authentic

Montessori and other interpretations, we can recognize what leads to promising results with children. Understanding the main elements of the Montessori approach and how they are best delivered is key. Not all parents may want Montessori education for their children. But as we discuss and examine the disparities, you'll get a better idea of what to look for. First, I will explain the differences between the authentic approach described in this book so far and the variations that confuse the public. And there certainly is understandable confusion.

Perhaps the most telling and humorous reaction I have ever received when I mentioned Montessori education was from an enthusiastic young woman who responded, "Oh, I *love* Montessori; I'm a Montessori ski instructor!"

I hesitated before responding, "Oh . . . What does Montessori skiing mean? I didn't know Maria Montessori ever skied."

She furrowed her brow and asked, "Who?"

"Montessomethings"

I was not aware of how *much* variation is being implemented in Montessori schools until I took a sabbatical year to see the schools for myself. I had been teaching and working at Forest Bluff School for twenty years, and I had heard about the variability others witnessed around the country. But up until my sabbatical, I had only visited Montessori schools that were very similar to ours, with the same international organization's accreditation, so I had not seen the wide fluctuation within the larger Montessori community. Visiting other schools was like coming out of hibernation, and I was excited to see what "Montessori" meant to many across the United States. While I assumed I would see some variety, I expected to see familiar learning materials and the basic framework of the approach. I expected to recognize the schools' classrooms as being Montessori classrooms.

I began my travels with a visit to an old acquaintance who had recently become the head of a Montessori school in Chicago. This private school for over two hundred children of ages three to fourteen appeared to be very popular and had a long waiting list.[3] The school's website was impressive; I was excited for the tour.

My first surprise was that my friend knew very little about Montessori as an educational approach. I wanted to be helpful, so I asked whether he had read about Montessori education and where he had gotten information. He explained that he had not read any of Dr. Montessori's writing or any books about the method, other than one parent's inspired account called *Montessori Madness!* The previous head of this school had given my friend a verbal introduction to the approach but agreed with his premise that some things about Montessori were "probably great" and other things "could be improved upon." My friend talked about several other educational methods and models that he found equally intriguing, some of which I had not heard of. I said that I would be interested to learn more about them, but I wondered, if Montessori was just one of many approaches in their school, why call it a Montessori school? Why use the label at all?

I quietly followed him on his enthusiastic tour, seeing room after room of children milling about; teachers filling out forms in the corners or reading to groups of children; children working with workbooks and computers, plastic puzzles and wooden blocks. There were a few recognizable Montessori materials on some shelves, but I saw none being used by the teachers or children. The classrooms, though cheerful, were also messy, loud, and chaotic. My friend and I stepped over papers on the floor in the hallways and squeezed past boxes painted as play props with piles of textbooks and folders sliding off them. Flapping, sticker-covered papers and cursory children's paintings hung on every wall.

At the end of the tour, I felt confused and disturbed by my friend's lack of awareness at just how unlike Montessori this environment was. I asked if he had any questions for me as an observer. He asked how I keep Forest Bluff School teachers accountable for covering a curriculum in our Montessori school. I answered that they learned in their Montessori training from the Association Montessori Internationale what curriculum to use, how to teach it through sequences of presentations, how to keep careful records, and how to plan their lessons every week. Doing all this was an expectation of the high standards of Montessori education.

He looked at me quizzically, so I tentatively asked, "Do your teachers have some kind of Montessori training?"

"Oh, yes . . ." he answered, "most of them have been teaching Montessori for twenty years or longer."

"Do you know where they got their training?"

He did not know specifically.

"Do you know the names of their training centers or types of training?"

Not exactly, my friend answered; he had some guesses, none of which rang a bell for me. I said nothing more, wanting to be polite and nonjudgmental. I was exhausted when I left.

There are many such schools, unfortunately, and I was just starting to discover what they looked like. I was beginning to realize how unaware too many school communities are of what authentic Montessori looks like and what it can do for children. The most unfortunate thing about such schools using the title Montessori when they do not implement the approach is, in my mind, that they inhibit the very traits Montessori fosters. In such a chaotic and cluttered environment as the one just described, where is the support for developing a sense of organization and a strong ability to focus? How do adults nurture engagement when they are not presenting the materials to learn with and demonstrating how to collaborate and when they appear so distracted? Where is the palpable respect in mannerisms and interactions, which is such a cornerstone of Dr. Montessori's approach? How can curiosity and resourcefulness grow without the materials that enable children to explore concepts on their own and to be independent from their teachers, textbooks, workbooks, or computer programs? Furthermore, if the teachers are not working with the Montessori curriculum to address all areas of knowledge, recording their presentations, and following up by reviewing the children's work with them, then how are teachers fostering the students' natural intellectual drive to educate themselves? And where are the children building their abilities to think and act independently in order to develop realistic courage?

The same day I saw this first school, I went to my next visit in a neighborhood called Auburn Gresham in the South Side of Chicago. I have to admit that I was now dreading what I might find since realizing how misrepresented Montessori could be. But what I saw next gave me hope and inspiration.

This second Montessori program was in a public school of roughly 485 children, ages three to fourteen. The majority of the school building was a conventional public school, but three classrooms at the end of the long hallway formed a Montessori lottery program within the public school. Fifty-five students were enrolled in this neighborhood school public Montessori program.

After my previous tour at the other school, I worried that teachers without a degree from a recognized Montessori organization would not be able to create the most important aspects of a Montessori classroom environment. But then came my second surprise of the day. Despite having no formal Montessori training, the teacher in the Primary classroom of three-to-six-year-olds was maintaining an environment I recognized at once as having Montessori qualities. I saw respect in the teacher's and students' grace and courtesy, the joy of inner freedom, and concentrated engagement with work. The room was uncluttered, orderly, and clean, and the atmosphere was calm and pleasantly industrious. Children sat at rugs and at individual tables, engrossed in their chosen work with an almost-complete set of Montessori materials available on the shelves. The teacher walked gracefully and carefully from one child to another, helping and encouraging them in their work and acknowledging their efforts with smiles and eye contact. She was gentle and attentive. I breathed a sigh of relief. Apparently, this teacher had regular meetings with a Montessori teacher trainer who advised her as a friend, and she had gleaned the spirit of the approach and some basic information on how to present several Montessori materials and activities. The previous teacher for this group of children had been fully trained, so the older children in the class had learned how to use the materials in past years and were now showing the younger children. I was encouraged to see some important aspects of the Montessori approach in action.

The third school I visited that day, in Beverly, farther down on the South Side of Chicago, gave me yet another scenario to ponder. As with the other two schools, these classrooms were not formally accredited by any Montessori organization, though every teacher in this church-housed city school had completed formal training with one of the two most established organizations in the United States. The founder, who gave my tour, was not formally trained herself but was clearly astute and well versed in Dr. Montessori's written work.

"I don't care if you call something this kind of Montessori or that kind of Montessori," she told me. "Good Montessori is good Montessori, and that's all we care about here."

I noticed right away that the classrooms and hallways were clean and orderly. The traditional Montessori materials were in good condition on the shelves at child level, and the furniture, rugs, and windows formed a pleasant, comfortable, but work-like atmosphere. The teachers were hard to spot at first, busily working with students who were all demonstrating respect and trust. I saw no workbooks, textbooks, or worksheets, just the Montessori materials being used and the children's work: colorful, creative, and carefully crafted charts; drawings; research reports; mathematical equations; and original timelines. Beautiful things were clearly happening in this school. Children were happily learning and building themselves.

These are three different examples of what we might call—somewhat tongue in cheek—"Montessomethings." Such schools are not affiliated formally with any accrediting Montessori organization that trains Montessori teachers or sets standards for Montessori schools to reach, and they may or may not mix in other educational approaches. There is clearly a wide range in this category, from classrooms that barely resemble Montessori to fairly accurate implementation. Clearly, we cannot make assumptions about these schools based on their Montessori accreditations or affiliations. Regardless, the unrecognized and unstudied variations, along with the lack of knowledge about the authentic Montessori approach pose real obstacles to defining and spreading the benefits of Montessori education to more children.

The Roots of Montessori in the United States: AMI and AMS

There are several organizations that represent Montessori and train teachers in the United States, but I am going to focus on the two chief ones. You may anticipate that the existence of these two accrediting organizations clarifies what Montessori schools and teacher training consist of. However, their history and their divergent interpretations of Dr. Montessori's work have actually furthered public confusion.

Even in the very early years when Dr. Montessori traveled and explained her approach, variations in Montessori practices sprang up. Dr. Montessori recognized right away that while her ideas were enthusiastically accepted by audiences in *theory*, many educators surged ahead without fully understanding how her findings translated to *practical* implementation. She also received criticism and contrastingly— but equally troubling to her—misplaced praise. The public fixated on Dr. Montessori, not her proposal, and viewed her as the creator of a new method of education. She insisted they were missing the point: the children were the ones showing what children are capable of, what their true psychology is, and she was merely the one who made the initial discovery. She called for scientific study of how children learn as a continuation of her observations. This research would transform education to match children's natures more accurately than most educational practices we have today.

Dr. Montessori's logical response to the public's misinterpretations was to establish an organization in 1929 with the help of her son and collaborator, Mario Montessori. The goal of this organization, named the Association Montessori Internationale (AMI), was to define the principles of the Montessori educational approach and to clearly uphold them. The purpose was to protect the authenticity of the philosophy and reliable implementation of the educational approach as designed by Dr. Montessori and her colleagues. AMI was to serve as the source for information about the Montessori approach in all its details.[4] The organization's most important aim was to train teachers to implement the approach authentically.

To serve this need, Dr. Montessori went to every country she could, giving numerous training courses for teachers and using language translators where appropriate. As a result teachers who traveled long distances to receive this training started Montessori schools all over the world. A dramatic ebb and flow of school openings and closures ensued. Through decades of international turmoil, revolutions, and world wars,

Dr. Montessori actively lectured throughout Europe, Asia, and the Americas right up until the day she died in 1952, while planning a trip to Africa. The Association Montessori Internationale continues to operate from its base in Amsterdam and has affiliates all over the world, including in the United States (called AMI/USA).

In the United States there is another large organization promoting Montessori education, founded by an American shortly after Dr. Montessori's death. In 1953 Nancy McCormick Rambusch, a highly educated young woman and a whirlwind of charismatic energy, became increasingly interested in Montessori education as an alternative to the conventional school model. Eagerly Rambusch traveled to Paris to attend the tenth International Montessori Congress, where she met Mario Montessori and conveyed her desire to promote the Montessori approach in the United States. Mario encouraged Rambusch to first complete the AMI teacher training in London, which she then did. With this training, Rambusch and others founded the Whitby School in Greenwich, Connecticut, as a Montessori school in 1958. Subsequently, Mario appointed Rambusch to be the representative of the Association Montessori Internationale in the United States. Six months later, Rambusch created an organization for AMI in the United States: the American Montessori Society (AMS).

From the beginning Rambusch's goal was to create an American version of Dr. Montessori's work, to further improve it by incorporating more recent theories and methods in education and to spread this version of Montessori to as many children as could benefit. Rambusch galvanized American interest through her public lectures, articles, media, and her book, *Learning How to Learn: An American Approach to Montessori*. This inspired the founding of many more Montessori schools in the United States during the early sixties. Rambusch's expressed desire to modernize and Americanize the Montessori approach is infused in her book and media interviews.

Over the next two years, Rambusch argued with Mario and AMI's appointed teacher trainer in the United States, Margaret Stephenson, on a number of details about the training format. Rambusch envisioned training courses with large faculties that would offer differing viewpoints, incorporating information beyond Dr. Montessori's insights and creating an atmosphere of experimentation and freedom for variety in interpretation. In addition Rambsuch wanted teachers to be able to train faster, making Montessori readily available to more American children and thus more appealing to the American public. In response Stephenson and AMI colleagues from Amsterdam countered that the training must be carried out at the pace, and with the detail, that would ensure quality and coverage of all necessary content. Stephenson also insisted that the course content remain authentic to the approach as was laid out by Dr. Montessori and AMI. The result of this disagreement was a total separation between AMI and AMS. The American Montessori Society has existed and thrived as its own organization ever since.

This split and the differences between the two organizations furthered, rather than addressed, the confusion in Montessori implementation. AMI and AMS have fundamental and practical differences that stem from their differing goals and assessment criteria.

Divergent Paths, Complementary Goals

AMI and AMS diverge specifically in how they train teachers and the content in their courses; their requirements for a teacher to earn a diploma; and their standards for school accreditation/membership. The results of these discrepancies are recognizable in the schools that each organization respectively accredits.

Because the Association Montessori Internationale was established to adhere to strict guidelines designed for effective results, the association approves its training centers with definite, specific standards. The teacher trainers undergo an extensive training program and are then individually assessed before being approved to become trainers.[5] The length of AMI courses, the course content to be covered, examinations for trainees, and the criteria and instruction needed to become a trainer are all delineated and controlled by AMI headquarters in Amsterdam. As a result of this consistency, a teacher who took an AMI training course in 1983 in one city will have the same course content as a teacher who took AMI training in 2010 in another city. This kind of regulation ensures certain outcomes and continuity for teachers and, consequently, for students. As implementing authentic Montessori is the central theme of the organization's culture, AMI's strength lies in upholding careful standards for such implementation, focusing on quality control and authenticity and deepening the understanding of the original Montessori approach.

The American Montessori Society, by contrast, sponsors training courses of differing lengths by trainers with different training backgrounds and expertise and delivers content that trainers decide upon individually. It thus offers variety that can be dynamic but problematic to finding consensus on what Montessori is and how to implement it. Instead, AMS's training format serves the goals of being inclusive, open to different ideas, and accessible. Among AMS's strengths are its ability to collaborate with other educational organizations and its approachability for parents and the public. AMS members spread the word about Montessori and actively reach out and bridge connections. In fact, education under the name Montessori has spread most widely in the United States through this organization. Without Nancy Rambusch's energetic effort to appeal to the American public in the 1950s and '60s, the name Montessori might not have spread beyond a hundred or so schools in the United States. The pioneering spirit of AMS continues to drive the culture of its members.

The differences between the two organizations can in fact be looked at as complementary strengths. Progress in promoting Montessori has been made when the AMI and AMS organizations agree on general guidelines for Montessori education. For example, in 2010, the then leaders of AMI/USA (Virginia McHugh Goodwin) and AMS (Richard Ungerer) collaborated to create a memo of understanding that delineated rubrics for public school use that define good Montessori practices. These initial meetings resulted in the formation of a new organization, called the Montessori Public Policy Initiative, with the goal of creating a bridge between AMI and AMS Montessori. Today, leaders from AMI and AMS continue to converse with one another, formally and informally, and to work together to benefit more children with the Montessori approach. In their dialogues with each other, both organizations reach for ways to improve their own shortcomings without sacrificing their unique strengths. The conviction that unites Montessori educators is an agreement that within reason *any* interpretation and practice of Montessori possibly does more good for children than most other educational approaches.

Being honest about how the two organizations have different goals makes their roles in the promotion and practice of Montessori education clearer. Acknowledging their differences is key. Rather than compete against one another in the current era, AMI and AMS complement one another because they serve different purposes for Montessori in the United States.

Differences Play Out in Implementation

You may wonder whether the difference between AMI schools and AMS schools is outwardly noticeable. During my travels to other schools in my sabbatical year, I observed AMS schools to see if I could recognize what makes these programs different from AMI-accredited schools. Here are a couple stories from my time touring these schools:

In one AMS Primary classroom, seven five-year-old children have puzzle maps spread out on rugs with large sheets of paper beside them, into which they push pins to create outlines of map pieces—like tracing but with hole punching. As the children each complete this exercise, they walk to the teacher and follow her as she checks in with others, until she comes to check their work and tells them whether they are "finished" and can go on to something else. Clearly, this is an assignment where all the five-year-olds are to do the same thing and the teacher made the choice, not the children. The children do not appear very focused or engaged, mostly talking to one another. The respect for self-directed behavior, which happens when children make choices and follow individual interest, is not evident. At the same time, something else in the room catches my attention: I am impressed that a specialist is expertly guiding an autistic boy through his activities and supporting his interactions with other students. This adds to my impression that despite not reaching Montessori's full effectiveness, this is an inclusive, lovely environment where children appear to feel safe and to enjoy learning together.

In another school, I admire an AMS-trained Upper Elementary teacher's friendly mannerism and animated teaching style. I am curious that she is showing a group of fifth graders how to multiply with fractions on a white board, while the corresponding Montessori materials sit nearby on a shelf. After complimenting this teacher's dedication and enthusiasm for her students and the lesson, I gently probe, "Did you not use the Montessori materials for fractions because you find that these students are ready for the abstract version, or do you never use the materials for this lesson?"

"Well, the fraction materials can only go so far . . ." she begins, assuming I agree.

I share my observation of how intently the students listened to her clear explanation during the lesson. But then I come back to the issue by asking what she *does* do with the Montessori fraction material.

"You just can't do much with the fraction material," she says, again as if I should know this.

"But," I persist, "what about division of a fraction by a fraction or multiplying fractions by whole numbers or multiplying fractions by fractions with the materials?"

She looks bewildered and doubtful. Clearly, entire sections of the Montessori curriculum have never been shown to her, which means that she has to teach from more traditional methods. Although her students do seem intent on doing the work their teacher is presenting, I think about the benefits of working with the Montessori fraction materials that they are missing out on. What is additionally concerning to me is that the teacher is seemingly unaware that such curricular content even *exists* in Montessori, and yet as an AMS Montessori-trained teacher, she represents these gaps in knowledge as limits of the approach to the public—including to the parent who is sitting with us during this conversation.[6]

Alone in the Classroom: What's a Teacher to Do?

Realistically, challenges to Montessori implementation occur for *any* individual teacher. While access to thorough training helps Montessori teachers start off on the right foot, the journey truly begins when they are alone in the classroom facing their tasks. Under daily pressures, no matter where teachers get their training or how much or little they receive, their own variations can creep into their interpretations and implementations. Working in Montessori-accredited schools with supportive staff leadership to encourage them to follow their training helps. But in many Montessori schools today, the pressure on teachers to use conventional workbooks and electronic tablets, give conventional tests, and prioritize other learning over the curriculum from their Montessori training can be intense.

Being a classroom teacher is challenging to begin with; when things are not going well in a classroom, anyone may also be tempted to try alternate methods or even to find solutions contrary to the Montessori approach. Without support from school leaders, colleagues, and dedicated parents, one's belief in Montessori can waver. In fact, there is much more pressure on Montessori educators, who are already going against the grain of cultural norms.

Being isolated and continually questioned or doubted can lead teachers to stir in bits and pieces of other methods in a desperate attempt to find something that will satisfy others. Some teachers might succumb to using traditional-style tests to determine what children are learning, dictate to children what to work on and give them assignments for classwork, or distribute workbooks or worksheets to get children to "do something." The students, unfortunately, are the ones who face the consequences. An incomplete Montessori approach, where some aspects of Montessori are present but not others, falls short.

Once this cycle begins, teachers can go for many years having never really experienced what children are capable of in Montessori classrooms. They may not witness the amazing changes in students or the calm, contented demeanor of children whose needs are being fully met at school. They may never witness the intellectual exploration that children delight in with the Montessori materials. Dr. Montessori's early descriptions may begin to sound like a dream, a fantasy. A teacher might conclude that all he was told in his Montessori training was implausible, or that children are "just different today" and can't do what Dr. Montessori demonstrated they could in her day.

A lack of continuity between classrooms (in the same school) is also a common issue that puts pressure on Montessori teachers. A teacher may be trained to give presentations to children of certain ages according to the expectations of their training's standards but might then have twenty students whose previous teacher neglected to show them the expected lead-up lessons. Teachers in this situation have to improvise to cover information that should have been covered when the children were younger and most receptive. If children have passed the sensitive periods for learning with certain designed materials, the next teacher has a larger hurdle to face in teaching things that the children missed in their previous level.

These pressures are all further increased when teachers do not receive support or guidance from a Montessori coach or a consultant. Within a Montessori organization such as AMI, reaccreditation consulting visits, occurring on a three-year cycle, are helpful in addressing these pressures, and certainly, AMS teachers turn to one another in their organization's tradition of mentorship. But ultimately, the leadership and the culture of any school must promote ongoing guidance and encouragement for the teaching team.

Accepting the Challenge into Their Own Hands

During my sabbatical travels, I stop in the doorway of a public Montessori school Elementary classroom and start talking to the teacher there. My eyes drift around the room, over the stacked boxes of plastic game-like materials and the piles of photocopied pages and textbooks stuffed in front of some ragged, dusty Montessori materials. I ask the teacher if she uses the Montessori Elementary materials very much. She shakes her head and grimaces.

"You know, the kids just don't work with those much anymore. Every year, I find that we're spending less and less time with them."

I ask where and when she had her training, and she mentions the local AMI training center. She then taught for more than thirty years, the last ten being in public school. I ask if she and the other Montessori teachers ever get together to talk about their classrooms or students.

"Not really," she answers, and then asks, "Why?"

As any training course is just the beginning of one's journey in the classroom, adopting an appetite for continuing to learn and grow is central to being a good Montessori teacher. Fortunately, teachers can always learn more by reading and rereading the written work that Dr. Montessori left behind. Without deifying Maria Montessori, as some have been accused of doing, teachers can respect her discoveries and attempt to implement her approach as closely as possible. Doing so increases teachers' comprehension of the working principles in action. Teachers who want to improve refer to Dr. Montessori's writing often.

What brings the approach to life is connecting it to the real experiences in the classroom. Teachers can reflect on their observations of their students and on the responses the children offer. Collaborating, discussing, and brainstorming with colleagues also deepens teachers' understanding and helps them to explore the approach together. A career in Montessori is a continual quest for deeper understanding, knowledge, and experience. Montessori teachers have to think, observe, try things, observe again, reflect, and communicate. This is what makes it such an exciting path!

Finding Dr. Montessori's Words Helpful: My Own Story

During my years at Forest Bluff School, my colleagues and I have found that every time we have had a problem with students, moving further into Montessori's approach, rather than away from it, is the answer. We discover solutions by studying Dr. Montessori's books, talking with each other, and trying exercises and approaches that Dr. Montessori described. Far from limiting teachers, the Montessori framework supports the adventure of discovery and reveals the territory for exploration and research. Successes occur because Montessori education points to human nature itself, not so much as a theory or a methodical practice but as a way to respond to the human spirit within each individual child. This is why I prefer calling Montessori an approach rather than a method;[7] Montessori is an *orientation* in how adults approach children and their self-formation. And when teachers embrace this orientation, they quickly discover that there is always more to learn about children, the ways they learn, and how they form their individual selves. Such work is exciting. Because every individual is unique and constantly evolving and developing their characters, the discoveries never end.

We've all got to keep in mind that internal liberty is at Montessori's very core. The educational approach is built upon the notion of freedom within the boundaries of nature. Dr. Montessori pointed out that nature itself has certain laws, such as gravity or the fact that particles move faster in response to heat. There are laws of nature in us as well, imbued with freedom for creativity. When very young children go through a sensitive period for order, they respond eagerly to being shown how to line up everyone's shoes in the morning, how to wipe up the last drop of spilled water, or how to bring each box to the very edge of its shelf throughout the room. They love to make everything look uniform and neat. The boundary, which is a natural law, is that sensitive period for seeking and creating order in the environment, and the freedom within it is the response to that urge and the ways it manifests differently in each individual child.

A common criticism of AMI-style Montessori is that people think it may be too rigid or its teachers too dogmatic. But if you really look carefully into Dr. Montessori's writing, you will find that the opposite is true: Dr. Montessori expresses humility and respect as she encourages teachers to observe children openly, watching the children's creative responses to life. What could be more creative than children forming themselves into unique individuals? I cannot find any places in Montessori's writings where dogmatic responses are recommended.

Every time I have retired at the end of a long day puzzling over what to do to help a certain student or another, one of Dr. Montessori's books, such as *The Discovery of the Child* or *The Absorbent Mind*, suggests some freeing way to reach that child. After reading I sigh with relief and then, with a newfound determination, head back to the classroom the next day—not feeling confined by the Montessori approach but liberated. Again, I attribute this to Dr. Montessori's focus on the ways that human beings naturally learn. The liberty of the approach is framed by a supporting structure: of prepared environments with a balance of freedoms and boundaries, delivered in a healthy manner by a prepared adult who serves as a model and a link to that learning environment.

I relate many of my own challenges in the classroom to those that others experience. This is a universal condition of working with human beings! Just as the previously mentioned public Montessori school teacher gave up as she found children less and less interested in the Elementary materials, I, too, have been tempted to give up on Montessori practices at times. When I was twenty-five years old and in my first year of teaching Primary at Forest Bluff, I had eight four-year-old boys who moved around my classroom like a windstorm, taking things off the shelf and laughing, ignoring me, and causing havoc. I had also six new three-year-olds, three of whom were interested in having power struggles with me every morning about whether they would wear their shoes or sit near me when asked to, and I had five super-bright five-year-olds who were disappointed that I had replaced their previous teacher. They wouldn't give me the time of day when I invited them to come work with me.

There were more children in the room, making a total of twenty-six, but those nineteen described above were the ones making me toss and turn every night. I tried to figure out what I could do to get them working and behaving. I considered some disciplinary approaches from a collection of books on my shelf. Some of these, I thought, made good points, but I wondered how to make them fit into the context of a Montessori classroom. There was no separate room to banish a child to in our school building, no other adult who could take a child away from the group, and no way to restrain or separate a child from the life of the classroom. So the remedies to misbehavior had to be found within the framework of Montessori.

I don't know what I would have done without the advice and encouragement of several other more experienced colleagues, who answered my many questions after school. These teachers patiently talked me through my options in a Montessori setting and reminded me to take the whole child into consideration. They guided me to keep looking for what might capture each child's interest to inspire concentration and that subsequent internal "settling" of personality in each child.

My other resources were Dr. Montessori's books and the albums I had written as part of my AMI training. When alone, I took comfort that Dr. Montessori seemed to have witnessed the difficulties teachers like me face in working with young children. In *The Absorbent Mind*, I found the following:

> A child has only to do something wrong or noisy; for example, throw himself on the floor, laughing and shouting, and many, or perhaps all the children will follow his example, or do something worse. This kind of "gregarious instinct" produces a collective disorder that is the opposite of social life, for the latter is founded on work and orderly behavior of individuals. In a crowd, the spirit of imitation spreads and enhances individual defects; it is the point of least resistance, where degeneration originates. The further this kind of degeneration goes, the harder it becomes for the children to obey a person calling them back to better things. But set them at once upon the right track, and an end soon comes to the manifold consequences of the single source of this disorder.[8]

This passage reminded me of the strong instinct in two-, three-, and four-year-olds to imitate others automatically. I realized then that their behavior was simply human nature playing out. Instead of getting upset, this passage reminded me to call on another instinct in young children: the desire to do good and to join others in community. Her words invited me to become the leader and do something about the situation.

But they also helped me to realize that such scenes will inevitably occur with little children. Teachers cannot expect perfection and dream up a fantasy of children always moving about the room respectfully and interacting peacefully. That can only be the *eventual* result of a lot of hard work and time. It is this acceptance of the reality of human nature that makes Montessori relevant to contemporary culture. Dr. Montessori continues on this theme by bringing in the teacher's role:

> When called on to direct a class of such children, the teacher may find herself in an agonizing situation if she is armed with

no other weapon than the basic idea of offering the children the means of development and of letting them express themselves freely. . . . The teacher must remember the powers which lie dormant in these very divinely pure and generous little souls. . . . She must call to them, wake them up, by her voice and thought.[9]

This advice helped me to think positively and remember that my interference and efforts must turn the children toward their better selves and inspire, rather than punish, them. These passages framed the situation and also my actions as a teacher. But one line further along gave me the courage I needed: "A vigorous and firm call is the only true act of kindness toward these little minds."[10]

This declaration made me realize I had to take charge and step in firmly. I had to act confidently and assuredly to get the children's attention and win their trust. I had to give them a leader to follow. And then, reading a bit further in this passage, I saw the freedom and creativity that the Montessori approach offered to me as a teacher:

The good doctor, like the good teacher, is a person. Neither of them are machines, merely prescribing drugs, or applying pedagogical methods. . . . It is for her to judge whether it is better for her to raise her voice amid the general hubbub, or to whisper to a few children, so that the others become curious to hear, and peace is restored again.[11]

Dr. Montessori then suggests different ways to appeal to children and help them to focus on their movements. Doing so settles them, engages them, and gets them thinking for themselves again. As I followed the advice of these passages and the suggestions from my colleagues, my little students gradually changed over the course of that year. The situation demanded my persistence and faith in the approach and in the children themselves, but it worked out!

This story reveals how teachers can use Dr. Montessori's writing to find a successful path for teaching with this unique approach. Rather than resorting to the nearest conventional method of putting children in time-out chairs or using other punishment-reward techniques that only temporarily—as research proves[12]—motivate good behavior, I was reminded by Dr. Montessori's writings of the successes possible when working with children from her positive approach.

Dr. Montessori used such words as *awaken* and *call* and referred to children's "little souls" and "spirits." Taken out of the context of her time and culture, these words can sound flowery and vague. But when working in harmony with human nature, educators cannot treat children like machines or subjects. Children, like their teachers, are full of potential and free will; if forced, they will never reach the spontaneous, chosen self-discipline that is possible. Such reminders of the purpose of this approach, interwoven into the more practical aspects of teaching, make Montessori work splendidly. Dr. Montessori inspires teachers with her writing in an important way; when I read her work, I was enveloped by a whole different mood, one that conveyed to my students that I believed they were capable and that we would succeed, together. This reoriented me as an educator to think creatively, proactively, and positively.

How to Spot a Well-Functioning Classroom

When Montessori is working well in a classroom, you will see the eight traits we have described exhibited by the students. You will also see some wonderful results in Montessori graduates. Knowing that variation exists across Montessomethings, AMS schools, and AMI schools, and being aware of their different strengths and descriptors, is key to understanding the Montessori landscape. But you may want a shortcut for how to get a feel for whether a Montessori classroom is functioning effectively in one visit. Here is a simplified way of checking for effectiveness. There are three qualities that a layperson can look for when they walk into a well-functioning Montessori classroom: respect, joy, and concentration.

Respect

First, ask yourself whether the interactions between the children, the adults, and the environment reveal sincere respect. Some signs of this are quiet voice levels, eye contact, careful movements, offered choices, taking turns to speak, and walking around—rather than across—children's

Young children develop self-mastery and independence by following inner tendencies: building the Pink Tower, caring for themselves in a prepared environment, and caring for items in the environment.
Top: John Dickson, middle: courtesy of Forest Bluff School, bottom: author's collection

The Solid Cylinders, the Pink Tower, and other Montessori Materials are arranged in an organized fashion on the Primary shelves. A bustling Elementary classroom shows children in action—joyfully engaged and focused, each with their own pursuits!

Top and bottom: author's collection

Montessori materials lead implicitly from one to another. Studying length differences with the Red Rods leads to work with the Number Rods, used for learning to count, compare, add, and subtract amounts 1 through 10.

Top: author's collection, bottom: John Dickson

Building the three-dimensional puzzle of the Trinomial Cube at age five is indirect preparation for exploring the algebraic equation and its interrelationships with labels for each component, explored here at age eleven.
Top: author's collection, bottom: courtesy of Forest Bluff School

Montessori students learn to help each other and work together. Here, a five-year-old boy helps a four-year-old classmate to read action commands; two Elementary children look up words from the Adjective grammar box command cards in a dictionary; two boys record their division process with Racks and Tubes material; two ten-year-olds find the square roots of very large numbers, record their process, and learn a way to guess their outcomes with the Peg Board.

Top: John Dickson, two middle: author's collection, bottom: courtesy of Forest Bluff School

Children in Montessori classrooms learn to independently direct their learning. Here, students confer with their teacher about the organization of their original illustrations and research chart on animal life; a seven-year-old gathers research; six-year-olds investigate botany samples from outside with the microscope, illustrating and recording their findings; a fourteen-year-old creates an artistic and factual chart about an aspect of US history.

All photos: courtesy of Forest Bluff School

Teachers in Montessori use lessons that continually build on lessons from earlier levels. An elementary teacher gives a group botany presentation on the parts of fruits. She dissects a real sample and writes the scientific names of each layer; after a presentation, children will do follow-up work. Below, students find and record answers for Division of a Fraction by a Fraction after their teacher gave them a presentation.

Top and bottom: author's collection

Montessori builds self-reliance and also community. An eighteen-month-old boy learns organization and focus by baking biscuits; two fourteen-year-old girls bake chicken pot pies from scratch to feed their classmates lunch.

Top and bottom: courtesy of Forest Bluff School

work rugs. The teachers bend down to the children's level and look them in the eye when speaking to them, and they have a certain grace to their movements, thereby extending courtesy to the children in a very natural and comfortable way. The teachers should be aware, kind, confident and gentle. These actions and qualities create an atmosphere that visitors will notice the minute they walk into the classroom.

Manners of grace and courtesy are important to maintaining good human relationships. Montessori teachers not only model cooperative manners for children but also demonstrate them in formal presentations. When addressing the younger children in such presentations, teachers move slowly, deliberately, quietly, and pleasantly so that children can really see and absorb the motions and manner. Such dramatization matches the characteristics and needs of little children and is therefore very effective. With older Elementary-aged children, Montessori teachers most often raise concerns about manners by dramatically acting out what *not* to do! This tongue-in-cheek humor appeals to the characteristics of Elementary children's reasoning minds and imaginations. The humor encourages older children to think about and discuss the reasons for manners and customs and, in doing so, to resolve their own shortcomings.

In one often-told example of a grace and courtesy lesson, Dr. Montessori saw that a very young child's nose was running, and she gave a slow, deliberate demonstration on how to blow one's nose with a handkerchief. The three-, four-, and five-year-old children gave her their rapt attention and broke into applause when she finished, and then eagerly began practicing by blowing their own noses. It occurred to her that the problem with young children's poor manners was not disobedience or intentional slovenliness but that no adults had taken the time to show them in a slow and visible manner that would appeal to their natures.

Montessori teachers learn to give grace and courtesy presentations on anything that needs attention: how to push in one's chair after standing up, how to roll up a rug or mat neatly, how to carry a material across the room, how to pass another person without bumping into them, how to walk around items on the floor without stepping on them, how to sit down smoothly, how to shake hands to greet someone, or how to wait for someone's attention. These actions all have to do with being mindful, aware of oneself and of others, and respectful of people, objects, and the environment.

Grace and courtesy can likewise be seen in the detailed movements of children's hands; when onlookers notice children pausing to pat the edges of their mats as they carefully roll them, and making each twist of their wrists deliberately and effectively, they know that some attentive teacher demonstrated this action slowly and perhaps in an exaggerated manner. Or maybe, the child saw this demonstrated by another child and learned the technique that way. Children may watch the same presentation, pick up on different points, and roll their rugs a little differently. But a general culture of care is visible in their mannerisms.

Montessori teachers demonstrate grace and courtesy lessons many times throughout every day, formally and informally. Such lessons may be described in their teaching albums from their training courses, but they can also be spontaneous and created by the teachers themselves, as living responses to the children's current needs. Teachers may invite the oldest children to demonstrate a grace and courtesy lesson for younger children, and children often do this on their own, without being asked. Children gradually internalize such manners and begin to exhibit them naturally.

When looking for respect in a classroom, you can very quickly pick up on the grace and courtesy that act as its outward manifestation. Are children moving about with awareness? Are they speaking in voices that do not disrupt children around them who are trying to concentrate? Are they refraining from interrupting each other's speaking or working? Are they placing things down carefully? Are the materials in good condition, revealing that children have been shown how to handle them with care? Are children helping one another—to put on an apron or tie a shoelace? Are they putting their work away when finished, and are their belongings hung up and put away neatly, instead of being strewn about on the floor? These are all signs that respect is a strong priority. Certainly, every class is in a stage of evolving; the teacher may have only begun with the children and might have much to cover before these signs manifest themselves. But within a few days of the teacher making grace and courtesy a priority, an observer should be able to see little signs here and there of children becoming more aware and responding to the atmosphere of care and respect that their teacher encourages. When you see signs of grace and courtesy everywhere in a classroom, then you know the teacher understands both the mechanics and the spirit of the Montessori approach.

Joy

Second, is there joy? True joy arises when children are developing inner freedom. Such freedom invites children to make choices, to follow inner drives to be active, and to pursue something they are curious about. Inner freedom is intertwined with developing self-discipline, such that a child can hold back from one impulse in order to choose another action. If the children are told what to do and are strictly controlled by an adult, they will not exhibit joy in their work. Likewise children will also not be joyful when allowed to do whatever they wish and indulge their every whim. Joy comes when one's mind and body are in sync, from having self-control and from independently carrying out self-directed actions in harmony with one's companions and environment.

You can tell when children are sincerely *joyful* and not just happy. Children can be happy because a friend gave them a piece of candy or because the baking exercise they love is available when they walk in the classroom. But a developed discipline for choosing one's actions and the joy that results cannot be handed from one person to another; these come from within and exist in harmony with that child's developmental needs. It is not uncommon to see a child skip unself-consciously across a Montessori classroom, suddenly hug himself with glee in the middle of an activity, or burst through the front door and down the hallway in a rush to get back to work after a vacation.

It may sound strange to hear that you can see this joy manifest in a Montessori classroom, but you can, if you have learned what true joy looks like in a community of children. And if this joy is absent, then you have a clue for what is lacking in that classroom. Perhaps the teacher is too controlling, dictating to the children what work they must do without giving guidelines or proposing suitable choices. On the other extreme, the teacher may not notice much of what's happening in the room, allowing the children to terrorize each other, abuse the materials, or do whatever they like. Looking for the children's contented joy is a way of finding whether teachers have a grasp on how to maintain the learning environment, enthusiasm for learning themselves, and the ability to support children in becoming internally independent.

Concentration

The final element you should see in a successful Montessori classroom is that almost every child is engaged in work with real concentration. I say "almost" because not every child will be at the same level of self-control; some children will most likely be in transition from one activity to another, on their way to something to concentrate on, lost in thought, or even just in the midst of an off day or moment. It's extremely rare that every child is concentrating in a room at the same time. But if more than four or five children are milling about, that's a sign that those children need more help from the teacher to engage in work. The teacher may not be contributing a major part of his or her role, which is to link the children to the environment.

When children are concentrating, they are not doing "busy work." Busy work is any activity that does not require engaged effort. The kind of concentration that we aim for in a Montessori environment is the kind that the late psychology professor Mihaly Csikszentmihalyi described as *flow*.[13] Flow is deep concentration that transforms us, that feels great and leaves us feeling refreshed. This concentration occurs when we become so involved in what we are doing that we may not be aware of things going on around us. Dr. Montessori found that children repeatedly go into this state of flow when their activity has a real purpose. The purpose may be visible, or it may be more internal and developmental.

For instance, a young child may be pouring water with great focus, back and forth slowly, from one pitcher to another. Her purpose is to perfect her own movements so that no water spills. She wants to find the way to do this, and to do it again and again. The child is so totally, internally focused on this activity that she may continue for ten minutes or longer without seeming to notice what else is going on in the room. The motions seem to fascinate her. She slows down and uses a sponge when there is a drop of water on the table. She looks intently at her hands and at the spout of the pitcher, learning how high to tip it, seeing the speed and trajectory of the water spilling forth from the spout. At the same time, the soothing sound of the water pouring in a steady stream guides her to monitor the speed with which she tips the pitcher. The child waits patiently for the last drop of water to fall off the point of the spout. She places the pitcher carefully down on the table. The details of how her movements affect this process are illuminated for her as she repeats, and repeats slowly, with her own momentum and determination. If the child is directed by an adult to do the activity, this deeper level of focus is not attained. Here instead, this girl is responding to her will to do the activity and to that inner guide that drives her to make her motions most effective.

The kind of concentration we are talking about here is specific. Children can *look like* they are concentrating, when they are actually just going through motions that someone has told them to repeat. Children might do this to pass the time, or to gain the attention of some adult who may praise or scold them. But their occupations do not resemble the deep concentration Montessori teachers are taught to recognize and to promote through their presentations. To accomplish an atmosphere of concentration, teachers must feel awe for the children's incredible development and the keys to the world this education reveals to their students. For instance, a teacher's appreciation for the Moveable Alphabet, which represents the human achievement of creating and using abstract symbols for the sounds of the human voice, translates readily into a child's engagement, focus, and curiosity as they pursue making words with it, with their teacher's enthusiastic support. If the children are concentrating by using Montessori materials in effective ways to extract their purposes, then we know that their teachers presented the materials with Dr. Montessori's recommended drama, awe, and intrigue.

When onlookers search for the respect, joy, and deep concentration that should exist in a Montessori classroom, they might also see the details that lead to these qualities: variety in the children's work during one's visit, three hours of uninterrupted time to work and learn every day, and a span of three ages grouped by the four planes of development. This grouping means that children are encouraged to work primarily as individuals if under age six and mainly in groups between ages six and twelve and beyond; such formats align with children's psychological characteristics. You will also see children engaging and focusing on their actions, an environment organized to encourage internal organization in the children, children responding to their curiosity—feeling courageous about making mistakes and collaborating to accomplish their goals—children being respectful to one another and the materials, and children being resourceful to collect what they need. The existence of such qualities serves as a guide for observers. My personal experience has been that authentically implemented Montessori, with these qualities of respect, joy, and concentration, provides the perfect conditions for children to develop those desirable eight traits.

Montessori's Compass for the Whole and All Its Parts

Understanding the issue of variation that predominates the Montessori landscape is important for those who wish to choose a school for their own child, become a Montessori teacher, start a school, or conduct research. Like any successful organization, each Montessori school must have a compass—a vision and clear principles and practices—to reach well-defined goals. In the case of education, the goal is to provide optimal conditions for children's natural development. The guiding compass in Montessori is the quest to find what works best for children and how they learn. My colleagues and I find that this goal points educators straight toward Dr. Montessori's profound discoveries.

We might ask ourselves: Is *a little* Montessori better or worse than *no* Montessori? Most people who see positive Montessori-like education environments will say that all efforts to become more Montessori-like should be encouraged. I agree, because what are widely known as best practices in education today, even in non-Montessori circles, resemble Montessori principles. Most Montessori-trained educators encourage the spread of Montessori-inspired teaching practices. I am in favor of this. However, my point is that the knowledge of authentic Montessori, and the major differences in the potential it can achieve, is worth aiming for. If people do not know or respect the differences between "a little Montessori" and the full implementation, the Montessori approach will never attract the close attention it warrants.

Furthermore the completeness of Montessori elucidates the approach's success. This only occurs when educators fit all the implementable parts into their schools to make a complete approach. Montessori teachers and their school leaders must ponder together, "What would be a *Montessori* way to handle this?" In this manner they must attend to the details in their schools, together. Teams of people thinking and working together can discover more than just one person can. And teachers need this support of communal focus. As explained in chapter 3, educators succeed by staying on track with what is best for their students, as it relates to age and characteristic. To do this, educators and school leaders cannot give in to one parent's personal desires or what's most convenient for themselves as adults over the needs of the children. Most important, educators need to flesh out the details of Montessori so that the approach comes to life.

Many Montessori educators may not be working in situations where they can control or decide the details of their school practices in optimal ways. In these cases, educators must start with what they *can* influence and keep working toward the children's best interests. If educators realize that children are capable of so much more when they have the best conditions for independent learning, teachers will be guided in the right direction. Because the true principles of Montessori match the nature of children's self-formation and the learning spirit that all children have, educators who aim for "best practices" will find their way to Montessori's approach. We have a compass: with authentic Montessori implementation, those eight traits that we have discussed visibly emerge in children.

The next chapter explores how public school educators are working through the challenges of implementing Montessori in perhaps the most difficult of situations: within government-mandated parameters and in the most rigidly conventional cultures in education today. When compromises must be made and external controls influence classroom procedures, how can educators inch toward the best practices for authentic Montessori? With major obstacles in the way, is it possible for teachers and administrators to pursue Montessori ideals? Are the results visible in the children? And is it worth the effort?

5

BENEFITING ALL: PUBLIC MONTESSORI SCHOOLS

Seeing a Contrast

On a morning visit to a Chicago public school that houses a small Montessori program, I walk down a hallway past a line of second graders, traveling as a class to use the bathroom. They abruptly halt as their teacher turns around, points, and shouts: "Hey! Keep your hands to yourself! Don't you look at me like that; get up here!" My heart quickens; I avert my eyes and hurry past. At the end of the hall, a sea of fifth graders comes stampeding up the stairs, yelling and pushing past each other roughly in jest.

I quickly stride over to the door of the Montessori classroom for three-to-six-year-olds and step inside. Immediately a world of quiet calm envelops me. The yellow walls are clear of the common clutter and overlapping posters. Natural light spills in from the windows. There are no piles of textbooks or scattered workbooks or worksheets on the tables. Instead, the colorful Montessori materials are displayed on low wooden shelves lining the walls, and children sit with their work at child-sized tables and beside small rugs spread out on the floor. The teacher smiles softly and speaks quietly to children as she walks slowly past them. One child is so at ease that she dances as she crosses the room to take out the Spindle Boxes, a material used for counting numbers. Another sits down at a small table and traces one Sandpaper Letter over and over with her tiny fingers, saying "*c*" to herself. The children exhibit the joy of independence and concentration. Their behavior demonstrates sincere respect among themselves and between them and their teacher. This is Montessori in a public school.

The contrast between the conventional school life in the hallway and the Montessori classroom is alarming to me. The students in this building are from the surrounding neighborhood, an area of boarded-up windows and potholed streets, with some of the highest gun violence in the city. And what is happening inside the school walls to help these children in their growth? If Montessori education is an aid to life, providing the way for children to develop traits for success and build themselves as people, then this neighborhood deserves the Montessori option like all neighborhoods do. The transformation that happens in children in a prepared environment—where adults link them to learning materials, inspire mutual respect with Montessori's grace and courtesy, and give freedoms with boundaries to help children become independent and responsible—is palpable here in this classroom. This points to the potential at the core of Montessori education.

In reading so far, you've learned what Montessori looks like in action, explored the framework that makes it work, and seen an example of how Montessori can be brought to life in a school. From the previous chapter, you now know that there are established ways to practice the authentic Montessori approach for the best results with children. The next logical question is whether Montessori education can be made available to all. In the public school world, where layers of bureaucracy and antiquated policies are the norm, does Montessori education have a place? Is it possible to make this model of education available to everyone, and will it work?

Evidence That It Works

The answer is yes. Quality Montessori can be, and successfully has been, made publicly available. Many public programs have shown that they can prepare Montessori learning environments for children with simplicity, humility, and focus, just as private schools aim to do. Can Montessori be made affordable? The website of the National Center for Montessori in the Public Sector (NCMPS) offers a sound timeline and recommendations for starting new public Montessori programs and mentions anticipated costs. It takes some initial funds to outfit classrooms with full sets of Montessori materials, appropriate furniture, and a trained teacher. But after the initial costs, public Montessori is an affordable and durable model. Districts save dollars per student in the long run because the educational format is consistently relevant over the years and does not need to add on social skills programs, or expensive technological equipment, subsequent textbook editions, or updated workbooks meant to address changing education fads. Once a district sets up a Montessori classroom with a trained teacher, then paper, pencils, and art supplies are the major annual expenditures. And of course all programs still need specialized help for children with greater learning, socioemotional, or physical needs.

The research collected from well-implemented public Montessori programs assures that children in public schools benefit from learning with this innovative approach. In a groundbreaking study released in October 2017, Angeline Lillard, at the University of Virginia's Department of Psychology, and her colleagues demonstrated that public AMI Montessori preschools in a high-poverty section of Hartford, Connecticut, elevated children's outcomes. The random lottery participants with recognizable differences in their performances showed that:

> Over time the Montessori children fared better on measures of academic achievement, social understanding, and mastery orientation, and they also reported relatively more liking of scholastic tasks. They scored higher on executive function when they were 4. . . . Montessori preschool also equalized outcomes among subgroups that typically have unequal outcomes. . . . This suggests that Montessori preschool has potential to elevate and equalize important outcomes. A larger study of public Montessori is warranted.[1]

This last point about equalizing outcomes is of great interest because it validates Dr. Montessori's suggestion that this educational approach helps all children to reach a higher potential. In fact, Montessori may particularly help level opportunity gaps, giving disadvantaged children a chance to get on equal academic footing with children from more privileged homes. This fact makes Montessori education a superior offering for public schools.[2] Other studies of public Montessori have been and are being conducted, but the results vary depending partly on whether the programs examined are practicing authentic Montessori, or are Montessori in name only. This again demonstrates why it is so important that people and researchers understand what to look for when seeking accurate study results or choosing where to conduct further research.

Why Montessori Fits in the Public Sector: The Universal Child

If she were here today, Maria Montessori would surely cheer the efforts of American educators who strive to make Montessori available in public schools. Dr. Montessori was known as a vocal advocate for underprivileged and marginalized people in her time. She regularly spoke in public forums for women's rights, for better treatment of the poor, for better infant hygiene, and for children to be respected. She reasoned that childhood was a special stage of human life, a time dedicated to creative processes of physical, spiritual, and mental formation, and that we must protect it tirelessly. Dr. Montessori proposed that doing so was the best way to improve the future for all societies. Even when her efforts were met with great resistance, Dr. Montessori persevered with courage. In extreme examples, when the regimes of Adolf Hitler and Benito Mussolini shut down Montessori schools, she was forced to begin again, everywhere she went.[3]

Dr. Montessori's educational approach is applicable to any setting because it is based on the observation that all children begin life with the same potential for growth. Although each human being has different genes, is afforded different resources, and grows up in a different home, certain shared qualities make us a species that can adjust ourselves to survive and even thrive. These universal gifts of nature—such as the absorbent mind and sensitive periods under age six—allow children to become a member of their immediate time, place and culture. As Dr. Montessori traveled and spent time observing and working with children around the world, she coined *universal child* to refer to this adaptability. Even in current times, Montessori educators witness and describe such potentiality in children.

Recognizing Universality

As I have not taught in public school settings myself, I share with you the experiences and insights of others who are deeply involved in Montessori public programs. Some of my favorite examples come from stories that two women, Anne Cox and Elizabeth Seebeck, shared with me. Cox and Seebeck volunteered for ten years at the previously described public Montessori program in Chicago. They had raised their own children and turned their energy into a dream of bringing Montessori education to children living in what the media might describe as a "distressed" neighborhood. Cox and Seebeck went to the public Montessori school almost every day—to support the teachers, to encourage students who might be having an "off" day, and to communicate with parents. They served the school as volunteers but were integral to the program's success. After they showed up consistently and without fail, the children, teachers, and parents came to view Cox and Seebeck as trusted friends and collaborators.

When I visited them in 2017, Cox and Seebeck were passionate about the idea that all children benefit from the Montessori approach. Cox told me, "Children are children everywhere, just like Maria Montessori said. My experience in the past ten years has been that no matter what they are dealing with, the home lives of the children do not dictate whether or not they can learn. And," she added, "*God knows* the color of a person's skin doesn't."

The children Cox watched over the years in the public school, whose population was predominantly Black, were intelligent and eager to learn, and as expected, they responded positively to the Montessori approach. When the program first started off, some children experiencing trauma at home exhibited challenging behaviors in the classroom. This tapered off as more and more of the children began to settle in and the older ones were eventually able to maintain the calm tone of the classrooms for the youngest children. Through the Montessori approach, the children gradually became more engaged with their work and began to focus and to respond to the organization in the environment by organizing themselves. They grew more curious about learning and courageous about trying new things, making mistakes, and learning from them. The children started to collaborate in their work and to show respect for their surroundings, other children, and their teachers. Over time the children became more resourceful in their schoolwork. As in any new classroom environment, these traits emerged slowly, but they eventually spread through each classroom community.

In my visits to this Chicago program, these traits were noticeable in moments such as this:

In a Primary classroom, I watch a four-year-old boy stand up during the class's group gathering and walk over to the shelf nearest to him. I wonder whether his wandering off might get him into trouble. His teacher continues to sing with the rest of the children sitting on the floor. I watch the boy take a haphazardly placed plastic apron off the shelf and kneel down on the floor. He rolls the plastic apron tightly and neatly, with slow rotations of his wrists, pinning the apron down with his fingers. Seemingly in his own world, with complete concentration, he carries out this spontaneous action and then carefully replaces the rolled apron on the shelf, where it will be ready for the next child to come choose that activity after group time. He returns to his place with the group. This boy is completely engaged and focused, showing respect for his environment and classmates with his self-directed tidying action.

This child is growing up in the same surroundings and attending the same school building every day as the conventionally taught children I had seen earlier in the hallway. I can't help but think of how he is developing self-composure, self-respect, and dignity in this Montessori classroom. All children have this potential and deserve the opportunity to engage with work, to focus, to organize themselves, and to follow their curiosity. They deserve to build courage, to learn to collaborate in their work, to feel the respect inspired by their teachers, and to build resourcefulness for whatever they may face outside the classroom walls.

The parents and teachers in this Montessori program tell me that besides their children having developed a love of learning and unparalleled academic knowledge, what they value most is the confidence their children are gaining from the Montessori approach. They consider the internal confidence to learn and to work with others to be the strong differentiating factor that make their children happier, more interested in the world around them, more eager to learn, and more ready to meet challenges in all areas of their lives. Their children are learning—in their words—"the Montessori way."

Public Programs: Never Put Your Drum Down

In some cities, public Montessori is well established and generally supported. But public Montessori programs everywhere, even the very best ones, face constant struggles. Montessori educators who are familiar with public programs unanimously shared this observation with me. In visits to more public Montessori programs in nearby Chicago, I found some of the most common hurdles in plain view:

A large Montessori magnet school serves 350 children of ages three to fourteen in the Chicago neighborhood called Bucktown. The young principal, who is in her second year there, welcomes me in. She is energetic and professional. She explains that two major struggles for her, besides all the usual challenges of running a school, are hiring enough qualified teachers for every one of her classrooms and obtaining funding for three- and four-year-old children, which is not covered by the district or state but necessary for a successful Montessori structure. This principal has to raise additional funds from private sources to fulfill this standard.

The school's charismatic former principal had spent nine years championing Montessori education throughout Chicago. Under his leadership, this public Montessori school became a solid institution with a vibrant community. After his departure in 2013, however, the school reportedly lost some of its Montessori character and strength under new leadership. The current principal tells me that she didn't know much about Montessori when she arrived a few years afterward, other than what she could learn on her own through reading and conversations with other educators. She wants to reinstall quality Montessori. She enrolled in a Montessori training course, but it has been hard to fit it into her busy work schedule. Her initial lack of Montessori knowledge frustrates her because she has difficulty holding teachers accountable or directing them to do things in a more "Montessori fashion." She finds that because many of her teachers have little Montessori training, such as brief online training, they are not on the same page about Montessori goals or how to reach them.

That same day, I visit a second magnet school in the heart of Chicago. I read about this school in the 1991 book *There Are No Children Here*, Alex Kotlowitz's story following the lives of two Black boys from 1987 to 1989 in the subsidized Henry Horner Homes. The school had a history of being run-down and disparaged. In 2006 it was turned into a Montessori magnet school serving children ages three to fourteen. Now, it is a popular choice for a diverse community of Chicago families in the surrounding area.

I find the current principal to be well versed in Montessori education. However, he also faces challenges. Trying to hire and retain teachers is his most urgent concern, but another challenge is getting his supervisors to allow his teachers to run their classrooms as Montessori programs. He tries to counter the district's requests for further standardized testing by sharing his own collected data reports of how well his students are performing.

Both principals mention the challenges of uniting a team of teachers who have differing information from their various training centers. Some of their teachers have AMS training, some have online training of some kind, two have AMI training, and others have no Montessori training at all. This last fact amazes me. I know from my own experiences that learning how to teach Montessori effectively requires the information, observation skills, and practice that training introduces. Having solid training and deepening one's understanding of the Montessori approach from original resources, as described in chapter 4, is imperative. After hearing about their varying levels of education and preparation, I wonder how many public school teachers are managing without the guidelines and support of the defined approach: the consistent curriculum to follow, individualized albums of how to present each lesson and their proper sequences, the described responses to look for in the children, and the necessary support of others with the same goals and similar practices. When I tour schools like these, the classrooms vary noticeably. Some have very few Montessori materials; others feature tidy, colorful shelves of Montessori materials. But in every room, regardless, only some children are concentrating or working with these materials, and the Montessori traits are inconsistent.

Despite this initial confusion, I see some encouraging signs that people are trying to make Montessori work in public school settings. From my own observations, these children are having a better educational experience than they might get from most conventional practices. I am also excited to hear that these school principals recognize positive outcomes in all their classrooms. The principal of the first school tells me that she noticed right away when she came to this program that "Montessori students are more inclusive, regardless of age; they help each other." She says, "I think it's because they're not competing with each other academically, so they can enjoy the task at hand and develop a joy of learning. Everyone's working on different things in a Montessori classroom. So they can focus on work independently and then share what they have learned with each other. This generates a collaborative spirit."

The principal of the second school tells me that he sees "kids being more human. They show their own personalities; these kids know who they are a lot sooner. It is huge to have choice, to have a sense of controlling one's own destiny from an early age. I see a love for learning, a joy. They are comfortable talking to adults, and they are not intimidated.

"One of the things I love about Montessori," he explains, "is that in conventional schooling, kids are taught, but about 70 percent of the time, they have to infer to make that final leap to understanding. Some kids just never get that, and so they fall short. But in Montessori, that never happens, because every child gets the concrete support right to the very end, when they can find the 'aha' for themselves. Montessori just makes sense. It gives children an intellectual identity that is just not comparative."

A few weeks after these visits, I meet with the CEO of the Office of Teaching and Learning for Chicago Public Schools and three of her colleagues at their headquarters on Madison Avenue. My goal is to discover what challenges they see for the Montessori programs. I want to understand why these programs are so undersupported. I also wonder why Chicago is so far behind several other cities with more authentic Montessori practices within their public schools. I do not ask these questions directly; I am grateful to have an audience at all and want to encourage Chicago to continue these Montessori public programs. The four city representatives tell me in the beginning of our conversation that their main concern is a lack of funding for such programs. I notice that although they value the Montessori programs, they seem unaware that the most imposing issue the Montessori principals spoke to me about is not primarily a financial one but rather the clash of the conventional school culture against Montessori's more in-depth approach to children's learning.

In hopes of inspiring these CPS leaders, I show some colorful photos of Chicago children working with the Montessori materials in their local public programs, and I share the positive things I notice. Wanting to encourage, I ask whether there is any way I could help or support these programs. The CEO asks, "As a Montessori educator, what do you think we need to do to ensure that these programs succeed?"

While I hadn't expected this question, I jump at the chance to speak on this. I list the first seven actions I've learned matter most:

1. **Start with children three years old or younger**; early childhood is the beginning of a learning cycle that cannot be replicated at later ages.

2. Have Montessori's designated **three-year age span** in each room with the same children and teacher so that older children mentor the younger ones. Younger students receive indirect preparation for their own learning by exposure to the materials the older classmates are working on (and older classmates additionally benefit).

3. Establish continuity for the original population of students, so that **children who have experienced the foundation of Montessori at the younger ages can progress from one Montessori classroom to subsequent ones**; teachers can then support each child in their progression through the connected curriculum.

This third point is so often ignored that I pause to demonstrate its value by showing a sequence of photographs of a boy working with the Trinomial Cube.[4] I explain that if a child of age five or six learns how to build the Trinomial Cube in the Primary Level classroom but does not get a Montessori Elementary teacher who is trained to present that material, then he cannot discover the algebraic formula with it in his elementary years and the sequence is lost. Then the Trinomial Cube remains just a physical puzzle of colorful blocks and doesn't hold the incredible power for this child to discover the algebra for which it was designed. Subsequently, if this child comes to the Upper Elementary classroom for nine-to-twelve-year-old children and has a teacher who is not trained to show him how to take it to the next level of algebra, which is to apply the decimal system to the material and eventually cube three digit numbers with the Hierarchical Cube, the student misses what comes next. Both student and teacher need to experience the Montessori base of each level to move on to the next, if they are to reach the potential the curriculum offers. This is a potential available to *all* students, and Chicago public school children deserve access to this learning progression with the complete Montessori curriculum.[5]

I continue my list:

4. Maintain an **uninterrupted work period** of three hours every morning. This is imperative if children are to develop concentration and have time to work with the materials and receive lessons.

5. Employ **Montessori-trained teachers**, support them to get the most complete training they can, and give them chances to keep learning more.

6. Designate a **spokesperson to lead the community of principals and school leaders** and get them together regularly to discuss challenges and learn more about Montessori. This leader pulls everyone together so that the public school district leaders can work with the Montessori programs as a unified group.

7. Work with Montessori-trained coaches from organizations such as Public Montessori in Action or the National Center for Montessori in the Public Sector (NCMPS). A well-trained coach can guide and support teachers and administrators with

Montessori-specific situations. These individuals help schools establish **Montessori standards to aim for and ways to assess and improve public programs** with information that pertains specifically to public Montessori.[6]

Only the fifth and seventh of these suggestions require financial commitments; the first four are pedagogical, having to do with fundamental Montessori guidelines.

Two years after the above conversation, some of these suggestions were put into place. But the progress for the programs is slow, and awareness of their struggles remains far from the eyes of parents and the surrounding communities. Several Chicago public Montessori programs have suffered major setbacks, such as losing trained teachers and battling school leaders who are not aware of Montessori's potential. One program I describe here is under threat of closing. I sincerely hope that as more state and local policy makers, public-education professionals, and citizens become aware of Montessori's benefits and understand how it works, they will actively support these programs for Chicago's children.

Starting Off in the United States: A Brief History of Public Montessori

Montessori public programs have existed in the United States for a long time. The first school was established in 1913 by Katherine Moore in Los Angeles just after Dr. Montessori lectured there. Others followed, although the numbers have fluctuated with openings and closures. Public programs bloomed in the 1960s and again in the 1980s. The most recent growth of public Montessori programs is notable in that more than half the public programs that exist today started up in the last two decades. Currently, more than 550 public Montessori schools educate children in the United States. It is the largest alternative to conventional schooling in the public sector. Consisting of magnet, charter, and regular district programs, some Montessori programs encompass entire school buildings, while others are embedded inside conventional public schools. Public Montessori continues to be on the rise, aided by the success of these programs, positive anecdotes from parents and students, and the emerging research that shows positive results for Montessori education.[7] Public Montessori programs have grown in several cities in a variety of ways. Some began as parent-led movements and others by Montessori-trained educators spreading the word. Some have focused on making a social impact in communities, and others have made authentic practices their top priority. Still others have worked on building the sustainability of Montessori programs in the public sector.

Many cities, such as Cincinnati, Milwaukee, Minneapolis–Saint Paul, Hartford, and Washington, DC, have positive stories to tell. Public Montessori programs have taken hold in the United States, and they are making a difference. However, the challenges these programs face in the public sector continually threaten to degrade their quality. Understanding these challenges is the first step to solving them.

Challenges and Solutions in Public Schools

The three most common challenges for public Montessori programs stem from the need for educators, parents, and legislators to understand Montessori's unique paradigm. But even once the paradigm has been made clear, these three areas must continually be addressed in public schools:

1. The need to change standardized testing practices that do not align with Montessori's approach.
2. The necessity for well-trained Montessori teachers.
3. The need for clear, informed leadership to maintain Montessori within public schools.

Before public school communities muster the determination to resolve these three main challenges, they must be given a clear understanding of what Montessori is and what it can do for children.

Explaining and Implementing a Different Paradigm

One can easily get lost in many details of why public schools may struggle to implement authentic Montessori. But the central argument is that Montessori's approach is the polar opposite of the conventional model our public schools are based on. This requires a paradigm shift in our thinking. As reviewed in this book's introduction, the fundamentals of public school in the United States were designed roughly 150 years ago during the Industrial Revolution to educate the masses. Children needed to be moved efficiently from room to room, and subjects were divided and delivered by lectures and textbooks and memorized by the children. The "product" in the end was presumably an educated child—meaning, one who has knowledge. The standard way to determine whether this result was achieved was to test the children to see if they could reproduce the exact information delivered to them. The conventional approach arguably does not demand total engagement, focus, organization, curiosity, courage, collaboration, respect, or resourcefulness. Nor does it encourage children to progressively develop these traits.

Because Montessori education helps children develop ways to acquire information through their own active investigations, it empowers children to learn for themselves. The emphasis is therefore on providing a rich intellectual environment, rather than on teachers feeding units of information in lockstep. In the Montessori format, the children are the learners, the world is their source of endless information, and the teacher is a guide to aid the process. An atmosphere of curiosity, intellectual pursuit, perseverance, and joy results. When the approach supports children as self-forming beings, human energy is freed up, rather than controlled or contorted, by the school system.

Thus, providing a Montessori model within public schools begins with explaining the very different approach to the appropriate stakeholders. Principals, teachers, policy makers, school boards, and parents need information on what Montessori is and how it works before they can embrace the approach and implement it effectively.[8] In public districts with some flexibility, Montessori programs are better able to follow independent pedagogical guidelines and succeed. This pays off in the long run: unlike other teaching methods that come and go—such as Whole Language briefly replacing Phonics for reading, the New Math of the Common Core Curriculum in 2009 replacing carrying/exchanging numbers in categories, or a new textbook or computer program replacing another—the Montessori approach remains relevant no matter the time or place. The approach does not go in or out of fashion, since it is based on child development. Montessori also works when implemented as a whole, with the full curriculum and philosophical approach intact and interactive. It is designed to be eventually applied across an entire school, from the earliest grades and into adolescence. Conflicts between the Montessori approach and conventional schooling play out in the three main areas mentioned: testing formats, teacher preparedness, and informed leadership. In each of these three areas, I will suggest remedies that lead to success.

Testing That Doesn't Work: Finding a Better Way for Students

Most educators agree that excessive required testing can disrupt children's learning. Even so, American public schools are drowning in a test-driven culture. And though we see Montessori students succeeding in life skills, executive function, social interactions, intellectual understanding, and eagerness to learn (abilities that conventional tests do not typically reflect), the children in most Montessori public schools are still required to take time out of their schedules to fill out standardized tests. On average, they outscore their districts, but the tests keep coming back to interrupt their learning time.[9] And sometimes Montessori students do not impress with their scores,[10] particularly if their Montessori program is being held back from reaching its potential. Problematically, poor test results can become the determining factor for whether any public program survives. Test scores drive the funding, and the funding decides which programs get closed or further restricted. Teachers and administrators know their jobs, and their programs depend on getting good scores on conventional tests. This cycle repeats, pulling Montessori programs away from their unique strengths, year after year.

The tests themselves are part of the problem. Quite simply, conventional standardized tests are designed for completely different metrics than those of Montessori and presented in a foreign format for Montessori students. Conventional tests are designed for a narrow curriculum that rewards memorizing abstract information and reproducing it. The Montessori curriculum, conversely, is developmentally based and interest driven, and it follows different orders for topics introduced, different timing for mastery, and different vocabulary.

As an example, Montessori students may develop high levels of understanding of mathematical processes from working with the materials. But understanding processes is not what current conventional standard tests tease out. Instead, standardized tests request answers to equations in formats that may differ from how Montessori children are taught. Although Montessori students begin working with mathematical processes years before students in conventional schools, they only learn to write these processes and their results down after much experience with mathematics; this may occur even a year or two after they have begun working with a particular mathematical process. Five-year-olds may learn to multiply four-digit numbers with their friends and teacher with the Golden Bead material, but they might not write the process down on paper in a traditional format until they've had a great deal of practice with this and several other materials. These exercises are learned with concrete materials, using fun learning games that involve several children and require a lot of movement, such as carrying trays of golden beads, bead bars, squares, and cubes across the room from the shelf supply to their rugs and back again when exchanging between the categories. Subsequently, cards with numerical representation are included in the exercises, which the children match with the corresponding concrete amounts. After much experience with these physically accompanied processes of mathematics, children begin to understand the process as represented by the numerals, which is more abstract. Through a series of exercises with these and other materials that represent the parts of the process with increasing abstraction, each child begins to comprehend, and then record, the numerals in their categories on paper. This may take many months or even a couple years, but the benefit is that when children do write the math on paper, they understand the process fully and are able to articulate it and use it for solving real-life problems.

Students also learn on individually differing timetables, depending on their specific interests and developing abilities. To summarize, with the AMI Montessori curriculum, children learn addition, subtraction, multiplication, and division with four-digit numbers when they are in preschool, but they compute with numbers of four or more digits using only paper and pencil when they are closer to fourth or fifth grade. For most children, that is when their independent knowledge of math is more secure and they have the maturity to demonstrate their knowledge through the abstract format of formal tests. This point can *only* be reached, however, if the children and their teachers were not interrupted or restricted from fully practicing authentic Montessori, from the age of three onward.

Montessori educators are conflicted when trying to implement Montessori thoroughly while required to test children conventionally to mimic a conventional teaching style. With pressure to perform on conventional tests, schools risk turning public school teachers away from their Montessori curriculum and manner of teaching in order to "teach to the test." When principals know this is undesirable, they may advocate for the integrity of Montessori implementation in the classrooms. But when administrators do not really understand the reasons behind the Montessori approach and do not have the impetus to promote its value, their lack of support can inadvertently demolish the programs altogether.

One public school principal tells me that she knows the conventional tests are not showing all that the Montessori students in her school know. She feels it's unfair to test them in a completely different format, but these tests are the standardized assessment her district requires. She knows that Montessori students learn concepts and information through their own experiences with the learning materials and each in their own unique way. Their expressions are therefore individual and do not always fit into a box designed for repeated memorization. This principal understands that as the students mature to their later elementary years, they develop ways to define and explain what is in their minds quite impressively. But acquiring this ability is a point of arrival, so the children cannot always translate what they are learning when tested every year. The problem is not particular to Montessori; *any* alternate educational program requires the flexibility to follow their own design within the public school system—otherwise, the program cannot be an "alternative" to the conventional model. Although she can articulate this issue clearly, this principal feels helpless to do much about it in her current public district. The tests keep coming.

Some Montessori educators argue that such testing does not belong in a Montessori environment at all because it clashes completely with the philosophy. Testing alters teachers' and children's goals and inter-actions. In a testing environment, for instance, students are set up to compete with one another. Competition often imprints fear into chil-dren's behavior with one another and with the teacher. It distracts chil-dren from developing their most positive characteristics, which is exactly why authentic Montessori programs are not designed to test children as conventional programs do.

Evaluative measures more suited to the Montessori curriculum and style do exist, however, and these could address the long-standing issue of testing in public schools. Certainly, teasing out what students know allows them to demonstrate their interest and depth of knowledge. Luck-ily, Montessori teachers do have ways of identifying children's compre-hension. All throughout their work together, Montessori teachers actively assess the children's progress. They primarily do so by observing the children when working. Montessori teachers learn in their training what signs to look for to determine a child's comprehension. They listen to what children say and watch what children do and how they behave. Rather than stop the flow of work cycles to formally administer tests, Montessori teachers assess and record children's progress several times a day in natural ways, even as they interact. Assessment happens, infor-mally and formally, when the teacher momentarily investigates a child's readiness for the next level of a lesson.

While abilities such as thinking on a deeper level and mak-ing connections between subjects are not clearly revealed by written multiple-choice tests, Montessori students *do* expose their abilities in conversation-style inquiry. *Every* presentation from a trained Montes-sori teacher begins with observation in the case of younger children and with some conversational eliciting of information in the case of older children. In the Elementary Level, for example, the teacher begins a presentation by asking a few questions such as, "Remember the other day when we talked about gravity? What do you remember about that?"

Having listened to the children's responses, the teacher may follow up: "Remember how . . . ?"

After assessing how much each child comprehended and retained, the teacher introduces the new presentation with something like, "Well, today we're going to see what happens when . . ." and the new lesson begins.

The students experience this direct and subtle checking in as normal parts of conversations. They learn to verbalize what they know, and they eagerly share their thoughts and insights in a natural way. This is arguably more like the real world, the way that adults in the workplace interact, help one another, and collaborate. Educators and parents need to be shown the futility of interrupting this valuable learning time by sitting the students down and making them fill in multiple-choice questions and write verbatim answers, especially when it can be replaced by more real-world formats of demonstrating one's knowledge. Typically, the students themselves show the benefits of this approach when conversing naturally with adults outside school. Montessori parents often witness their children's insatiable quests for more information and see their desire to pursue knowledge outside school for pure enjoyment. Montessori's "testing style" actually fuels learning, rather than pitting children against one another in competition for grades, demoralizing them with scores, or training them with preselected topics for study.

When Montessori students are required to take standardized tests, their scores also may not reflect their comprehension for another, more internal reason. If teachers have not learned in their training how to help children to express their comprehension, they may not be covering this important final step. Certain AMI Montessori teacher trainers have told me that bringing children to the point of verbalizing what they are doing is a very important last step in working with the Montessori approach. This must be done delicately, in a manner that matches the characteristics of each age and individual. This last step is called the *third period* in Montessori's Three Period Lesson, a three-step process of, first, revealing or discovering information, second, practicing with it, and finally, expressing one's understanding.

It is not enough, these AMI trainers say, to just show an elementary-aged child a Montessori presentation and then observe that they understand how to work with the material correctly. With children over the age of six, the teacher should at some point tease out what the children understand verbally and help them to find the words to describe their experience. For example when a child has worked on long division with a material called the Racks and Tubes, the teacher should—when appropriate, as in their weekly one-on-one meeting—help him or her talk about the basic steps and give the process the name *division*.

For example, students might clarify in their own words: "We subtracted the amount we used, which is here in these beads on the board, and over here we wrote this same amount on paper as a subtraction equation." Students get accustomed to saying the large numbers they are working with as well: "So our equation was seven hundred forty-six thousand, eight hundred twenty-four divided by six hundred twelve, which equaled one thousand, two hundred twenty with a remainder of one hundred eighty-four."

It is impressive to witness what children as young as six or seven years old learn in quality Montessori classrooms, but if they cannot eventually articulate what they are doing, their abilities may not be recognized. Pausing to support this articulation is the trained Montessori teacher's final step. Crucially, this process and its timing cannot be forced; children are willing and even eager to joyfully and generously share what they know with one another and with adults when not forced, graded, judged, or manipulated. In other words, Montessori teachers learn not to reward, praise, or punish to motivate children. They don't find a need to. Instead, they learn ways through their training to support children's natural drive to acquire knowledge and to develop skills. In fact, allowing children to choose when they want to challenge themselves with tests would be the most Montessori-like approach to the timing of test taking. Even better, the children—with their teachers' help—could create their own ways of checking their knowledge and demonstrating it for whomever needs the proof that they are learning.

To find ways to live with the current testing culture in public schools, some Montessori programs have reached compromises by asking their district leaders to collect test scores less often, so that children can be tested at the end of third and sixth grades rather than, say, every six weeks. Because the Montessori curriculum is covered over time in three-year cycles of a child's growth instead of in multiweek units, it makes sense to hold off testing what students have learned until they have completed one of these three-year cycles. These are the most logical testing points in a Montessori program. District leaders may agree to this when the test scores at such determined intervals are satisfactory.

In the meantime some principals, teachers, and public school leaders have become familiar enough with the Montessori curriculum to identify what is covered and to reconcile it with the conventional test content. Educators must realize that although the exercises have different names, everything that's necessary to cover is there in the AMI Montessori curriculum—with very few exceptions that are easily remedied. Elementary AMI teacher trainers direct trainees to find these correlations in an effort to help them prepare for public school settings before they graduate. Currently, the NCMPS and AMI websites list correlations between the Montessori curriculum and standard conventional ones, though Montessori teachers still need to address some individual differences at state levels.

Standardized test taking really gets at the roots of the dysfunction that exists in conventional schooling. By using other appropriate ways to demonstrate Montessori programs' efficacy, not only will Montessori educators be able to work within the high standards of their Montessori curriculum freely, but they could also lead conversations of how to improve conventional schooling practices. When and if our nation moves away from an across-the-board standardized testing culture, Montessori is poised to flourish in the public sector.

A Need for Montessori-Trained Teachers Who Continue their Learning

Another component that determines a public Montessori program's success is having thoroughly trained Montessori teachers. It takes time, funding, and effort to become fully trained.[11] And yet, as you learned in previous chapters, training is vital to a teacher's ability to implement the Montessori approach effectively.

The public sector requires that teachers have state certification. Teachers are then left to complete Montessori training in addition to this certification, often with little support or encouragement. Because so few teachers have the time or means to acquire both state certification and Montessori accreditation, many public programs can only hire state-certified teachers who have little knowledge of Montessori. Fortunately, some states supplement selected Montessori teacher graduate programs by granting trainees their state certification upon graduation.[12] This recognition started when AMI and AMS partnered in 2010 to form the Montessori Public Policy Initiative (MPPI), which still drives such progress today. As a result Montessori-trained teachers can more easily work in public schools in several states. MPPI diligently works to spread the availability of this option to more states and succeeds in doing so every year. A master's in education is also granted by some colleges and universities as an extension of certain Montessori-teacher training courses. Another validation some Montessori training centers have acquired comes from the US Department of Education, through the Montessori Accreditation Council for Teacher Education (MACTE). Once teachers have sound Montessori training, they have the foundational toolbox they need to teach throughout their careers in both private and public schools.

To implement Montessori education effectively within the public school system, principals and teachers must continually seek out steady sources of information, guidance from experienced Montessori consultants, and opportunities to further their own education about Montessori's approach and implementation. Montessori training courses, conferences, and subsequent refresher courses are available for public school teachers and principals, provided they are given district funding and the time to attend. Such experiences benefit students directly. Every teacher needs a toolbox of resources to pull from when facing challenges in the classroom. Building one's toolbox is paramount, and it's a process that never ends for teachers in any setting. Montessori is an approach that fosters lifelong interest in learning and, as such, encourages adults to keep growing alongside their students. Engaging, focusing, and organizing are actions that teachers help children learn in part through emulation. When adults are curious, courageous, collaborative, respectful, and resourceful, they enable children to develop these qualities too.

The Montessori Teacher's Difference: Conflict Resolution and Self-Regulation

With their unique orientation, Montessori teachers are able to approach problems with students differently, and this is particularly notable in public school settings, where conventional classroom settings may restrict teacher's options. At one city school, I see Montessori teachers speak often with their students individually and as groups about ways to stay calm when they feel strong emotions. These conversations fall naturally into the grace and courtesy lessons that are integral to the Montessori approach. Children learn from watching each other, and because there is a three-year age span in each classroom, younger children always have older role models to observe, while older children get the pride and practice of demonstrating for and helping others. Program directors, teachers, and assistants help this child community to change how they handle conflicts.

Despite the challenges children and their parents might experience at home or elsewhere, they learn peaceful and supportive ways of interacting and working in Montessori classrooms. Parents are grateful when they see the differences in their children, and they experience the benefits of changed behavior at home. With the emphasis on caring for one another in Montessori classrooms, children don't give up easily on one another, because their natural empathy is encouraged and put into practice. In this way, public programs can become more than a school. They are communities that evolve as the children grow.

When discussing children's more challenging behavior in classrooms, volunteer Anne Cox cautions, "The children were difficult at first, believe me. In the early days, if a boy fell off his chair, the whole class would burst out laughing. Our Montessori teacher, Ta Promlee-Benz, was so upset by this. The children saw how sad she was when they were mean to each other. Ta talked with the class every day, and when a child was hurt, she taught children to say, 'Are you OK? Can I help you?'"

Cox says that Promlee-Benz got them to say it out loud, and it became a script. Because Promlee-Benz was so earnest and the children respected her, they imitated her.

Having an available phrase relieves the children from a default reaction of laughing and poking fun when someone is hurt; now they have an alternative. This is the grace and courtesy lesson that these children needed in moments of confusion. This approach presumes that children can develop their self-regulation and compassion. The teacher engages the children, demonstrates how to show respect and curiosity, and invites them to exercise their skills of resourcefulness.

Program volunteer Elizabeth Seebeck tells me, "Another thing in the early days was that the rules of the street sometimes came into the classroom. A kind of war would break out every time someone bumped someone else, whether intentional or by mistake." When the adults stopped the children and tried to talk to them about it, it became clear that the children's response was not a matter of pride but of perceived survival. According to Seebeck, "We told the children, 'Everyone has to feel safe in order to work here. We're all safe in here. When you're in this classroom, you don't have to push back.'" The children were able to understand and accept alternative choices of what to do when pushed in this environment.

The Montessori-trained teachers also asked the students questions about how to resolve the conflict to get them thinking, and then invited them to share their ideas for solutions. This way, students were invited to engage in the process and become more resourceful.

When facing serious, more threatening behaviors, Montessori public schools must create or use systems that teachers can implement easily, just as in any conventional school program. Procedures need to be spelled out, agreed on, and supported in practice. Teachers and school staff best serve children when they have a united plan of action to follow for the more extreme difficulties that may arise.

When specialists and non-Montessori-trained professionals enter Montessori classrooms to help with conflict resolution or with any greater needs students may have, these adults benefit from some orientation to Montessori's educational approach ahead of time. It is critical that they respect the children and their Montessori ways of working. Orienting specialists beforehand helps everyone forge communicative relationships. Montessori teachers learn valuable insights from other professionals, and vice versa. A good leader recognizes the importance of introducing teachers and specialists to each other in order to foster their relationships and explain the Montessori approach. Doing so goes a long way in ensuring like-mindedness for success in the classrooms.

Most Montessori teacher trainers spend time in their courses discussing situations that may arise for trainees who will be teaching in public schools. Understanding other school professionals' roles and how to work with them are elements of preparation that most Montessori trainers recognize. Also important is the time trainers spend talking about working with children with greater needs, children from households with various levels of income, children for whom English is not their first language, and children of differing abilities, religions, cultures, and ethnicities. These factors are important in any inclusive school setting.

Montessori Teachers and Students: Getting Ready to Learn

Montessori teachers use the classroom structure to reach each child in the community. A significant benefit of Montessori's approach is the flexibility it gives teachers to do this. I will elaborate by giving an example of how Montessori's structure lends itself to meeting individual social and emotional needs. One of the most challenging times of a school day for children can be the entrance, which is a transition of getting ready to learn.

AMI-trained Elementary teacher Ta Promlee-Benz explains that she begins every morning in her public Montessori classroom by observing when and where any one child is ready to engage with work. When the children first come in to start the day, they may be dealing with some strain from outside of school; they may be totally shut down or, as Promlee-Benz says, "not available to learn." In a conventional classroom, the teacher's timetable would force her to start a lesson that might pressure an unready child to learn a particular lesson. Doing so would increase that child's discomfort, making the teacher's efforts counterproductive.

"But in Montessori," Promlee-Benz says, "I can give a child some space to start working on something the child chooses. There is always something productive to do in a Montessori classroom, always choices. There are also many interesting things to watch other children working on. Children learn to settle themselves so that they are ready to learn."

When Promlee-Benz observes the signals that a child is open to learning, she invites him or her to join a lesson one-on-one or includes them in a small group to work. "If I couldn't do this, I would have to fight all day long to get some children to be ready at the time and place they were supposed to be. I wouldn't be able to work *with* them."

A Montessori teacher's observation skills and flexibility allows him or her to find when each child is ready to learn. When approached sensitively in this timely manner, children find that engaging with work can be a remedy for their discomfort. Work of some kind typically settles them and satisfies them. Montessori children come to look forward to that feeling of engagement and begin to seek out interactions with their teacher and the materials. This repeated experience fosters an eagerness to learn.

Promlee-Benz also finds that the flexibility of the Montessori classroom allows time for each child's comprehension to blossom; children have time to think, to observe, and to reflect. They are not required to waste time shuffling between rooms or switching between teachers for each subject; they do not suffer institutional interruptions of their thought flow or concentration. Promlee-Benz concludes, "In Montessori, we are tuned in to each child. This helps with misbehavior and also with comprehension."

Such qualities make Montessori an attractive model for public school teachers.

Challenges Principals Face: Becoming Strong Montessori Leaders

There are several challenges that are unique to public Montessori school principals. To begin with, most public school principals and school leaders lack the information they need to lead Montessori programs effectively. Without clearly defined, appropriate Montessori standards, principals, parents, educators, and supervisors at public schools sometimes do not even recognize that their own programs are not reaching Montessori's potential. If they are aware, they often do not know why the programs are falling short or how to remedy the situation. For example, many principals are assigned to Montessori programs without knowing ahead of time that conventional testing does not align with Montessori's format. They are also rarely informed of the range of Montessori training for teachers. With pressure to collect tests and to put state-certified teachers in their classrooms, public school principals usually don't have time to check teacher credentials in the "Montessori category."

In addition principals have many other responsibilities and limitations that relate to the Montessori programs' success. They have to juggle schedules for all the classrooms that fit the lunch, recess, and "specials" requirements of their public school district. Carving out a three-hour uninterrupted block for classrooms can be a tremendous struggle and, in some individual cases, impossible. Finally, many principals have to raise funds to enroll children under the age of five because not all states give public funding for educating very young children. Montessori programs are designed to begin with children aged three or even younger, which can be a very big challenge to fund. When five-year-old children enter the Montessori programs without having had the previous years of early learning experiences designed to match their first developmental period, the classroom lacks the basic characteristics that make Montessori so effective.

Principals who see benefits from the Montessori approach often work hard to solve these issues of testing, training, scheduling, and funding. After all their efforts, however, there is often little time left over to see to the details of implementation in the classrooms. And the difference between so-so Montessori and quality Montessori for the children lies, quite simply, in the details. With numerous distractions, the lack of attention to the details of implementation holds some public programs back from becoming the authentic Montessori environments that can produce impressive results.

Another challenge to public Montessori school principals occurs when district leadership changes hands. A knowledgeable superintendent might protect a Montessori program from testing pressures and allow principals to schedule three-hour work periods and to group students by three-year age spans. But this person might be abruptly replaced by a new superintendent who comes in and tells the program leaders to change things to fit the conventional model. They may not understand Montessori or respect it.

Changes in leadership happen frequently in public schools, and this can adversely affect the Montessori programs. When a new leader charges ahead with an agenda that does not align with the testing exceptions, teacher training, scheduling particulars, or funding specifics of Montessori programs, any well-established and successful Montessori school, even one with hundreds of students from ages three to fourteen, can go downhill within just a few years.

The answer is to keep explaining and advocating for Montessori at all levels, constantly and comprehensively. Everyone in the school system has to take part: teachers need to understand and believe in what they're doing, principals need to understand and believe in what the teachers are doing, superintendents have to understand and believe in the Montessori approach, and the district board members must be supportive as well. If one of these links in the chain fails, the others can carry the program forward for a brief time. But if more than one of these links breaks in close succession, trouble is inevitable. Continuity within a school system is especially important for children, who might spend as many as eight years of their education in one public school. Because the Montessori model is built for continuity, it can be a sound answer to many of the problems in conventional public schooling. However, the characteristic continuity must be protected and maintained by the school leaders.

Strong leadership, good communication skills, and fundamental Montessori knowledge make for a good public Montessori principal. Currently, the conflux of leadership skills *and* Montessori knowledge in one person is rare. A principal with no Montessori background, however, can still understand what standards are necessary and support them.[13] To be effective, a principal who is not well versed in Montessori must partner with a Montessori-trained person on staff whose role is to explain the approach and support the teachers in its implementation. This Montessori-trained person becomes the source for a clear narrative and specific anecdotes that the principal can access to advocate for their program to the superintendent and to the district leaders. Both aspects are necessary for programs to succeed.

District directors can help school principals by protecting the flexibility of Montessori classrooms and by holding the programs to measurable Montessori standards. District leaders and school boards must advocate for supportive policies and the funding, both public and private, for three- and four-year-olds to enter public school, for teachers to get full Montessori training, and for high-fidelity implementation in the classrooms. Principals can create schedules that allow teachers and students to eat in their own classrooms together more regularly, reduce how many times students have to move between rooms for classes, and eliminate announcements and other interruptions during work cycles. These changes allow for the daily three-hour uninterrupted work period that is so essential to the growth of self-control and fuller concentration for the children. Such involvement from leadership gives students the chance to follow their individual, intellectual interests with joy and to develop their study and work habits—capabilities that will extend beyond their school years.

Integrating Children with Greater Needs

One of the most common challenges for any public school setting is integrating children with greater needs into the classrooms. The principal must support teachers to work with all their students. Conventional classroom teachers must have resources for children suffering from trauma, lacking prosocial skills, or with major differences in their cognitive, emotional, mental, or physical abilities; likewise, Montessori teachers must have resources that support every child. Montessori settings, because they are more flexible and designed to meet individuals' needs, are a good option for public schools, if they have the specialists that each child needs. Without necessary assistance for children with greater needs, Montessori classrooms could be disrupted in ways that affect all the children, while leaving some without the extra attention they deserve. School principals need to keep an eye out for these situations and bring in specially trained experts to help.

The inspiration of Dr. Montessori's educational approach originated from her early work with children with greater psychological and physical needs.[14] Thus the insights and guidelines in her writing are often applicable to students with exceptionalities. Work has been conducted to bring both Dr. Montessori's and Mario Montessori's insights regarding children with greater needs together with current research, and more of this work is underway.[15] Maria's and Mario's guidelines are helpful, but public school teachers also need the latest information on how to respond most effectively to children with greater needs and how to help them in classroom communities. This is the way to successfully build classroom communities that work together. When it comes to children who learn differently, many teachers have demonstrated that Montessori's format and culture make it possible to integrate children of different abilities and needs effectively. As long as public Montessori teachers get the same support as those in conventional classrooms, the flexibility for individual differences within the Montessori framework may lead to even more successful outcomes for children.[16]

Finding a Way

So what can anyone do at the grassroots level to bring the Montessori approach into local schools? Parents have made an impressive influence on public schools to provide quality Montessori programs. If one wants to spread Montessori education, they can first share what they know about this option with other parents and explain what it can do for their children. This is best done by listening, observing, and seeking to understand what any community of parents wants for their children before recommending Montessori. Most parents, of any background, are intrigued when they hear about the traits that Montessori helps children build in themselves: those of engagement, focus, organization, curiosity, courage, collaboration, respect, and resourcefulness. Because these traits prepare individuals to explore and acquire knowledge and to work together to solve problems more creatively, we know that children in all settings need them. And the most important component in the Montessori spirit is to prioritize *children's* needs.

Advocating and Making It Happen

I have three suggestions to pass along from people I have met who have implemented Montessori in the public sector.

- First, talk to public school boards at the district level to incorporate Montessori in public education. Familiarity with the approach helps—if board members are parents or grandparents of Montessori children or have been Montessori children themselves, they may already be enthusiastic about Montessori as an educational approach. In districts where this is not the case, invite board members to come see successful Montessori programs or host a viewing of images or videos of children working in these settings. Many observers become enthusiastic supporters once they have seen a Montessori classroom in action with their own eyes. Every relationship counts; every connection can make a difference. Constantly nurturing relationships and committing long term to keep it up gives public Montessori traction.
- Second, find a Montessori-trained educator who can guide schools with their implementation standards and strategies. This could be an organization or an individual coach who is willing to nurture and support the area schools. They must have a history of positive experiences from inside the classroom and the ability to clearly communicate the Montessori approach in practical detail.
- Finally, establish and support local Montessori teacher training centers. A big step to maintaining Montessori public programs is to feed the public school system a steady supply of Montessori-trained teachers. As mentioned, keeping fully trained teachers in the classrooms can make or break quality Montessori in the public sector. For the children, these efforts pay off. Those who witness how students really do develop important life traits will tell you that their public Montessori program makes a difference. In quality public programs, the results can be astounding.

Transforming Lives: Parents Speak Up

Parents want the Montessori alternative in the public schools. Existing programs have long waiting lists because families hear by word of mouth that those in the programs notice positive results in their children. And as public Montessori supporter and volunteer, Elizabeth Seebeck tells me, "I have never seen a parent who doesn't care deeply about their children. Parents at the public Montessori school where I volunteer come to every school event they can. They want to know how their children are doing in school, and they want to be involved."

Parents take note when their children seem more excited to go to school, work through their social struggles more quickly, want to be kind to others, feel confident and proud, seem more interested in reading, and want to talk about what they're learning.

At one public Montessori program, parents expressed very passionately what they saw happening. Anne Cox tells me,

> One father is this very stern man and he never says much, but at a parent engagement night—which can be filled with tear-jerking testimonials—he speaks up. Finally, it gets around to this father, and we all wonder what he's going to say. He gruffly says, "I don't know *what* you are doing in there. But whatever it is, keep *doing* it. My kid had no light in his eye before he came here. You put the light in my son's eye."
>
> One uncle came in to a parent night. This nephew of his could be a bit brazen, but I told him when he walked in, "I just love your nephew," and he looks at me sideways, like I must be joking. But after Jarel gives him this presentation of his Montessori math materials—Jarel is very proud of his work and explains the whole thing, does a beautiful job—the uncle comes up to me and says, "I can't believe he's doing this." He is astonished and really moved by what he has seen. Many parents tell us they wish they'd had school like this, wish they'd been able to learn in a Montessori school. Their memories of school, in general, are not happy ones. So there's a trust issue. But they see the difference in what their children are experiencing right away.

Seebeck adds, "The parents here see that Montessori is a different way, a better way, to learn. They see their children love to learn here, that they are not afraid of school; they are happy and thriving in ways their parents never had a chance to."

Cox adds, "We can see that the parents find support here too. A mother just told us, 'I feel now like my kids are OK, because of this school. I can go ahead and get a job now. I can go back to work.'"

I ask one mother, whose daughter attended a public Montessori program from a young age until age twelve, what difference she thinks Montessori made for her. She tells me that in high school, her daughter continues to show traits she developed as a Montessori student:

> She questions things; she's always trying to find out what the real facts are. I think that's so important in today's world. Montessori set the foundation for her learning. It gave her critical thinking skills. She thinks of new strategies for learning. Also it's in her mannerisms: she's more eager to learn, she's always on the honor roll, she focuses more, she's more interested in learning new ways to approach her work. I think with Montessori she got the *whole* of education, not just depending on what the teacher tells you but learning to trust your own ability to research your interests and to ask "Why?"

She concludes, "I don't want my kids to just believe anything they hear."

This mother knows the importance of respect for oneself and for the truth and of developing the curiosity, courage, and resourcefulness to seek it out. This really shows in the children themselves; Montessori public school students in this public program tell me, "In Montessori, I feel good about myself."

The Takeaway on Public Montessori

It's important not to dismiss these stories as just lovely anecdotes from a few inspired people and a receptive community. It's true that some of the positive things happening in Montessori public programs may also be achieved in non-Montessori communities. But the difference with Montessori is that from the core of this educational approach, its academic and cultural lessons—the embrace of math, language, science, art, and all subjects as necessary to making our lives better, and helping the flow and harmony of life in the cosmos—inspire profound respect and gratitude for humanity and the natural world. This core encourages positive responses in children to learn and grow. The lessons emphasize the beauty and balance in the natural world, positive human contributions, the ways we have overcome challenges throughout history, and the ways that humans and nature have worked together. In Montessori environments, children and their teachers create communities where people respect themselves and each other because of the style within the academic lessons.

The design and presentation of Montessori lessons ignite a self-corrective ability inherent in human nature. Children therefore are released from external control, and the development of their self-control is engaged. This is exactly how children become agents of their own learning who are comfortable in their abilities, striving to improve, and free from fear. They do this with the materials that are designed to allow individuals to build their knowledge without viewing mistakes as humiliating and without being constantly corrected by others. They become courageous, and with courage, children are able to fully exhibit kindness and generosity to others around them. The best of their natures emerge, and they have the energy to learn how to treat each other in ways that feel best.

Children weave through the Montessori curriculum guided by their interests and by a teacher who has the flexibility to meet each child's different learning style and abilities. They acquire academic knowledge but in a fully integrated way, where the curriculum relates to all aspects of their life experiences and vice versa. As awareness of the benefits of Montessori education grows, public programs will progress more swiftly and with guidance, their implementation can become more accurate, authentic, and effective over time.

After a visit to a public Montessori school where parents told me how their children were benefiting from the Montessori approach, I wrote these notes in my evening journal:

> Clearly, a sincere attitude of respect—the hallmark of the Montessori approach—fosters relationships and builds community. It is not just the academics that these public school families

appreciate, although they can clearly see that their children are learning so much and are constantly curious and excited to learn more. What is pervasive and struck me as I made the long journey home through the city's traffic and rain is this: When Dr. Montessori said this is 'an education for life' and 'an education for peace,' she meant that the dignity, grace, and courtesy that these children and their parents are able to cultivate in a Montessori environment change their lives. The teachers show them what it feels like to be respected for who they are and how to be respectful to one another and to themselves. Change is happening through the education of the children—the very place Dr. Montessori pointed to as the epicenter for societal transformation.

While I was working on this book in 2019, two amazing women who actively promoted public Montessori, Jacqueline Cossentino of NCMPS and Chicago volunteer Elizabeth Seebeck, both tragically died of cancer. I dedicate this chapter to them, with hopes that Jackie's work and Elizabeth's stories will inspire readers to bring this liberating form of education to more public school children.

In the next chapter I will discuss the primary place where every parent can participate in Montessori's approach for their children: at home. When parents adopt the paradigm that children actually form themselves, parents are eager to prepare their homes for their children to get the most out of the Montessori approach. The ultimate goal of supporting children to become engaged, focused, organized, curious, courageous, collaborative, respectful, and resourceful is not limited to what happens inside schools but extends outside them, into the wider world.

6

IN THE HEART OF THINGS: EMBRACING THE APPROACH

Bringing It Home

After learning so much about the positive effects of Montessori education in schools, you may be eager to know how to bring the principles home to family life. Naturally, children's abilities to engage, focus, and organize and to be curious, courageous, collaborative, respectful, and resourceful develop through many experiences not limited to their time in school. Thankfully, the Montessori approach offers guidelines that can be transferred easily to home life to benefit families. Parents can embrace the paradigm that children form themselves within the four planes of changing characteristics and needs, then prepare the home environment, model behaviors, and provide choices and boundaries to foster responsible independence. Anyone—even people whose children do not attend a Montessori school—can raise their children with Montessori values and see many positive effects.

For some parents this may require that they adjust their thinking; Dr. Montessori saw that parents, like educators, tend to underestimate children's potential to learn independently through exploration and action.[1] But once this is pointed out, most readily agree that the Montessori mind-set and approach reinforces children's independence at home and fosters those eight important traits for life. Children often respond by showing at home the respect, joy in learning, and concentrated interest that their Montessori classrooms encourage. Although school and home environments differ in their roles, the two complement each other. And when children can meet their developmental needs through the Montessori approach in school *and* at home, they realize their fullest potential.[2]

Raising children in a Montessori-inspired fashion can be as simple as removing some temptations while providing others. In one example, a Montessori family in the Midwest avoids cell phones, tablets, screen entertainment, and video games for their children at home—as some high-profile Silicon Valley families apparently do.[3] The children in this particular family watch an occasional movie, making that a special treat. On this day, their mother Karey is about to cave in and let her eleven-year-old son, Sam, watch a movie after three days of being home with a cold.

When Karey returns from work late that morning, she opens the door to her son's room and gasps: there's Sam in his pajamas, holding a plastic golf ball in his hand and standing over an eight-foot-long contraption made from hundreds of wooden Kapla blocks.

"Mom! Look at this!"

Sam places the ball carefully at the opening of a tunnel, and it rumbles through the contraption, gradually descending with multiple changes of direction. The ball finally rumbles out at the opening and hits little pencil stubs standing like bowling ball pins. This display of simple engineering and architecture was completely devised by Karey's preadolescent son.

"Very cool!" his mother exclaims and smiles broadly.

She closes the door gently as she backs out. Karey leans against the doorframe for a moment and thinks, *Wow, all that creativity probably wouldn't have happened if he'd had entertainment to watch.* By considering some Montessori fundamentals such as preparing the environment and giving choices and boundaries, Sam's parents set the stage for such ingenuity to percolate and come to fruition. When there was nothing to entertain him but books, ordinary objects around the house, and his own creativity, Sam had to be resourceful. He engaged in building with the blocks and focused for a time, and he acted on his curiosity to see what he could make happen with the blocks, ball, and pencil stubs. He organized his thoughts and actions to build a structure that would balance and move the ball forward. His application of the Montessori paradigm was unconscious, just as his mother did not intend for him to build something while he was convalescing. She did not instruct him or even give him ideas. But she did, as a parent, play an instrumental part in what Sam chose to do: she decided to leave her son with books, blocks, and other nonelectronic means of self-entertainment at home that morning while he was resting; she had prepared the environment with the means, the time, and the freedoms and boundaries that supported the emergence of such an activity. In such a simple way, a parent can foster creativity and all the eight traits we have been talking about by providing the conditions that allow children to make decisions about what to do with available tools in their immediate surroundings. It's a way of saying, "I believe in you. You can think and do for yourself." And parents can do this with a lightheartedness that says, "Have fun in life!"

A Montessori View for Parents: The Paradigm

The Montessori approach helps parents learn to get out of their children's way, where appropriate, by allowing children to have direct relationships with their surroundings without needing adults every step of the way.[4] In the past two decades, numerous books and articles by psychologists practically beg parents to let their children develop independence. It isn't always easy for parents to let their children act for themselves, without directing them, controlling or interfering with the process, or commenting on their performance. After all, this may have been the role that adults in many parents' own lives played when they were children themselves, and so it feels familiar to do the same. The result may be children who are not so eager to collaborate with the adults in their lives.

But even more troubling, children who are at the age when they should be able to make their own sandwiches, clean their clothes, and make their own decisions are impeded. Instead of being shown how to do these things and given reasonable responsibilities, children are routinely encouraged (and sometimes pressured) to spend hours playing a sport, to do more homework, or to find entertainment with technology. In other words, while most parents are providing physical care, doing the decision-making, holding down a job and caring for the household, the children are not involved or included. Such customary parental behaviors often stem from a generous desire to relieve children from the burden of responsible work, to make them happy, and to ensure their success in a competitive world. But in these cases, important life skills fall by the wayside, and with them the self-reliance and those eight traits that lead to realistic competence in all areas of young adulthood. Many wise parents recognize this fact once they are shown some practical ways to remedy the situation.

Dr. Montessori proposed that the answer is to begin with very young children who are just forming the foundations of their personalities. She recognized that human beings have inner guides that propel them in their growth and urged adults to work with, instead of against, these inner guides to promote children's healthy development. When parents truly accept that children form *themselves*, and are not formed by others, they begin to recognize the numerous, subtle ways that conventional culture often promotes the misconception that *adults* are forming the children. This paradigm shift is important because parents' thoughts about their children unconsciously manifest in expressions, decisions, and actions. It is liberating when parents realize they can raise their children as they choose, with conviction even as others do differently. They can embrace an approach that honors natural human development.

As a parent myself, I recall an example where the Montessori approach guided my parenting response when our son was just starting to walk. When he was a very active thirteen-month-old, our son, Stanley, would lunge across our driveway at full speed, legs scissoring, his little shoes slapping the pavement. Naturally, we worried that he would fall and hurt himself whenever he did this. But instead of swooping him up, restraining him, or grabbing one of his arms to steer him, we searched for a way to help him be safe without interfering with his need to move.

We knew from Montessori that he needed to find the limits of gravity and strengthen himself, with his joy and energy propelling him. We wanted to respect his focus for learning to walk on a hard surface and allow him to engage in it.

To solve this problem, we helped our little boy dress in anything that had a hood, like a sweatshirt or raincoat before going outside. One of us bent over and held the hood in one hand, careful not to pull on it or interfere with his motion in any way. Stanley rose to his feet and began his crusade. When he started to fall, we didn't provide resistance unless it seemed at the last minute that he was about to smack his face on the pavement. We let Stanley tip and right himself, or land on his palms, again and again, only catching him when he might hit the ground dangerously hard. Eventually, he didn't tip at all.

There is an art to this kind of steering and collaboration, and it takes parents' time and attentiveness. But my husband and I also had fun helping our child enjoy his own powers. Marveling at little Stanley's courage and his abilities, we could lose our worries about the world and just be with him. He found his own way, and more than physically benefiting from this practice with his gross motor skills, Stanley came to accept our help as collaborators. My husband and I saw this process as a great training ground for the dynamic that was healthiest for us as a family. As parents we were there to help if something really harmful might happen, but we didn't unnecessarily block Stanley's free movement and self-driven discovery of his wonderful world.

It might be hard for some adults to collaborate with their young children's physical explorations as the previous example suggests. For my husband and I it felt intuitive. But I do relate with parents having to adjust their approach to raise their children with Montessori's paradigm; it was not so easy for me when our son was a teenager and our "not interfering" had to manifest in a more abstract way, such as mental exploration and choices. My husband and I knew from pondering Montessori's orientation that it was still important that we stay out of our son's way as he learned certain things for himself.

One cold morning, when I was in the midst of working on this book, sixteen-year-old Stanley jumped in the car to get a ride to the train station at 5:30 AM (This is when I went to yoga, and Stanley liked to get the early train to his Montessori-inspired high school in downtown Evanston and work on his computer at a nearby coffee shop). Right away, I couldn't help myself. I began listing all the ways I thought he could have been better prepared:

"Stanley! It's twenty-seven degrees outside and you don't have a coat or a hat. You're going to get sick!"

Grunted response.

"Are you actually going to work or just 'surf' on your computer?"

Strained silence . . .

I kept going: "It bothers me that you hang out with the same two friends all the time; you need to . . ." And on I went, all the way to the station.

The next day, Stanley rode his bike the three miles to the station—in the snow—before I awakened. That's how strong the need to be one's own person is, especially for adolescents. I blew it!

I later apologized for my morning car lecture. I told Stanley, "I'm trying to let you be, but sometimes I just can't help it! I guess I don't want to see you make the same mistakes I did at your age. At least make different ones."

Stanley grinned at me and said, "I know, Mom, but I need to make mistakes for myself, OK? I'm fine. Stop worrying."

I knew, I knew. This was the way we had raised him! But it was still hard. I told myself, *What is the worst that's going to happen? He gets sick, he feels cold, he finds that he doesn't have as many friends, or he gets a worse grade or doesn't learn as much in school as he could have. But then he will self-correct and change his course.* I wanted our son to pay attention to the feedback his surrounding world would give him, not rely on me. I knew this, as hard as it was to act in sync with this realization. It isn't easy to trust that children can learn for themselves.

When parents embrace the paradigm that children actively form themselves, they are no longer the center of their children's worlds. Just as Dr. Montessori proposed that the teacher should not stand in the front of the classroom and be the central source of knowledge for the students, parents also have a slightly different role to fulfill, that of trusted consultants rather than constant controllers. This authoritative (vs. authoritarian) style of parenting is more effective in the long run. It is not easy for everyone to make this shift in their interactions with their children, so for most of us this is a gradual process of trying and trying yet again.

However, do not mistake this to mean that the children are in charge of the adults! Maria Montessori was very clear that children must respect the authority of adults, and parents are a child's first experience of this dynamic. Parenting with confidence and being firm when necessary gives children security and demonstrates how they, too, will need to set limits and boundaries for themselves someday. The point here is that when children are treated with respect as developing beings, they more easily find their place in the family with dignity and confidence as contributing members.

An encouraging observation is that parents who bring the Montessori approach to their families succeed more than they fail. Montessori educators can provide a wonderful resource and can give parents very specific advice to use at home. When they begin this approach with infants and very young children, parents can start out as they intend to continue, adjusting along the way to match their children's developmental abilities as they mature. This sets a course for children to become more engaged, focused, organized, curious, courageous, collaborative, respectful, and resourceful at home. Parents can allow their children to engage with the world around them, to focus and organize themselves, and to become more resourceful; they can provide a supportive environment, model behaviors, and give freedoms that expand as children get older. A parent's job is to watch out for the most harmful dangers, knowing that children develop good balance and a healthy respect for what might hurt them by experiencing the smaller mishaps and learning from those. The result is that children build their own repertoires of experiences—and learn how to avoid truly harmful situations of their own accord. Looking at this logic through a Montessori lens, there's power in allowing children to develop realistic relationships with the world around them, with its very real freedoms and limits.

Three Pillars of Montessori in the Home

I encourage parents to think about the three pillars I use to explain Montessori's framework. The three pillars show us where to channel our parenting energy, and they can apply to children anywhere. As you'll recall, these three pillars are the prepared environment, the prepared adult, and freedom with boundaries. Beyond loving and caring for their children, the first important thing parents can do is arrange their home environments to support their children's budding independence.

Pillar I: Prepare the Home Environment

First, parents must pause and consider how their home environment is set up. Parents can ask themselves: Can my children find the necessary utensils for making their own sandwiches? Have I shown them how and helped them to do it? Are the ingredients within their reach? Is the spreading knife the right kind and size for their age? Is there ample time in our schedule for the children to make their own sandwiches? Have I shown them how to clean up afterward, and are my expectations simple enough that they can accomplish this? In addition to these considerations, for these changes to work parents must let go of their own perfectionist standards and instead learn to say, "You did it! Thank you!" when children accomplish these tasks to their abilities.

Dr. Montessori pointed out that children have different needs than adults do. Children's bodies are different sizes, and they have different abilities at each age. These realities have to be considered and respected. Parents need to adjust adult environments to make them suitable for children, but in doing so, adults mustn't remove every challenging aspect of a child's experience. Instead, we have to search for the right amount of challenge for each child's abilities and, in a Goldilocks fashion, find the one that fits just right.

Once parents begin on this path, they can be encouraged by seeing their children delight with increasing independence. The next step is to revisit how the home environment is set up and make adjustments every few months, knowing that children will grow and change both physically and psychologically. Most often this means that children need a new challenge to match their growing abilities because they master those they have already practiced over and over. At other times an adjustment might be called for when children are going through a tough time, need more support, or show they cannot handle as much freedom or the usual expectations. On a day a child is sick or hasn't slept well, for instance, a parent might help prepare his or her lunch, even though this is something the child normally does independently. For all ages, the routine and schedule that parents plan for their family is an essential part of setting up the home environment. Nap times; mealtimes; times to rest and reflect, read and study, exercise and be in nature; and other daily routines are also necessary and vital parts of every child's and young adolescent's informative surroundings.

Whenever something at home isn't going well with children, instead of punishing them or getting upset, a Montessori parent's first response can be "Is there something I can change *in the environment* that might fix this problem by supporting my children's current needs better?" Then, while the children are at school that day or asleep in the evening, this parent may get the chance to move a few things around in the kitchen to make them more accessible (or less, depending on what is needed). They might exchange some smaller items for larger ones or set up a new food preparation activity that is more engaging than what was available before.

Supplying child-sized items and spaces for smaller children to join home life—from the first years of their lives—gives children the message that they are respected as participating members of the family who are building their independence and who can contribute to the group. In the kitchen, for instance, a low child-sized table and chair, a low cabinet of items that children can use to help prepare food, and a set of their own child-sized plates, cups, and utensils can be life changing for the whole family. Making sure a sturdy step stool is accessible and that child-safe items can be reached gives small children respect and reasonable autonomy.[5] Everything about this preparation invites each child to engage in caring for themselves, the family, and their home.

For children from one to five years of age, it is especially important that objects be appropriate sizes and down at the proper eye level.

A Montessori Toddler or Primary classroom might have sinks, toilets, and even refrigerators that are down at toddler height so that students can use these appliances easily and as independently as possible. The tables are low, and the chairs are built precisely for children's body dimensions. The trays, plates, mops, brooms, and even the sponges are all tiny, to fit small hands and short arms. Montessori educators even make certain that the lip of each tray is compatible with little fingers, that handles turn easily, and that objects have the weight and shape that facilitate ease and early success. Parents cannot always make such detailed adjustments to their own homes, but they can still carve out some deliberate opportunities for their children to succeed in meaningful ways.

For children between ages six and twelve, parents do not need to provide such small items or separate their things into accessible spots. Elementary-aged children typically want to sit on adult-sized furniture and, as their hands and bodies grow, use adult-sized cookware. What they need now are new challenges, such as learning how to turn on electrical appliances and use them safely, how to follow recipes in cookbooks, and how to care for their own things, including their own laundry.

For adolescents, the home environment should be even more adult-like, and responsibilities should extend beyond the home and into the larger community. For instance, adolescents can grocery shop for the family and take on small tasks that their parents normally do. It is just as important in this stage of life that adolescents engage in the life of the family with actions that require some organizing and focus. As they practice courage and resourcefulness in many such situations, they gain a deserved respect. Their involvement becomes gradually more adultlike and appropriately challenging.

At Forest Bluff we encourage parents to focus on the child's bedroom and the kitchen first, with the bathroom and entryways next. After this, parents can set up smaller spaces throughout the house. For instance, they might place a low shelf or a basket with a few toys in the corner of the living room or common room for a young child. Slight adjustments may be enough for children to meet their own needs and be successful in their homes. The house does not need to be transformed completely, in other words, into a child's house! But it should be clear that children are also important persons who are active alongside the adults.

Pillar II: The Parent as Link and Model

The next step is to model for—rather than dictate to—children. Parents are the models for manners and decision-making in each family. Young children, in particular, watch their parents and internalize what they see them do. If their parent carries a plate with two hands instead of one, young children are more likely to imitate and carry a plate in that manner (and they'll be less likely to drop it, and will be therefore more independent). Such a desired result gives parents reasons to model best behaviors even when it is not convenient, because it pays off in the long run. Parents can also make a point to say "please" and "thank you" cheerfully, treating their young children the way they would like them to treat others. This is a deliberate demonstration of respect, which children internalize. If such behavior is consistently modeled, very young children tend to copy the adults around them because they are in an absorbent phase of their development. They do not do these things just because adults tell them to; they do them because they see them done by the adults they love.

By the time children are older, between the ages of six and twelve, some basic coordination and judgments are established. Children these ages want to—and are capable enough to—carry multiple things at once. In this stage children watch their parents not as much to learn how to move and act but more to learn how others *think*. Six-to-twelve-year-olds watch how adults think things through and see how they manage their emotions. They notice what their parents think of other people, of lying, of being truthful, and of other conduct. This is the time for telling stories of heroes, discussing myths, and modeling reflection and empathy more overtly. Parents need to give children at these ages more independence to think on their own and to work through their social interactions with their immediate peers.[6]

When they begin adolescence around age twelve, children look for how their parents manage living in the adult world with its adultlike themes and challenges. Parents then become models for how to plan a trip and drive a car; decide how much alcohol, if any, to drink; pay taxes, the rent, or a mortgage; and form and express political views. These are things parents are always modeling, whether they mean to or want to. Adolescents need support to try out positive and realistic adult experiences such as apprenticing, starting a first job, balancing a bank account, and interacting with adults outside the family. For example, they can make phone calls and inquire when band practice starts, compare plane ticket prices, schedule their own doctor or dentist appointments, or order takeout food. Collaborating and conversing with adults gives adolescents a few years of training wheels so that they can gradually increase their independence and resourcefulness toward adulthood.

Besides modeling, parents also serve their children of all ages by actively linking them to the finer points of life that they don't want their children to miss. When Montessori teachers actively link children to those finer points in the classroom, they do so by drawing children's attention to a certain detail of an activity. They whisper, they point, and they demonstrate a keen curiosity in a particular object or action. This draws children into deeper engagement with their surroundings. Like a servant to the spirit, rather than a tour guide, parents also link their children to their favorite aspects of living, like teaching their children to pray, to stop and inhale the sumptuous scent of the cookies pulled from the oven, to tilt their heads back to look in awe at the night sky, or to feel snowflakes on their cheeks. These are times of laughing together, passing the tissues during a movie's sad scene, or sighing after reading a beautiful poem. Many moments are also opportunities to show strength, resilience, or courage in the face of challenges, such as when parents pull themselves together after receiving upsetting news, help a stranger with their grocery cart in a parking lot, carry something heavy with effort, brave bad weather on a nature walk, or give and receive hugs. When parents do such things transparently and without having to think about them, they provide valuable gifts for their children.

In today's world of technological distractions, many of these moments can and will be lost if children have screens constantly drawing them away from their immediate surroundings. As a Montessori educator, I cannot stress enough how important it is to keep screens and technology out of the way during the precious years of childhood while children are forming themselves. No one yet knows the full impact of screen devices and their use on children's normal development, but the research that has come out so far does not encourage increased screen time.[7] This is important to keep in mind for everyone who cares about fostering independence, self-regulation, and high social and intellectual aptitude in young adults. Because common technology is now so easy to use, there is no reason to think that it needs to be introduced to children so that they will understand how to use it later. For the time being, screen time is too much of an obstacle to children's healthy development for me to recommend it here. Linking children to the real environment and to experiences that ground human beings and connect us to each other are premier priorities for parents.

Pillar III: Providing Choices and Boundaries in the World

The Montessori approach to balancing freedom and responsibility—or synonymously, choices with boundaries—gives guidance and substance to parents' decisions. When parents understand that independence evolves in a gradual spiral of increasing freedoms and adjusting limits, then giving choices and framing situations with boundaries for their children makes sense. Rather than offer a dogmatic list of dos and don'ts, the Montessori approach gives just the right amount of scaffolding with broad ideas, flexibility, and room for parents' and children's personalities. The approach is realistic, timely, and always relevant. It does not go in or out of fashion. This balance is based in human nature and allows for individuality, which is why it works so well for families.

In any situation, a parent can think about the freedoms by asking: Does my child get time and space each day to follow their own interests? What choices am I giving my child? Are they age appropriate? Am I giving just two or three choices, instead of an overwhelming, infinite number? Am I open to considering an appropriate, acceptable option my child proposes?

Parents also can consider the boundaries that the environment provides naturally or that adults hold in place. They may reflect: Do the boundaries support my child to make good choices? Are the limits clear and consistent? Does my child respectfully take no for an answer when I have to say no? Or are these boundaries so confining that my child has no freedom to make a choice now and then?

Some boundaries are fixed: children must get sleep at night, eat nourishing food, and use a seat belt when in the car. Children, like adults, must follow civic laws and respect nature's laws, societal limitations, and parents' personalized limits. Learning to do so is a vital part of social life and character development. By balancing appropriate freedoms and boundaries, parents help their children of all ages feel respected, collaborate, and engage in the world around them. Peaceful family relationships result from this structure.

Even so, parents do not need to follow every single suggestion a Montessori educator offers for their home lives in order to experience success. There is a range of specifics that the Montessori approach envelopes, and every family is unique. At Forest Bluff School some parents are more restrictive at home than the school might advise or, by contrast, allow their children much more freedom than we suggest. Sometimes children act differently at home but are able to adjust to classroom expectations when in school. It is most helpful, however, when the expectations and provisions at home and at school are compatible. They do not have to match perfectly, but the more similar they are, the easier it is for the child to transition between the two environments with the least stress. Parents who treat their children with respect and collaboration that mirror their classroom experiences reap the most benefits from this school choice. Montessori is an approach toward life that creates continuity for children's full development as people, everywhere they go.

Most often parents who grow in their understanding of Montessori welcome suggestions for parenting, and they align their approach at home. Parents typically want to learn ways to support their children in understanding what is expected of them in a classroom environment where choices and boundaries give opportunities to grow in independence every day. If there are initial challenges with parents and their children, they often evolve into successes through teamwork and communication with Montessori educators. This partnership is encouraged by the very fact that Montessori education is designed to be *an education for life.*

Considering the Four Planes in the Family

Now let's dive into some age-related specifics for each stage of childhood, following one of Montessori's most helpful insights for parents: the four planes of development. To recap, Dr. Montessori identified four major stages of childhood and called them the four planes of development. They are called *planes* to describe the consistent characteristics that plateau for roughly six years, divided by dramatic changes in physical and psychological growth between each plane. These planes—birth to age six / young childhood, ages six to twelve / the elementary years, ages twelve to eighteen / adolescence, and ages eighteen to twenty-four / young adulthood—have definite characteristics and differing needs; therefore, the prepared environments, adult interactions, and balance of freedoms and responsibilities must adjust to the specific stage of a child's development.

When applying the three pillars I've described to the home, parents need a very basic understanding of the differences between each plane of development. Of course every individual child is unique, but they all change dramatically as they grow through these subsequent stages in some predictable ways. This fact encourages parents to adjust their homes and parenting to match their individual child's developmental characteristics and needs, and in the case of multiple children of differing ages, to do so simultaneously. This sometimes means treating siblings in the same family and home differently. What helps a three-year-old may not help the six-year-old in the same family, and both children will differ greatly from the fourteen-year-old sibling. Although it may sound obvious, it is not always intuitive to consider developmental stages and expectations.

If two siblings are three and five, they are in the same plane of development, so the environment, parent modeling, and offered choices and boundaries will be similar. But when two siblings are just above and below a plane of development in their ages—say five and seven—the five-year-old will most likely be showing signs of being in the first plane and will need very different choices and boundaries in the environment than the seven-year-old, who may be developmentally in the second plane. They may be only two years apart, but their needs and characteristics are more different than two siblings who are as much as three years apart but in the same plane.

Parents find that consciously considering the four planes is extremely helpful; the planes make clear why reasoning with a two-year-old or a four-year-old is a waste of energy and why teenagers are past the point for storytelling to be the most effective format for imparting moral values. Knowledge of the four planes helps parents to know when and where to put their energies and how to deliver them most effectively.

This may sound complicated, but typically things unfold quite naturally once parents embrace the general ideas. In fact, with the challenge of adding new members to a family, parents may even find that things get easier in some ways. A parent of five children tells me,

> With my first child, I had the time and energy to set up the home environment and show her how to do things. I enjoyed setting everything up just right and spending time with her. But as I had more children, it became harder and harder to give each one that much attention. What I love is that my older children want to show the younger ones how to do things, and because they are Montessori children themselves, they are more patient and thoughtful than I could ever be! They never overstep; they are so respectful; they show their younger siblings how to do things slowly and really stand back to let them try things for themselves. The children seem to know what kind of help is best.

In such ways, entire families benefit from Montessori's approach at home.

Early Childhood: Birth Through Age Six

How do parents put the Montessori principles into play in their homes? Parents of a two-year-old, for example, consider what a child of this age needs with Dr. Montessori's observations of young children's characteristics as an initial guide. They then set up a home environment that meets these needs, model behaviors in a way that appeals to the characteristics of this age, and provide freedoms and boundaries that perfectly support a young child's developing independence.

Children under age six need reality and as much of it as parents can offer, so removing fantastical distractions and physical obstacles helps them. First, the bedroom needs to be childproofed for safety, matching a child's age, personality, and abilities. Then parents can create an environment that encourages activity and engagement by placing a mattress on the floor (in place of a crib) so that their young child can get in and out of bed as soon as physically possible; in this way, they start the day in a child-safe bedroom upon waking. With a bed on the floor that they can safely climb down from, one- and two-year-olds see themselves as active participants, capable of interacting directly with their surroundings without requiring adult assistance to do so. They also might have a tiny bureau only two feet tall with two drawers holding just a couple of outfits to choose between and try to put on.[8] There may be several books in a basket on the floor or a few toys on a low shelf, such as stacking blocks or a box with geometric-shaped slots in the lid and corresponding shapes inside it. In the mornings young children can get to these things and amuse themselves reflectively without interruption for some time. Starting the day this way is quite different from having to cry out to get an adult to come lift one from a crib, being dressed by an adult, being put in a bouncy seat or playpen, and being given some toys.

Think about the perspective a child is given in these two scenarios. One has a lot of free choice and the other is entirely adult-dependent. In both, some collaboration and gradual learning of life skills happens. The orientation of the first (Montessori-informed) example affects not only the child but also the parents, as they think about the child and their evolving role as the adult in this little person's life. In the Montessori-informed scenario, the child is a participator, capable of doing some things for his or herself, who will, with help, become gradually more independent over time. The adult is a helper for—not the director of— what the child chooses to do.

In the kitchen parents can put a child-sized table and chair on the floor in a safe area so that as soon as children are walking, they access this area for eating meals and helping prepare foods in the kitchen.[9]

This sends the message, "You are a collaborating member of this family, and you have a place where you can be actively involved in preparing our family's meals—we value your actions!" Children are more likely to carry their own little plate over to this table when they are able and to clear their dishes after the meal when they are shown how to. Because little children love to be active and have an interest in sequences and processes, such activities of order and specific steps appeal to them. Children especially love to participate when they see others around them also doing these actions. They are eager to engage, developing their ability to focus their energies and to collaborate.

As long as other distractions and obstacles do not interfere, parents will find that children are drawn to these family routines and that they find great joy in them. Possible obstacles and distractions might be verbal interruptions, ringing or beeping smartphones, or a television turned on in the background. Young children have an immense capacity for developing concentration, but it is still fragile until well practiced through the early years. Parents help young children to flourish by consciously protecting spaces and times in their homes for reflective, purposeful activity.

Parents can establish their relative roles by collaborating with their young children from the beginning. The parents' role is to demonstrate and to help. If the adults have tendencies to micromanage or perfect children's every move, they can counter this by deliberately getting busy doing their own adult work alongside their child. For instance, parents might prepare a small colander with strawberries and a steady step stool at the kitchen sink, with a child-sized tray on a low table so that their two- or-three-year-old can wash and cut the strawberries when naptime is over. Then the adult can help their child begin the activity—but once a child becomes absorbed in any stage of the process, the parent should turn to prepare the other parts of the meal in their own space at the countertop, so that they are busy and not hanging over their child's every move. In other words, an adult is there if needed but *not any more involved* than he or she needs to be.

Finding this balance is individual and varies with personality. Parents can consult with a Montessori teacher for more specific information, read Montessori books and blogs, and view quality online Montessori videos. As parents absorb elements of the Montessori approach, they hone their interactions with their children. The reward of developing a collaborative relationship, based in mutual respect, makes the effort to learn and incorporate this Montessori approach at home so worthwhile for both parent and child. Parents get to watch their children build a strong foundation of character and become active learners capable of making choices and of contributing to their families. The children build a solid mind-set for their lifetimes.

When parents enroll their young children in a Montessori school, they can also consult with their children's teachers about how things are going at home. This close communication that begins in the early years becomes an ongoing practice of teamwork throughout the parent-school relationship. All families are different. Some parents tend to try to force or push their children, and others may be so permissive that their children take advantage of them. Neither extreme might show the results hoped for. Most parents can benefit from getting customized pointers that help steer them to success early on. Of course, it's never too late to begin this teamwork and to welcome suggestions from Montessori teachers, no matter the age of one's children. Any family's parent-child dynamic is a work in progress and no one—no one—gets away without struggles. Parents, myself included, have to accept our own imperfections and be open to ideas and changes. As Montessori teachers get to know their students and their parents, they can help immensely by making alternative suggestions so that parents can find what works best for their own families.

Having attended presentations about how to bring Montessori into her family life, one mother of a three-year-old and a five-year-old tells me, "Montessori has allowed our children to exercise their free will so that they become more apt decision makers and contributors, even at a young age. In some instances it is more demanding because I am responsible for [helping them to be] active participants in our home life rather than a passive bystander. We recently visited a family friend at their house, and while getting a tour of their home, my daughter started helping the mom make the beds. My friend, who has three children, was astonished, and Montessori became a topic that day. In a fast-paced world with ever-changing values, I appreciate that our children get practice being responsible and accountable human beings from an early age. I believe each will have a well-developed acumen due to the self-efficacy they developed through their Montessori experiences."

The Elementary Years: Ages Six Through Twelve

For elementary-aged children, the home and interaction with adults is quite different, reflecting the needs and characteristics of this stage. Now capable of a great deal of independence in the kitchen and able to care for their own hygiene, elementary children need age-appropriate challenges. For example, they can learn to cook a simple dinner for the family once a week by picking a recipe from a cookbook, writing down the needed ingredients, and helping to shop for them. They can lay the necessary items out on the counter and learn how to cook with the stove top and oven—the latter two with adult supervision. (Think of the resourcefulness, organization, and focus developing here!) This activity can be kept simple and still be effective: A seven-year-old boy might choose to make hotdogs, baked potatoes, and salad every time it is his turn to cook. But eventually, he will probably get bored with this menu, realize he's mastered it, and move on to other simple recipes such as homemade mac and cheese. By the time he is ten, he might progress to making salads and grilling outside with his parent's supervision.

Having to contribute a meal each week might feel like a chore to some elementary-aged children. Even so, we have seen that they are proud and feel valued for their contribution, to a degree that far outweighs their parents' initial hesitation to ask their children to undertake this responsibility. Young people become quite competent and develop an appreciation for cooking, especially if they have a parent who also enjoys time in the kitchen. The key here is to collaborate, support, and encourage where needed. When children occasionally feel overwhelmed, it does not hurt for an adult to show compassion and help them out, or even fill in for them now and then. In fact, doing so models how to be a good member of a team. In reverse, a parent might even ask their child to cover the adult's night of making dinner. A parent's sincere gratitude makes children realize their contribution is real, not phony. This builds strong, collaborative families.

Again, adults have to make time for this weekly contribution to the family. When our daughter, Lillard, was eleven years old, my husband and I made the mistake of allowing her after-school schedule to get too busy. This left her no time to regularly prepare a weekly dinner. It quickly became the most stressful year for her. We learned our lesson, and so did she! Reducing her after school activities the following year so that she had two weeknights when she could cook or help with dinner made a huge difference in her mood and confidence. Spending a little time in the kitchen paid off by also grounding her to better handle all stresses with school or social life. She drew on this source of confidence, knowing that she was capable of caring for others through regular contributions at home.

I cannot emphasize enough how strongly this connection with family through contribution to the home life influences children's well-being. Although it may be counterintuitive for many people, Elementary-aged children whose families keep them involved in sharing household responsibilities are more responsible and diligent with their homework, sports, and other commitments as well. These children are confident and capable—components of self-value that are even more important than the life skills themselves.

Intellectually engaging activities are also important aspects of home life for six-to-twelve-year-olds. They can spend time playing board games, drawing, painting, building things, looking at a detailed atlas or globe, perusing magazines such as *National Geographic History* or *Scientific American*, and reading fiction and nonfiction books. Making these items available to children at these ages gives them much to think about, explore, and create. Borrowing from libraries, sharing with other families, and collecting from used book sales or flea markets are great strategies for accessing and recycling such items.

The elementary years are the ones that many adults best remember from their own childhoods when they built forts, swung from branches, played games outside with neighbors, rode their bicycles, and exercised their imaginations for hours at a time. But parents must allot ample time for all this to happen. Children cannot play if there is no downtime built into the schedule for occasional boredom, and thus for creating something to do on their own. Children who have more free time for spontaneous play during these elementary years often develop appetites for focusing and following their curiosity as they grow older. They become creative and innovative young adults. In a world where both of these traits are highly valued, parents are wise to be mindful of the number of hours spent on organized sports, programs, and after-school lessons, and to remember to protect some time for their children to simply think, play, and explore. By doing so parents provide boundaries for their children and, at the same time, give them freedom to build themselves as the human beings that they are.

One mother of five describes her seven-year-old son as a typical Montessori-raised child:

> Alvie got really interested in airplanes. He read about them, thought about them, talked about them, even wrote a report about them at home from information he collected. He taught himself about aerodynamics and experimented with making paper airplanes. Then one day I saw him outside in our yard with a feather he found. He collected some small sticks and used tape to attach them to the feather to make a flying machine. I told him, "I don't think that's going to fly, buddy," but he was undeterred. He was out there for *hours*. Sure enough, eventually he made this contraption so it would fly. It flew beautifully! One thing I think is remarkable was his patience at experimenting with this. He wouldn't give up. I think many kids would have given up or lost patience. Working at something he was completely interested in, with such perseverance—that definitely comes from growing up with Montessori.

Dr. Montessori tells parents, "The wise mother will remember that play time is never wasted."[10] She explains, "So long as a child is actively interested in what he is doing and there is no harm in his activity, he is definitely working on his own development. Besides any new idea he might be grasping, he is developing concentration and self-discipline."[11] During these elementary years between six and twelve, boys and girls dive into such explorations and teach themselves so much, when their parents provide homes that allow for it.

Adolescence: Ages Twelve Through Eighteen

As children enter adolescence, their family environments expand further to encompass the wider world. It isn't enough to have atlases around the house or exposure to cultures and religions through family or the books that they had when younger; now adolescents need to be invited into adult communities outside their families. They crave opportunities to be treated more like grown-ups and to interact in a more mature way. This is the natural time for the transition to adult life to begin; in many cultures and times, adolescence was the stage when boys went off to hunt with the men for the first time or girls had to take on new responsibilities alongside women in their communities. In a different sense, today's young adults need opportunities to try out their budding abilities in apprenticeships or internships with mentoring adults outside their own families. Learning about the realities of being responsible, such as showing up at a workplace even when one doesn't feel like it or completing a job to the satisfaction of an employer or adult mentor, is informative at this stage of life.

A good example to explain this might be a thirteen-year-old who takes a Saturday job working in a neighbor's store. The adolescent can process payments, help customers, take orders, or answer the phone. He or she can be treated as a valued worker while still having the support and guidance of an older, wiser person. In our own family, my husband and I told our teenagers when they turned twelve that the next few years would be "skill-building" years. We cautioned them not to expect payment for their work at their ages. Their very first jobs of choice— babysitting and working in a hair salon for our daughter, assisting a boatbuilder and working in an outdoor-equipment store for our son— were not paying positions, at first. Over time our adolescents developed their skills for interacting with customers. They followed directions and managed adult relationships without our involvement. They called their employers when they were too ill to work and repeated tasks when their first attempts fell short. When they were roughly fifteen years old, each of their employers spontaneously volunteered to start paying them; by then, our children had developed the maturity that adolescents are completely capable of when given such training opportunities. They were "hirable," with years of basic experience under their belts. In addition, the money they earned meant much more to them, and they were inclined to spend it wisely.

Adolescents are still not fully developed adults, however. They need to enter this world gradually, with incremental expectations and responsibilities. In today's world, where thirteen-year-olds are often seen hovering over screens together, very self-conscious about their appearances and perhaps a bit surly toward adults, it can be hard to believe that when the environment supports them in a Montessori fashion, these same teens eagerly engage with the real world around them. But truly, the deeper nature of adolescents manifests positively when they have a sense of purpose and connection to the physical world, not just a virtual one.

As fitting for her era, Dr. Montessori suggested a lifestyle for adolescents that involved farming chores and the creation of a microeconomy where the teens could sell farm goods and develop an understanding of how society functions. This firsthand experience would prepare young people to appreciate the appropriate role of new technology and to realize how to use it effectively to further human progress. It seems logical that Dr. Montessori would choose a gradual and cautious approach to technology in education and at home. Although Dr. Montessori considered the basic technology of her times to be some of the greatest achievements of human creativity, she certainly would have advised that parents choose the boundaries and freedoms for children as carefully in this area of life as in any other. Technology's proper and helpful role in the lives of adolescents must be deliberately thought out. The landscape of the technological world should be no different from any other environment adults prepare for younger people with choices and with limits that support healthy development.

One Montessori-oriented family demonstrated how technology can be approached just like any other aspect of the environment with prepared boundaries and choices. This particular family realized that when their son, Jack, entered high school, he would for the first time need to use a laptop on a daily basis for his schoolwork. Jack's parents deliberated on how they could set this new situation up so that their son could be as independent as possible. They discussed with him ahead of time the decisions for freedoms, boundaries, and when and how they would intervene or make adjustments. Then Jack and his parents went to a store to pick out a laptop together for his high school years. His parents installed restrictions into the computer's settings that served as boundaries, such as hours that the computer would shut off (9:00 PM) and turn on (7:00 AM), so that sleep hours were protected. They set certain website topics to be blocked (such as porn or movies/games) and the number of hours a day that the Internet would be accessible, in hopes of removing the temptation to spend more time than necessary surfing. These parents gave their son the clear understanding that this computer was for schoolwork and communication, not a toy for entertainment. As the result of sharing their own priorities and asking Jack to come up with his own, Jack begrudgingly created a four-sentence contract for his computer use, which his parents approved:

1. Don't let the computer take the place of conversations with friends and family.
2. Only use the computer for schoolwork, communicating about assignments, or learning.
3. Use it downstairs in the kitchen or library (not in my bedroom upstairs).
4. My parents have the right to take the computer away or restrict it if I break these rules.

It was very hard for these parents to then watch as their fourteen-year-old son struggled to restrain his desire to watch YouTube videos rather than focus on his schoolwork. They learned quickly that the lines of Jack's computer use were blurred by his need to access the Internet to fulfill many assignments for school. They often couldn't tell whether his computer activity was for school or for amusement.[12] His parents' priority that he continue to develop his excellent focus from his years of Montessori education was challenged by the fluid nature of his computer use.

Regardless of the initial struggles, Jack's family found that by continuing to use a Montessori framework of preparing and resetting the environment and adjusting the choices/freedoms and boundaries/responsibilities, they were able to make progress. They had set up the situation with the computer thoughtfully and collaboratively, and they had their mutually agreed-upon expectations to refer to. Within a year, Jack was much more focused again, even with his computer use. He had the knowledge and experience from his earlier years in Montessori to revamp his self-control. This shows how any parenting decision relates to principles of preparing the environment, modeling, and balancing freedom with boundaries.

Montessori educators and parents recognize that *how* such boundaries are delivered—especially to adolescents—is perhaps even more important than the fact that they be set. Just as a wavering, guilt-ridden parent of a two-year-old sends the message that they aren't sure of their decisions, a parent who is too wishy-washy or, contrastingly, who uses too forceful a manner will influence how any adolescent responds to a proposed boundary. In the teen years, parents need to be more transparent by taking the time to explain their adult reasoning and to respect their adolescent's desire to experience how the adult world works. Montessori-informed parents know that this feeds a real need that adolescents have for developing their worldviews. Decisions are best when adults can explain how they are fair and sound in their minds. This doesn't mean, of course, that adolescents won't argue with a parent's reasoning. In fact, establishing themselves as being different from their parents makes this a likely reaction. But adolescents cannot learn about the adult world without parents sharing their reasoning with them, which can be done with legitimate authority and mutual respect.

With this in mind, the family spoke openly with Jack about why they were setting certain boundaries and shared the specific boundaries they actually set for themselves with technology use. They encouraged their son to follow suit and design some of his own ways of curtailing his use. For example, when they gave Jack his first cell phone at age sixteen (and his job paid enough for the monthly bill), his mother showed him how she changed the setting on her own smartphone to discourage her from texting or checking for messages at every intersection while driving. She also showed him the Do Not Disturb setting that she used from 8:00 PM to 7:00 AM so she wouldn't receive calls or texts at night. Adolescents can see that their parents first set such limits for them, and then deliberately lift these limits when adolescents replace such limits with their own self-imposed limits. This is how adolescents gradually become adults through that same expanding spiral of freedom and responsibility that occurs in Montessori classrooms. As Jack's independence increased with driving a car and making his own decisions about setting boundaries for himself, his parents were encouraged to see him needing less and less of their intervention in his life. When a young person receives such respectful help from their parents, they tend to return that respect right back.

Young Adulthood: Ages Eighteen Through Twenty-Four: Reflections and Results

When children become young adults, the most noticeable results of being raised in a Montessori family become apparent. Montessori-raised adults aged eighteen and beyond engage in the world around them and in their own learning, and they show a strong ability to focus their attention, organize their thinking, and remain curious about many topics. They are courageous about their mistakes and collaborative with their professors, friends, and family, respectful of others, and resourceful whenever they have problems to solve. While increasingly on their own in college and in the workforce, young adults give us numerous examples of how their years of Montessori from both school and home manifest.

I find it interesting to hear Montessori graduates reflect on how this approach to education helped them in life. In a light conversation with some Forest Bluff graduates in their early twenties at a wedding reception for their classmate, a young woman named Meagan tells me that she attributes her organizational skills to her Montessori background: "I always take time to put my apartment and bedroom in order. I like to find a place for everything. I think it's because Montessori taught me to do this, to organize your space and prepare before you begin something."

Another graduate, Kathy, tells me that she notices her brother, who also attended Montessori school, approaching his relationships with other people in an organized way.

"How do you mean?" I ask.

"Well, when he and his girlfriend were having issues, his approach was very systematic. Not in a cold way, I don't mean that—it's like . . ."

She pauses to think and continues, "He went through the logic of what they had already tried and what they might try next. He proposed it in a way that made sense. He essentially created a plan to avoid repeating the same mistakes."

Marion, standing next to her, pipes in, "Yes, I see this, too. My friends are a bit chaotic in the way they go about things, almost as if they don't learn from their past experiences and put it together moving forward. My friends who are Montessori graduates are just more thoughtful, and I think this is because we learned to approach things in a more organized way. We didn't see this until we were older, but Montessori gives you a more logical, organizing way of thinking, from younger ages."

"I'm also curious to learn new things all the time," Kathy says, "Whereas I see my friends who didn't go to Montessori just learn what they *have to* for their jobs, and that's it."

Montessori graduates seem to reflect even more deeply on the results of their education as they get older. At a Forest Bluff School alumni event, a thirty-five-year-old graduate reports, "The curiosity that is sewn into the fabric of who you are in the Montessori classroom serves me very well today [as an engineer]. In Montessori you're encouraged to pursue your passions and encouraged to wander and just try and understand the world on a different level. I have a curiosity for my business, for my industry, for the core tenets of what's important, for my role, and this really helps me. When I find down time, I'm trying to learn more and get better at what I do. I trace that back directly to my Montessori foundation."

I have often heard young adults attribute the ways they see the world and their inclinations to collaborate, to follow their curiosity, to engage in their jobs, and to focus on what they care most about to having grown up with the Montessori approach both in school and at home. This is where people grow up learning to respect one another and to use their own resources before leaning on others.

My own two teenagers tell me that a big difference they notice between themselves (as Montessori graduates) and most of their peers in high school and college (who did not attend Montessori schools) is in their sources of motivation to excel. Our daughter tells us, "I think I'm self-motivated to do well in school, but most of my friends seem to do their work because their parents are pushing them or they're afraid they won't get into a good college. They are so stressed out. When they get a B, they say, 'My parents are going to kill me,' and they're crying. It's all external pressure, and I don't think it's good for them, it doesn't seem to be working, all that extra stress. And when that external pressure is gone, what will happen?"

Intrinsic motivation, which the Montessori approach employs, is undeniably more effective in long-term outcomes when compared to extrinsic motivations. There are many foundational studies that prove this and elaborate on the point.[13] Anecdotally I can attest as the parent of two Montessori graduates that giving the message "This is *your* life, you must do with it what you think is best" has paid off. Telling our children "I think you're wonderful" and "I see you have unique strengths" and, ultimately, "I believe in you" goes a *long* way in parent-child relationships. Dr. Montessori is often quoted for saying, "Have faith in the child." She really meant it. Her entire approach confirms this mantra. A strong belief in children's abilities to create their own lives and to reach their full potential manifests in how Montessori educators and parents treat children everywhere—in school and at home.

The Parent's Heart

I love hearing parent reports when they see the effects of Montessori in their own children. One parent of two girls who attended Montessori school until high school tells me,

> The two things I never heard when my children came home from school are, "Can you help me with this?" and the exclamation "I can't *do* this!" When we were children ourselves, I remember saying these lines regularly. I remember being frustrated with homework assignments, feeling confused and helpless. But instead of getting overwhelmed or being insecure the way we were as children, my girls seem to have this incredible sense of being empowered, of being capable. They don't panic so quickly; they go into problem-solving mode when things get tough.

Having faith that the Montessori approach will lead to worthwhile outcomes, requires commitment, like anything of long-term value. This mother hadn't always felt confident in her choice of Montessori, because the path through any school is imperfect, even in Montessori schools. What helps in such a case is that the Montessori approach asks us to look beyond the day-to-day; Montessori's emphasis on continuity and taking the long view of children's gradual development gives families perspective through a challenging time.

This same parent says to me,

> I tell other parents, "Don't leave your Montessori school just because you are having one bad year with a certain teacher or social group. Try to address it but work through it, so your kids learn how to." I got some good advice from a friend who was a Montessori teacher in another city when my girls had occasional challenges. She told me, "You're there for the Montessori approach, and you'll be glad in the end if you help them go all the way through the program." That has been so true! Everything worked out in the long run. All the little problems—that one mean classmate, the one teacher my one daughter didn't click with—they all passed. The important thing was that the Montessori approach was always still there. I had friends who left, and it was so hard to watch them go. Every time, I wondered if I was doing the right thing. But now I see that those kids are not as solid, as happy, as interested in learning, or as confident as mine. That's all the Montessori in my girls. I am so grateful that we stayed with the approach all the way through for those most important long-term benefits.

The community of parents at Forest Bluff School saw the difference in their children's behavior at home in spring 2020 when our school had to close for the last two months of the year in the COVID-19 pandemic. The Montessori-trained teachers tried to inspire their students to continue their independent learning at home by suggesting interesting activities.[14] Unsurprisingly, most children did not need much prodding. Having already established self-guided activity at home as a norm, families now incorporated school-like activities into their repertoire. The children got right to work. They astounded the adults with their creative ways to keep learning:

- Children used scissors, tape, wire, beads, and everything from cereal boxes to tinfoil to make learning materials that mimicked the Montessori materials in their classrooms; they made Bead Frames to do math problems and wrote synonyms and antonyms on cards for matching, as examples.
- They labeled items in their homes by writing on small pieces of paper and placing these all over the house.
- They counted objects they found and even categorized them.
- They made little boats from tinfoil and tested their designs and speeds in a neighborhood ravine.
- They designed paper airplanes and made graphs to compare their aerodynamics.
- One nine-year-old examined stock market reports in the newspaper every day, drew graphs of the information, and tracked it with the daily news about the spread of COVID-19.
- A twelve-year-old built a representation of the three branches of government using Legos.
- An eleven-year-old wrote a report on philosophy, sparked by looking at his father's philosophy book collection.
- Another depicted Andy Warhol with a wig and full character monologue for classmates on Zoom.
- A fourteen-year-old took her family "to Mexico" for an evening by handing them paper "boarding passes," arranging the living room furniture to be "airplane seats," cooking a Mexican meal, decorating the kitchen, and playing Mexican music for them.

Montessori children tend to be inventive and self-motivated at home. From these shared examples, it is clear that Montessori is not just an approach to education; it gives children a unique and expansive approach to life itself. What makes them "Montessori children" is that they are all unique individuals, their most complete selves, ready to give to the world. Dr. Montessori explained that this original, individual expression comes from receiving appropriate support for human development at each successive stage of life.

I will conclude this chapter with one more story—one that, for me, describes the epitome of Montessori education extending into home life. One day a mother at Forest Bluff School stopped me in the hall-way to tell me: "My family and friends do not understand why I drive fifty minutes each way, just to bring my three boys to this Montessori school. They say, 'The schools around here are fine, why are you put-ting yourself through all this driving?' But I tell them that this is not just a school. Montessori doesn't just teach things; it helps children to develop as human beings.

"I have so many stories of where I see this. A week ago, I was cook-ing, and I was alone with the three boys [ages two, five, and seven] because my husband was traveling. We don't provide any screen enter-tainment, so they just need to come up with their own ways to amuse themselves during these times. My oldest comes over and asks, 'Can I read my report to you while you're cooking?' He pulls over a chair and sits down on it next to the stove and starts reading. It was incredible! It was like fifteen pages, all his own words, all these facts about the ice ages and geology of the earth. I'm amazed, because he's only seven!

"Then another night, I am reading to him about the earth and this word *Pangaea* comes up. My seven-year-old's eyes get really big, and he says, 'Wait a minute! I know that word!' He runs all over the house collecting books that have this word and shows me. He tells me he wrote about this in his report and it's in each of these books about the earth. So he's connecting information, he's thinking, he's building his mind, all the time.

"It's like a dream come true to my husband and me to see our chil-dren so happy to learn. My friends tell me they can't get their children [in regular school] to do their homework. It's like a war for them, every night. But because of Montessori, my children love working, writing these big reports, and they're so excited to do math and to learn every-thing that they can at school and at home, wherever they are. Montessori supports them to be interested in the world, in everything. Seeing this drive in our kids, it's such a joy for my husband and me. Our kids are *so* excited to learn and to push themselves. They are *on fire!*"

Conclusion

A REVOLUTION IN THINKING

THERE IS AN URGENT NEED to address and solve great problems in our current world. As these problems evolve rapidly, we have no choice but to accept the changing nature of life's conditions. This has become more apparent than ever with pandemic viruses, the speed of technological advancements, and instability in our societies and in our natural environment. To be adaptable our children need to frame and understand problems by first observing and recognizing the contextual reality before designing solutions that effectively match their observations. This thoughtful, scientific approach addresses all areas of life; the approach in education should be no different.

Dr. Montessori pointed out, "Most pedagogical theories are based on vague philosophical plans. I would suggest that we start from something concrete, which can be really studied and observed."[1] For this concrete start, she looked at the children themselves and urged us to see what their behavior reveals about their characteristics and needs. From there, she designed an approach to match what can be studied and observed. We are wise to follow this example. The ultimate goal is clear: "The essential reality of every living creature is that it must be adapted in order to survive and our schools should pay some attention to this fact."[2] Developing traits that serve this ability to adapt, to be ready to think, act, and improve our world even as the times change rapidly around us, must be the goal of education.

The next generation can only make a difference if they are prepared to approach the world's problems effectively. Prerequisite is experiencing an educational approach that cultivates traits that support adaptability in thought and action, traits such as the eight I've highlighted in this book: engagement, focus, organization, curiosity, courage, collaboration, respect, and resourcefulness. The Montessori approach to education is designed to do just this. It is rooted in the scientific observations of children's needs and characteristics that when respected at each stage of life, optimally foster positive human development. Dr. Montessori created an educational approach with a complete curricular framework that allows for the discovery and pursuits of individual interests, one that matches children's universality. When practiced authentically, this approach is comprehensive, interdisciplinary, and attentive to the continuum of one's growth from childhood to adulthood.

As you head off with what I hope is a new appreciation for Montessori education, remember that this approach requires a willingness to depart from long-standing biases about children's learning and their education. Montessori is, above all else, a call to revolution in thought and attitude toward children's education. This revolution is based on two discoveries: children form themselves by their own powers, and they do so through their active interaction with their environments. These truths clarify that adults' roles both at school and at home are to prepare learning environments with freedoms and boundaries. Adults must cultivate in themselves a prevailing attitude of respect for the inborn capabilities of children and gratitude for the achievements that these capabilities make possible for humankind. Ultimately, the next generation's ability to adapt to changing times, places, and cultures stems from traits that must be fostered, rather than stifled, by the educational approach in our schools.

To Serve the Complete Human Being

One of the most important aspects of Montessori education is its sensitivity to the human need for individual freedom in development. Every society is made up of individuals who are each unique and whose interactions define society: "One cannot develop the individual outside society and one cannot have a real society unless it is formed by individuals"![3] Dr. Montessori saw that allowing children free interaction within prepared classrooms would naturally foster their developing morality: "For, the meaning of morality is our relation with other people and our adaptation to life with other people. Therefore morality and social life are very closely united."[4] Children can only develop empathy—that essential quality for peace in the world—through their interactions with each other in positive environments.

Notably, while some educators use the classroom to imprint the ideas that they themselves believe will solve world problems, Dr. Montessori took a different approach. She saw that any educator's approach of indoctrination breeds an inability to think for oneself. In young people, this leads to apathy, or even vulnerability to strong personalities promoting their own ideas, which might silence opposing views or, much worse, encourage genocide, destruction, or war. For this reason, and because of her experiences during her lifetime, Dr. Montessori did not encourage indoctrinating students with ideas—any ideas. She had faith that children could and would be capable of deciding for themselves what is preferable when exposed to environments and adults that help them in positive development. Her approach teaches children to think *for themselves* because the answers are never given by the adults; answers lie in the surrounding environment and in the physical materials, for the students to discover in their own ways.

In this vein, it is imperative that people realize that the Montessori approach cannot be franchised or regulated, because what makes it work is its base of freedom for individual creativity. This means that teachers, like children, must be free to respond to what they observe. Dr. Montessori provides guidance within her approach, and she points the way for educators to respond to the children in front of them. Teachers can only work in this approach when they are free to give spontaneous lessons, to follow the children's interests through the curriculum, and to give the children what they need in any given month, week, hour, or minute. Thus, teachers also must have freedom for their individuality. This approach is based in human nature, not in any formula or outwardly imposed dictations. This is why every school will differ slightly, and every classroom too. Montessori cannot be rapidly mass-scaled like a corporate business. Schools must begin with the youngest children and grow *with* them, in order to stay focused on Montessori values and prioritize quality over quantity. This is the way to reach the potential of the approach so that children get the carefully prepared environments they deserve. Dr. Montessori said to *follow the children* in their needs, developmental characteristics, natural behavior, and interests, and that is what her approach leads us to do. Individual freedom is at the core. One individual school at a time, responding to the community of children, is how the Montessori approach works.

Furthermore, she saw that when children are treated with respect and supported to develop self-discipline with freedoms and realistic responsibilities, they feel peaceful and generous toward one another. A sense of peace seems to arise from the Montessori approach, which heralds respect for individuality and fosters collaboration with others simultaneously.

That education should help humanity become more peaceful was an overarching theme in Dr. Montessori's public speeches. She urged people to make a study of peace: "How strange it is that there exists no science of peace, no science with an outward development comparable at least with the development of the science of war in the matter of armaments and strategy."[5] And she knew that the way to address our worldwide divisions lay in our commonalities, especially those centering on the future of our children. To focus on education was her answer: "The educator's sense of responsibility could succeed in creating universal cooperation, provided the point of departure is an interest in the child. There is no force that can unite men of the world other than love for and interest in the child."[6] Our children— and their universal needs—have the potential to create bonds between all peoples.

But Dr. Montessori was a realist. Her urgency came from acknowledging the worst in human nature manifesting all around her on a grand scale. Her ideas arose with awareness of the horrific practices of intimidation and cruelty committed by the regimes of Joseph Stalin, Benito Mussolini, and Adolf Hitler. Partially in response to this exposure, she was passionate in urging educators to consider children's invaluable individual construction as whole and unique human beings to be core to education's purpose. She wrote, "Not in the service of any political or social creed should the teacher work, but in the service of the complete human being, able to exercise in freedom a self-disciplined will and judgment, unperverted by prejudice and undistorted by fear."[7] Dr. Montessori ultimately realized that a peaceful world can come about only when children are raised in developmentally responsive environments with adults modeling gracious behavior and with freedoms balanced by responsibilities. By focusing our energies into these three pillars of children's lives, adults have a task that is based in simplicity and reality. The task is clear, and it is attainable.

Dr. Montessori's message about the potential role of education is timeless:

> Man is free, therefore, of the bondage of heredity and possesses the great potential of latent spiritual energies that will develop in accordance with the possibilities offered by his environment. I cannot repeat often enough that man's destiny is not ruled by fate. In the psyche of the child a most potent nucleus of powers exists that can be negatively or positively influenced by the environment. This certainty is a source of great tranquility and above all, contributes to the orientation of our actions in the field of education, which is therefore amenable to every hope.[8]

The environments we create for our children matter greatly in helping them to reach their potential for the future.

The Human Task

As for the children themselves, and their responses to learning with Montessori's child-centered approach, their self-actualization occurs naturally. Having their senses fed with the Montessori materials when they are very young and having absorbed the grace, courtesy, and respect in their social experiences in the first plane of development, children enter their second plane of development ready to look outward to society. As they next learn about the evolution of our planet, all living creatures, and human history, each child naturally comes to ask, "And what about me? What is my purpose? In what way will I affect this world, and do my part?" Dr. Montessori called this one's cosmic task because it is ultimate and fits into the larger context of the world and universe. Each person's task is unique and may be small and specific or grand and far reaching. All is up to the individual, decided by oneself. This is often an unconscious conversation, which may manifest only privately and internally, but one that every human being may seek. It is a natural point of arrival, and Dr. Montessori proposed that education, if it is to be a real help to life, must allow children to ponder the question of their purpose at whatever ages it naturally arises in them.

Even though it is unconscious, yearning to find one's place in the grand story of life—a deep and necessary quest to find purpose—inspires action and provides direction. Dr. Montessori recognized children's inevitable questions and offered the means for them to find their own answers. Determining their paths as they build themselves as individuals, Montessori students become citizens of the world, each eager and ready to do his or her part in collaboration with others. This ability to see outside oneself, coupled with a desire to empathize with those who may live far away or have very different experiences of life, primes young adults to move our civilization forward.

Realize the Potential!

If we realize the potential of Montessori, we can realize the potential of humankind. The Montessori approach is firmly based in profound respect for each child's task of forming himself or herself. This respect for the child's self-formation is perhaps the most differentiating characteristic of the Montessori approach, the one that parents notice when they first walk into a true Montessori school. Parents realize the respect teachers have for children in the wording they use to speak to them. They see it in the way teachers bend down to look each child in the eye when they greet him or her, the way adults listen as often as they speak, the choices they continually give to children, and their direct, thoughtful manner.

Dr. Montessori described the adult's role as one of service to children, rather than as master of them. Adults prepare children's environments and provide what they need, but refrain from constantly telling the children what to do. Instead, adults show and assist. The children are free to create themselves from the positive environment that is provided. Montessori teachers and parents support, guide, and respect the spirit within each child. They recognize the inner guides and urges that propel children to form themselves. Dr. Montessori saw all children in this way, and she asked each of us to do the same—to observe and to learn, a process that is deep and never ending. She implored us to never stop wondering at the miraculous processes at work in each child.

If we embrace this outlook, we can raise generations of children who possess the life skills to meet every challenge. Most problems that we face today are human problems, and having been created by human beings, they can be solved by human beings. Dr. Montessori believed in humanity's underlying goodness. She proposed that if we are humble, we may understand that solutions for our errors can be found in a new direction for education.

Montessori's educational approach will help our youth develop inner strength with traits that enable them to adapt to life and to further human progress. Dr. Montessori implored: "One of the most urgent endeavors to be undertaken on the behalf of the reconstruction of society is the reconstruction of education."[9] Revolutionizing education is the way forward. Let us accept the challenge. Montessori is the approach worthy of the infinite potential within *every* child!

Epilogue

"WHY?": CURIOSITY DRIVES LEARNING FOR LIFE

A FOURTEEN-YEAR-OLD MONTESSORI STUDENT NAMED Kaitlin expressed her gratitude for the Montessori approach in her graduation speech in June 2019. At Marin Montessori School in California, her teacher suggested students begin their speeches with the words "I believe." Kaitlin knew right away what she would write:

"I believe in the importance of why. Every kid goes through this stage. 'Why is the sky blue?' 'Why is the grass green?' 'Why do dogs have tails?' 'Why do we need bones?' As a kid, I was curious about everything. Looking out the window during car rides especially piqued my curiosity. Sitting in the backseat with my sister, I would pipe up once in a while with my usual why questions, and my mom would do her best to answer them. One day, after my mom had finished answering my third or fourth question, my little sister, who was probably about four years old, all of a sudden asked, 'But mommy, how do you *know* that?' and without missing a beat, my six-year-old self turned to her and said, 'Lexi, Mommy knows *everything*. That's why she's always telling Daddy what to do.'

"Now, eventually many kids' curiosity fades as they enter into the demands of school. However, in Montessori my teachers encouraged my curiosity. I learned not to simply accept information I didn't understand and move on. I learned that it's *good* to ask questions and to look more deeply into the answers. To fully understand a concept, I need to know . . . you guessed it—why. At Montessori there were very few limits to what I could pursue in the effort to satisfy my wonder. For example, in fifth grade a friend and I, interested in wild animals, decided to start an 'animal study.' During our research we became enthusiastic about tigers and saving them from extinction. Very soon our 'animal study' turned into a 'tiger study,' and we organized a bake sale to raise money for the cause. We even proposed a field trip to the San Francisco Zoo, which our teacher approved. We planned a trip for the two of us, found a parent chaperone, and visited tigers in real life. This is just one example of a time Montessori allowed me to take my latest interest and run with it.

"A later example was just last year, in eighth grade. For one of my personal odyssey projects I chose to recreate one of Pablo Picasso's abstract paintings to scale. Ever since I can remember, I have loved art, particularly drawing and painting. When I was so young I could barely walk, my grandma would spread newspaper all over her kitchen floor and plop me down with some fingerpaints, where I'd happily create for hours. Years later, in eighth grade, after much research and consideration I decided on Picasso's *Girl Before a Mirror,* a fascinating five-by-four-foot abstract. My personal odyssey included building the frame, stretching the canvas, and painting the piece itself. I'd always wanted to paint on a large scale but never made the time to pursue it. Montessori provided me with yet another perfect opportunity to follow my interests and explore something I might not have otherwise.

"Throughout my time in Montessori school, I have been an eager learner. I want to know the reasons behind the rules, and develop a deeper understanding of any topic introduced to me in a lesson. Math is a great example. If I don't understand a concept in class or remember how to solve a certain equation for the homework, it isn't enough for my friends to just show me how to solve it. I immediately respond with, 'Why?' I can't move on without *fully* grasping the concept.

"Marin Montessori has kept me inspired and fostered my curiosity. Two whys I've never asked at Montessori are 'Why do I have to go to school?' and 'Why do I have to do this?' I've never used just books and papers to study. I've always been taught through visual learning with materials I can touch and through immersive experiences I can't forget. Whenever I'm assigned a project or begin a new class, I'm excited. I wonder: *Where can I take this?* Or, *What will I learn?* I'm so grateful to Marin Montessori for always nurturing my curiosity and encouraging me in whatever I've wanted to explore. I'd like to thank my mom for always believing in me and always being someone I can talk to. I'd like to thank my dad for pushing me to be the best person I can be and for encouraging me to immerse myself in my work. I'd like to thank my friends for always being there for me and supporting me through everything. I'd like to thank my sister, Alexis, because we make a great team and for never failing to make me laugh every day. Lastly, I'd like to thank all of my teachers because I know I wouldn't be where I am today, or who I am today, without all of your support and encouragement. Thank you for helping me to reach my full potential, even when it was hard for me to see that I could get there, and *of course*, for helping me find the answers to more of my whys. I've never lost the imagination and excitement that I had as a little girl finger painting on the floor in my grandmother's kitchen or riding in the back seat of the car asking questions as they came to mind. I believe that my time here at Marin Montessori School has not only fully prepared me for high school, but it has given me an enthusiasm for learning that I will carry with me through the rest of my life. This I believe."

After reading these words, we should be even more determined to give children an educational approach that nurtures, rather than thwarts, their innate desire to learn. Let's give them an approach that works. Give them Montessori.

ACKNOWLEDGMENTS

THANK YOU, JIM, FOR BEING the best husband in the world and a friend like no other. You know how much I love you! Thank you, Dad, for modeling how to be honest and open to people, and to show sincere respect to every human being you encounter. You and Mom supported me all through this project and in all my work and life. Mom, you've been a mother, but also one of my very closest friends and a fantastic colleague as well. I am grateful for my sisters, Lisa, Lynn, Pam, and Angel, for your support and the laughter through the tears. I am so fortunate.

I send special gratitude to two people without whom this book might not exist. The first is Virginia McHugh Goodwin, who gave me courage and told me I could do it. You read my earliest, rambling draft and called it my "magnum opus" and then enthusiastically asked for each draft for six years until it was finished. That's a true friend! The second is Cynthia Morris, my incredible, invaluable writing coach. You have supported me in all the ups and downs of the creative process but also in life's waves, and you have taught me how they are intricately intertwined. You are the angel everyone needs in order to learn to believe in themselves and tackle this creative and spiritual journey armed with love, fortitude, and joy. Thank you for always saying just the right thing right when I needed it.

Thank you to friends and colleagues who read drafts for me, gave feedback, and urged me forward: Graham Cook, John Kuhns, Jeanne

Nolan, Janet McDonnell, Gary Goodwin, Jenny Turner, Merle Gordon, Claire Foster, and Margaret Kelley.

Thank you to all who shared their words and stories with me: Cary Roloson; Kaitlin and Alexis Gasner; Erica Allen; Stephanie Daggett, Ta Promlee-Benz, Anne Cox, the late Elizabeth Seebeck, and the parents, teachers, and staff at Oglesby Elementary; the late Jacqueline Cossentino; Keith Witescarver; Tim Nee; Gerry Leonard; Gretchen Hall; Phil Dosmann; Marsha Enright; Dakota Prosch; Alex Phillips; Erica Kittle; Lisel Taylor; Joe DiCarlo; Stew Fuller; Ann Marie Nedeau; Reeve Waud; Alexandra Sturm; William, Caroline, and Elizabeth Duckworth; Caroline Gillette; Katherine Krey; Jefferey Boucher; Sophia Smith; Daniel Patterson; Luke Corsiglia; Ford Johnstone; Marilina Becirovic; Victoria Roos; Shubhik DebBurman; Sue Kowlzan; and Katy Linde. Many, many other Forest Bluff families have all contributed to this endeavor, and more than you can imagine. If you went to Forest Bluff or were a parent there, you're in the fabric of these pages!

Thank you to all the AMI trainers and the wider Montessori community who have given me a heart-led home among you to grow and develop a passion for humanity and a fully rewarding career. I am grateful to Lynne Lawrence, Judi Orion, Maria Teresa (ChaCha) Vidales, Ginni Sackett, Silvia Dubovoy, Alison Awes, Jamie Rue, Andrea Fleener, Jennifer Shields, Erin Smith, Kerey Lontz, Elise Heneke-Stone, Laurie Ewert-Krocker, Sharlyn Smith, Monte Kenison, Carol Hicks, Uma Ramani, Jenny Hoglund, Vibhuti Jain, Molly O'Shaughnessy, Connie Black, Greg MacDonald, Allyn Travis, Phyllis Pottish-Lewis, Guadalupe Borbolla, Baiba Grazzini, Jean Miller, Hilla Patell, Nimal Vaz, J. McGeever, Merry Hadden, and so many others. Your work is invaluable! I am thankful for those who had a great impact on me but are no longer with us, especially Kay Baker, Hildegard Solzbacher, Renilde Montessori, Peter Gebhardt-Seele, Annette Haines, Silvana Montanaro, and Margaret Stephenson.

Special thanks to two very important mentors, David Kahn and John McNamara. You are irreplaceable in the world of Montessori in North America, especially in pioneering the adolescent level with remarkable contributions. I also want to also thank current executive directors Ayize

Sabater of AMI/USA and Munir Shivji of AMS, Tim Seldin of IMC, Rebecca Pelton of MACTE, Denise Monnier and Wendy Shenk-Evans of MPPI, Sara Suchman of NCMPS, along with the editors of Montessori journals and leaders of organizations that tie us all together and keep us informed and growing professionally.

Thanks to fellow school and organization leaders and authors for your inspiration and camaraderie: Patty Eggerding, Jennifer Hanna, Kate Sargent, Sam Shapiro, Michele Shane, Maggie Radzik, Mary Lou Cobb, Maura Joyce, Kathy Minardi, Ben Moudry, James and Sarah Moudry, Cathy Swan, Shazia Abdulla, Michael Waski, Donna Goertz, Jacqui Miller, Mary Reinhardt, Eder Cuevas, Junnifa Uzodike, Simone Davies, Elizabeth Slade, Koren Clark, Floyd Creech, Sep Kamvar, Catherine Massie, Ray Girn, Mira Debs, Sheri Bishop, Gina Lofquist, Dave Ayers, Lucie Tamasova, Sylvia Arotin, Alan Preece, Audrey Perrott, Jacquie Maughan, Diana von Rosen, Carrie Lang, Jesse McCarthy, Anna Perry, Beth Norman, Debby Riordan, Julia Volkman, Zahra Kassam, Jane Mills Campbell, Susan Stephenson, and many, many more contemporaries whose work, knowledge, and dedication I admire. The list just keeps growing every day, so if you're reading this, you're on it!

Thank you to Lynn Jessen for urging Forest Bluff school to always reach high, to Haley Tate, Laura Earls, and Forest Bluff directors Matt and Sarah Robbins, Regina Cyvas Sokolowski, John Dickson, Abbey White, Peter Dutko, Debbie Secler, Kaiti Andersen Reigelman, Melanie McEneely, Maggie Kelly, Nalisa Ward, Stacy Keane, Anne Mahon, Keri Godon, Rachel Coad, Iuditha Jager, and gosh, there isn't enough room to name every one of you, but if you worked at Forest Bluff at any time, consider your name HERE! We worked so closely together over the years, and your stories, observations, and insights are in here. Your partnership contributed greatly to this book.

A very special thank you to Carolina Montessori, Joke Verheul, and Alexander Henny for your tireless work of revealing Maria Montessori's words and work to the world. And thank you, Angeline Lillard, for your inspiring quest to research the benefits of Montessori education with sound science and honest analytics. The four of you are more needed than ever!

In the literary world I want to thank Altie Karper for reading an early draft and giving me expert advice and encouragement. Thanks to Shannin Schroeder at Cup and Quill for helping me restructure and clarify my message; to Adeeba Arastu, Sanjeev Rau, Tina Koenig, and Megan Valli Minnick; to Rebecca Makkai, Jeanne Nolan, and Sue Boucher for guiding me in choosing my publisher; to Kara Rota for taking a chance on a first-time author; and to Michelle Williams, Frances Giguette, and all the team at Chicago Review Press, who've been so attentive and professional. With your positive, welcoming, and upbeat tone, you treat your authors like friends.

Thank you to Susan Rivera, to my "right-hand woman" Ysenia Deleon, and to Alberto Torres: You are part of my every day. The wisdom, friendship, support, and assistance you give means the world to me.

You may think it silly, but I have to acknowledge the four-legged friends in my life, who comfort me and bring me strength and joy in every step. I won't mention names since they'll never read this.

And last but not least—*NOT LEAST!*—thank you, Stanley and Lillard, for being your true selves, for knowing who you are, and for offering your talents to the world. You give me hope for the future.

NOTES

Introduction

1. The United States still lags well behind other countries in science, math, and reading scores, and despite reforms, the trend is worsening, not improving. See scores reported by the National Assessment of Educational Progress (NAEP), https://nces.ed.gov/nationsreportcard/.

2. There are very few such schools. For instance, roughly 160 Waldorf Schools exist in the US, and this is the oldest and second-most popular alternative model. Montessori, which I will discuss as its own category, leads by a landslide, with over 4,500 schools in the US and over 20,000 in the world.

3. For reports on the shortcomings of progressive approaches, see studies by Loveless, 2001; Egan, 2002; and Mayer, 2004, listed in the bibliography.

4. Maria Montessori, *From Childhood to Adolescence* (Thiruvanmiyur, Chennai, India: Kalakshetra Press, 1973), 103.

5. Erica Moretti, *The Best Weapon for Peace: Maria Montessori, Education, and Children's Rights*, (Madison, University of Wisconsin Press, 2021).

6. She was the first woman to graduate from the medical school at the University of Rome and one of the first female doctors in Italy. She was, according to some sources, one of three women in her university class.

7. "Defectives" was the common term used in Dr. Montessori's day.

8. Rita Kramer, *Maria Montessori: A Biography* (Cambridge, MA: Perseus Publishing, 1988), 110-111.

9. See the introduction to Dr. Montessori's book *The Formation of Man* (1955) where a discussion of this point makes her feelings clear. She did sometimes use the word *method*, though it's hard to know whether this term had the same connotations of "rigidity" and "prescription" in Italian as it often does in English.

1. Montessori in Action

1. She traveled through twenty-three countries in her lifetime as far as we know, although some were not established as independent countries at the time.

2. *Flow* is a term in positive psychology, first described by Mihaly Csikszentmihalyi in 1990. I will discuss this term further in chapter 4 with a discussion of Montessori's emphasis on concentration.

3. Dustin's Montessori teacher had demonstrated this wiping motion from the left side of the table to the right, in straight lines; this is indirect preparation for the organization of words and numbers for the processes of reading, writing, and in most cases, mathematics (in the country he is growing up in). Dustin expresses this general pattern with his wiping motions.

4. Subsequently, a three-year-old notices the water on the floor and runs to get a small mop, which she rubs over the wet floor and then replaces on its hook next to the child-sized sink.

5. While younger children will imitate or repeat information regarding time, or recognize a symbol on a clock, they typically cannot recreate the concept of time in their minds or explain such abstract concepts the way that these older children do.

6. The alphabet we use for English originated in the Middle East with peoples who spread and added to it as they traveled. Children in a Montessori school in another part of the world will hear a different origin story that invites them to explore their own language's written symbols. In this way, the Montessori curriculum adapts to culture and country.

7. In this particular Montessori school, children must be in the class for at least a year before they will be oriented in how to safely walk through the town to the library without adults, in a group of three or four peers. So a six-year-old would not walk to the library quite yet.

8. This story has an addendum: The older children in the nine-to-twelve-year-old class hear this "Communication in Signs" story in the same month from their

own teacher, which they heard several times when they were younger in the six-to-nine class. Each time, the story is limited to the basics. This is deliberate, so that there is always plenty more to learn if children want to pursue any topic on their own, and in this way, their research is always an original, exciting exploration for them. The teacher-prepared charts that accompany the story are cursory, for example. So this time when they hear the story, the nine-to-twelve-year-old children decide to create their own charts that map out the details of every language, and they make extensive charts. This is a great example of how children, as they mature, continue to explore topics and increase the complexity of their work extensions by choice. The younger children see the older children's work going on in the hallway, outside, or in their classroom when they walk in to borrow something. They are excited to see the connections between their work and that of older students, and that everyone's explorations are unique. This creates an intellectually and socially diverse and vibrant community life.

9. This is so imperative for children under age six because they are learning through their sensorial explorations of the world. This is the only manner in which young children can create a base for understanding the qualities of the real world. Montessori is unique in recognizing this biological fact and designing a curriculum entirely focused on giving the keys to this foundation.

10. Angeline Stoll Lillard, *Montessori: The Science Behind the Genius* (Oxford, England: Oxford University Press, 2017), 28–33.

11. In this adolescent Montessori program, every student prepares for trips by participating on student-run committees to learn adult skills for interacting with the outside world and to care for each other. These include the Safety, Gear, Food, Finance, and Transportation Committees.

12. Students do this during the three hours of daily work time allotted for all areas of study: algebra, geometry, essay and composition writing, vocabulary, annotating literature, independent study projects, US history/government, and planning work, trips, and activities.

13. From working with experts in any field, adolescents learn skills and develop sincere appreciation for the different kinds of work people contribute to a society.

14. There is much more than courage involved in Montessori's use of the word *valorization*, but I am simplifying the concept for the purposes of this book. For more, see the appendices in Dr. Montessori's writing in *From Childhood to Adolescence* (1973).

15. Montessori, *From Childhood to Adolescence* (Thiruvanmiyur, Chennai, India: Kalakshetra Press, 1973), 108.

16. This and the careers of Montessori alumni are great areas for further research studies. In one study, University of Virginia researchers interviewed twelve alumni from a culturally diverse Montessori preschool in Washington, DC, and found:

> One was a lawyer, working at a large firm on commercial real estate contracts. One worked for the U.S. government as a health policy program analyst and resided in Scandinavia. Two women worked in science/math, one as a neuroscience graduate student and the other as a statistician leading a project team. Revealing themes of entrepreneurship and creativity, among the alumni were a web designer, a digital marketer, a professional stage manager (the youngest interviewed, at 25, who had majored in theater arts and graduated just 4 years previously), and a professional dancer (who also taught dance and choreographed—the oldest interviewed, at 40, who was among the earliest attendees of the school). Three were food services entrepreneurs. One had opened five restaurants in the last 10 years, another had started a chain of restaurants "from the ground up . . . [that had all] survived so far," and the third was just starting an Instagram private chef business on the side while working as a chef for the United Arab Emirates. One who owned restaurants also owned real estate in Norway, where he currently lived. Another graduate worked in quality assurance, supporting disabled people in their employment; she aspired to open a roller-skating rink.

   The results of this study may or may not be attributable to their Montessori experiences as very young children, but the descriptions do seem noteworthy. See the full study, Angeline S. Lillard, Jessica Taggart, Daniel Yonas, and Mary Nia Seale, "An Alternative to 'No Excuses': Considering Montessori as Culturally Responsive Pedagogy," *Journal of Negro Education* (in press).

17. These are classic findings. There are spurts of brain growth that indicate "major increase in the complexity of neural networks" around ages three, seven, and twelve, as well as stages of lesser growth that indicate periods of synchronization. See Herman T. Epstein, "Correlated Brain and Intelligence Development in Humans," in Martin E. Hahn, Craig Jensen, and Bruce C. Dudek, *Development and Evolution of Brain Size: Behavioral Implications* (New York: Academic Press, 1979), chapter 6.

18. Jill Sakai, "How Synaptic Pruning Shapes Neural Wiring During Development and, Possibly, in Disease," *Proceedings of the National Academy of Sciences of the United States of America*, June 24, 2020, https://www.pnas.org/doi/10.1073/pnas.2010281117.

19. Dr. Montessori considered child development from in-utero through the mid-twenties, and she developed her educational approach for children from birth to age three and from age twelve to age eighteen more thoroughly than I relate in this book. For more resources about Montessori for infants and very young children, see *The Montessori Toddler* by Simone Davies, *The Montessori Baby* by Simone Davies and Junnifa Uzodike, and *Montessori from the Start* by Paula Polk Lillard and Lynn Lillard Jessen. There are also several articles at MontiKids.com and Forestbluffschool.org/blog about these early ages. To learn more about Montessori's thoughts on adolescence, see *Montessori Today* by Paula Polk Lillard and *From Childhood to Adolescence* by Maria Montessori, particularly the appendices.

20. For adolescents working on farms, the cycles that last entire seasons and even years demonstrate the patience and foresight that are required in adulthood.

2. The Framework That Makes Montessori Work

1. Montessori children have the ability to concentrate on their work and to stay focused as a direct result of their years of practice in the Primary level. This is what makes them capable of such collaboration and independence at these Elementary ages.

2. These numbers vary across Montessori settings in different countries and cultures. There are successful Montessori classrooms with much higher numbers of children and one teacher in the United States and in many places around the world. The numbers given here are more common in the US today.

3. While mornings are optimal, it is beneficial to have a second three-hour work period later in the day, or to have more afternoon stretches of work time that are as close to three hours as possible. Logistically, because one three-hour period per day is usually attainable in the mornings, this is a requirement for Montessori environments.

4. Becoming familiar with how long a meter is on a sensorial level aids children as they grow older and need to picture how far several meters are, or the fractions of meters. The metric system is the universal language of measurement

around the world. Knowing the meter length well gives children confidence and orientation.

5. Established in the San Lorenzo district of Rome in 1907.

6. Maria Montessori, *The 1913 Rome Lectures* (Amsterdam: Montessori-Pierson, 2013), 20.

7. Montessori, *1913 Rome Lectures*, 21.

8. Maria Montessori, *The Formation of Man* (Amsterdam: Montessori-Pierson, 2007), 38.

9. Montessori, *Formation of Man*, 21.

10. Maria Montessori, *The Discovery of the Child* (New York: Ballantine Books, 1990), 149.

11. Montessori, *Discovery of the Child*, 304.

12. Montessori, *Discovery of the Child*, 305.

13. Montessori, *1913 Rome Lectures*, 74.

14. Montessori, *1913 Rome Lectures*, 74.

15. Montessori, *Formation of Man*, 10.

16. In just *one lecture*, for example (called "Intelligence," discussing the ability of children to develop and further their intelligence, given April 18, 1913, and recorded in *The 1913 Rome Lectures*), Dr. Montessori mentions Alexander Bain, a Scottish inventor; the *Inferno* by Dante; Ronald Ross, a British medical doctor born in India who won a Nobel Prize for discovering that mosquitoes transmit malaria; Christopher Columbus; Alessandro Volta, an Italian physicist known for the invention of the battery (although in this lecture she refers to his exploration of Luigi Galvani's discovery of the electric impulses that can be conducted through frog's legs); Isaac Newton; Galileo Galilei; Denis Papin, a French physicist who invented the pressure cooker and modeled the first piston steam engine; and Albrecht von Haller, a Swiss anatomist, physiologist, naturalist, and poet—among others! This demonstrates how well read and in touch with the highest levels of intellectual and social human progress Dr. Montessori was. Her spontaneous pulling from memory and drawing of connections revealed an active mind, one that inspires.

17. Dr. Montessori's curricular ideas were also developed and realized by her collaborators, mainly Mario Montessori, Camillo Grazzini, Adele Gnocchi, and Anna Maccheroni. These individuals and others have worked with the

Association Montessori Internationale to ensure that all additions interconnect and adhere to the Pedagogical Committee's highest standards. (AMI's Pedagogical Committee is also currently called the Scientific Pedagogy Group). The robust curriculum that AMI delivers today reflects this collaboration and gives Montessori an intellectual depth that results in stimulating, superior learning environments for children.

18. Montessori, *Formation of Man*, 42.

3. An Effective Model

1. Maria Montessori, *Maria Montessori Speaks to Parents: A Selection of Articles* (Amsterdam: Montessori-Pierson, 2017), 5.

2. Lynn Jessen was already AMI trained and had taught in other Montessori schools.

3. The Sumerians were the first civilization in Mesopotamia and the first that we know of to have a writing system, called cuneiform. In the Montessori Elementary curriculum, the teacher presents this information to encourage research of this and other early civilizations.

4. As a side note, what made this event more surprising was that I had never proposed that the children sing to the flag. The national anthem was one of many songs in our classroom's songbooks. So this was Tara's idea to ask her classmates to surprise their teacher this way, quite spontaneously. They wanted to show their teacher that they had finished the cleaning on their own and decided to do something they deemed ceremonious.

5. We have many ways of addressing spelling in Montessori, such as helping a child to make their own booklet of words or giving lessons on how to arrange words in alphabetical order and then search for them in a dictionary, on how to group similarly spelled words together, and so on.

6. Exceptions are made in unusual circumstances, such as when a parent is hearing impaired, is traveling in another time zone, or has a challenging work schedule.

7. In Forest Bluff's community there have only been a few parents who could not find times to attend formal events. In such cases we try to meet with them individually and check in several times a year by phone to keep them up to date. We align our events with the majority of parent schedules.

8. Grandparents' Visit in December, Fathers' Visit in February, and Mothers' Visit in May.

9. More about this in chapter 6.

4. Authenticity

1. Waldorf schools were designed by Austrian philosopher Rudolf Steiner (1861–1925). The first school was founded in 1919 in Germany. The first Waldorf school in the United States was founded in 1928 in New York City. Waldorf schools can only use the names Waldorf or Steiner if they follow Steiner's model and are accredited by the Association of Waldorf Schools of North America. This protects those methods from being exploited or unfairly represented.

2. Montessori schools that are registered with certain organizations have standards for accreditation, but they vary.

3. Of the three schools described in this chapter, two are private and one is public. All three are predominantly non-White, debunking the myth that Montessori mostly attracts White, wealthy families. (The reference to the demographics of these three schools is in *no way* correlated with the theme of this chapter, however.)

4. Today, AMI is the international leader in Montessori education. It collaborates with like-minded organizations to meet key policy positions globally and offers courses for diverse populations, such as Indigenous communities, elders with dementia, and children in vulnerable places (e.g., children in African refugee camps are served through a program designed to provide equitable access for all children called Éducateurs sans Frontières).

5. Becoming an AMI trainer is akin to getting a PhD or a medical degree. The trainer-in training consists of a three- to five-year period of rigorous preparation studying in Montessori theory, how to present the materials, how they interrelate and what their multiple purposes and uses are, and study under a mentor who trains teachers. No other Montessori training program in the world holds this high a standard for its trainers. This is what continues to delineate AMI from all others.

6. Another AMS-trained teacher might have all Dr. Montessori's fraction-material lessons from a different AMS training course, so this is not necessarily representative of the organization's standards. Part of the problem is the inconsistency between AMS training centers to date.

7. Dr. Montessori and many others have used both terms. The term *method* implies that this is a methodical approach, which it is not. In actuality, Montessori offers guiding principles and practices with freedom and flexibility for individual children in relationship to their teachers and peers.

8. Maria Montessori, *The Absorbent Mind* (New York: Dell, 1967), 262.

9. Montessori, *Absorbent Mind*, 262.

10. Montessori, *Absorbent Mind*, 262.

11. Montessori, *Absorbent Mind*, 263.

12. For several examples in modern research, see chapter 6 of Angeline Lillard's *Montessori: The Science Behind the Genius*, 3rd ed. (New York: Oxford University Press, 2017).

13. Csikszentmihalyi is the author of the classic book *Flow: The Psychology of Optimal Experience* (New York: Harper & Row, 1990).

5. Benefiting All

1. Angeline S. Lillard et al., "Montessori Preschool Elevates and Equalizes Child Outcomes: A Longitudinal Study," *Frontiers in Psychology* 8 (October 30, 2017), https://www.frontiersin.org/articles/10.3389/fpsyg.2017.01783/full. (As of 2022 a national study is already underway.)

2. Significantly, this study was conducted in "high-fidelity Montessori classrooms," which means that only Montessori activities were in the classrooms and that the teachers were thoroughly trained to present these activities in the traditional manner that Dr. Montessori demonstrated to be most effective. At the time of Lillard's research, these classrooms were accredited by AMI.

3. Mussolini opposed Montessori for spreading ideas about individual liberty and freedom of thought. Initially, Mussolini praised the Montessori approach for the disciplined and orderly appearance of the self-controlled students. He and Montessori were on agreeable terms, and he supported the spread of Montessori schools, such that they appeared to be collaborators for a time. But when Mussolini proposed indoctrination, he and Dr. Montessori clashed.

4. You might recall the Binomial Cube progression explained in chapter 2, under The Learning Materials.

5. Another common breakdown in public Montessori programs results from misunderstanding this sequential continuity from preschool, through to middle

school: When public programs are forced to accept older children without the base that gives them necessary preparation, new (older) children may still benefit in some ways and can be an asset to a classroom. Too often, however, they actually lose out, because they cannot make up for the lost years of practice. This disadvantages students, the classroom community, and the teacher, who has to spend time and energy straddling many divergent levels and having little time left over for those who are developmentally in sync with the level of the curriculum. Montessori works best when accepted as a whole-school model, with continuity from young ages all the way through eighth grade and sometimes beyond, replacing the year-by-year conventional curricula and matriculation practices.

6. NCMPS also provides useful tools and guidelines through their website for public schools.

7. Angeline S. Lillard, "An Association Between Montessori Education in Childhood and Adult Well Being," *Frontiers in Psychology* 12 (2021) https://doi.org/10.3389/fpsyg.2021.721943; Lillard et al., "Montessori Preschool Elevates and Equalizes."

8. It is also helpful to view the research on Montessori outcomes. See studies listed on the National Center for Montessori in the Public Sector website, the American Montessori Society website, or the Association Montessori Internationale website. Other sources include the Center for Montessori Research at the University of Kansas and the Early Development Lab at the University of Virginia.

9. Allyson L. Synder, Xin Tong, and Angeline S. Lillard, "Standardized Test Proficiency in Public Montessori Schools," *Journal of School Choice* (August 2021): 1–31, http://dx.doi.org/10.1080/15582159.2021.1958058.

10. Public Montessori observer Phil Dosmann reports that children from low-income urban homes often need additional support. For example, they may need more practice learning how to analyze data to solve math word problems. But in general Dosmann reports that regardless of income level or ethnic background, public Montessori students tend to do very well on social study and science tests. This is because of the Montessori curriculum cultural subjects and students being allowed to do research and follow their interests. They also tend to do well with writing; though if English is their second language, this can challenge some test takers. In other words, children who do not score highly on standardized tests may have a variety of circumstantial factors contributing to such results. Another longtime observer of public Montessori

students, Floyd Creech, reports seeing Montessori students—including those from low-income backgrounds—outperforming their peers in conventional public schools in their same districts in South Carolina. There are studies suggesting these observations, but more research needs to be done.

11. There are scholarships available to offset training costs provided by private institutions and funds like the Margaret Elizabeth Stephenson (MES) Fund. When weighing costs, states can also measure what it costs to train and certify teachers for conventional teaching and consider replacing those programs with Montessori training for their public school teachers in the Montessori pipeline.

12. Where states have done this, there is much more—and better quality—Montessori public education. For a good example, look at Wisconsin, a state where legislation—in large part due to the work of longtime Montessori advocate Phil Dosmann—has been passed to provide a licensing track for teachers getting their Montessori training.

13. There is a substantial three-week AMI training course for school principals and anyone interested offered by several training centers in the United States, which is called the Core Principles Certificate Course. This course gives principals the basics they need to support programs effectively.

14. See Dr. Montessori's reviews of the work she did with children from 1898 to 1907 as a medical doctor serving children with greater physical and psychological needs, specifically the references to her discoveries in her early written work, such as *The Montessori Method* and *The 1913 Rome Lectures*. Dr. Montessori was very inspired by the work of Édouard Séguin, who is commonly described as a father of special education. Dr. Montessori's approach incorporates practices, such as breaking down activities into multiple individual steps, reducing the language used in a lesson, and including multiple senses to explore, that benefit children with greater needs as well as neurotypical and exceptional children.

15. See the special-education work of many contemporary Montessori educators all around the United States, as well as the work of the Montessori Medical Partnership for Inclusion, which highlights the collaboration of Mario Montessori and Theodor Hellbreugge.

16. It's helpful to note, however, that the format of a Montessori classroom does require children to have a certain level of physical and mental independence in order to utilize the environment. The success for a child with greater needs

depends on the resources of their Montessori school and teacher, as well as the population in the classroom. From my personal experience, the situations where children are not succeeding in a Montessori classroom are when they are physically or mentally unable to progress noticeably with *some* level of independence, at least in *part* of each school day. Developing individual independence is the goal for all children, regardless of whether they have exceptional needs, so trained adults aim to "fade out" at the moment a child can do something independently. If a child is at risk of hurting themselves or others or if a child needs unremitting direction from an adult—physically, socially, or cognitively—in order to function, progress toward independence, or benefit from the classroom environment, then a Montessori classroom may not be the best choice. A child's self-esteem is an important factor in his or her development; it should always be the determining factor in whether a Montessori classroom is the optimal choice. If a school cannot provide what a child needs, that child will be best served by moving to the one that can. By itself, in other words, the Montessori approach cannot guarantee every child's success. However, Montessori environments could be incredibly effective for children with greater needs and therefore an excellent choice for public school districts that aim to serve all their children with deserved respect. The worldwide Montessori community continues to grow with training workshops and excellent information for teachers about how to include and support children with greater needs.

6. In the Heart of Things

1. Maria Montessori, *The Formation of Man* (Amsterdam: Montessori-Pierson, 2007), 45.

2. Books, puzzles, art supplies, blocks, musical instruments, household items, and simple toys are best for a Montessori home life. Children need time to explore and create with the objects they find around their homes and surroundings. Nothing fancy or expensive is necessary. This is why I do not advise purchasing and having Montessori classroom learning materials at home; the Montessori materials are meant to be specially presented in the school environment by the trained teacher for their best use. Duplicating these materials at home backfires when children lose interest because of how they were presented at home, or treat them as if they were toys. The materials in one's classroom should be reserved for classroom learning and serve as keys to the world. The whole point of the materials is to help children *notice* the keys, the important

aspects, to *apply* out in the real world, which includes home. Outside the classroom, children very naturally apply such keys to their real-life situations. The materials are designed to support the children abstractly in this way and are meant to be shared with a large group of peers. Having Montessori materials at home dilutes their purpose.

3. Recent research shows negative effects of technology overuse, and many parents have witnessed addictive behaviors result from screen time.

4. In this chapter, *parent* could mean grandparent, foster parent, guardian, or any other caregiver who supports a child's life from outside of school in the ways described.

5. For many more suggestions and ideas, see Paula Polk Lillard and Lynn Lillard Jessen's *Montessori From the Start: The Child at Home, from Birth to Age Three* (New York: Schocken, 2003) and the Forest Bluff School blog at https://forestbluffschool.org.

6. This refers to in-person interactions with friends but not to online interactions, which of course necessitate close adult supervision and guidance. Because online formats cannot give children the autonomy they need to practice, in-person play and conversations are more suitable for raising children with Montessori benefits.

7. See: Carr, Nicholas, *The Shallows: What the Internet Is Doing to Our Brains* (New York: W.W. Norton, 2011).

8. Boxes and bins can be used to serve such purposes as well; one does not need to spend a lot to show their children that they care to make their room attractive, accessible, and inviting. Simple and tidy does the job.

9. Such furniture can be made simply or, if necessary, supplied by sturdy crates and step stools; the most important features are safety, size, and attractiveness.

10. Maria Montessori, *Maria Montessori Speaks to Parents: A Selection of Articles* (Amsterdam: Montessori-Pierson, 2017), 19.

11. Montessori, *Maria Montessori Speaks to Parents*, 23.

12. Savvy children can find ways to circumvent computer restrictions, so it helps to consult a skilled technician.

13. For starters, see the work of Mark R. Lepper throughout the 1970s, 80s, 90s, and 2000s; more recent meta-analysis studies, such as Christoper P. Cerasoli, Jessica M. Nicklin, and Michael T. Ford's "Intrinsic Motivation and

Extrinsic Incentives Jointly Predict Performance: A 40-Year Meta-analysis,"
Psychological Bulletin 140, no. 4 (July 2014): 980–1008, https://doi.org/10.1037
/a0035661; books and articles by Alfie Kohn; and ample research cited in
Angeline Lillard's chapter titled "Extrinsic Rewards and Motivation" in her
Montessori: The Science Behind the Genius.

14. When it became clear that the stay-at-home order was going to last more than
a few weeks, Montessori schools around the world began designing online
learning formats using Zoom, FaceTime, and other platforms for communicating with students from home. The best ones were live and interactive.
Most (private) Montessori schools were open for in-person learning the
entire 2020–2021 school year and beyond. This demonstrates how nimble
and adaptable the Montessori educational approach is, even in the most challenging of times.

Conclusion

1. Maria Montessori, *The 1946 London Lectures* (Amsterdam: Montessori-Pierson
Publishing, 2015), 87.

2. Montessori, *1946 London Lectures*, 87.

3. Maria Montessori, *Citizen of the World: Key Montessori Readings* (Amsterdam:
Montessori-Pierson, 2019), 19.

4. Montessori, *Citizen of the World*, 19.

5. Montessori, *Citizen of the World*, 111.

6. Montessori, *Citizen of the World*, 106.

7. Maria Montessori, *To Educate the Human Potential* (Thiruvanmiyur, Chennai,
India: Kalakshetra Press, 1991), 3.

8. Montessori, *Citizen of the World*, 107–108.

9. Maria Montessori, *The Formation of Man* (Amsterdam: Montessori-Pierson,
2007), 69.

BIBLIOGRAPHY

De Stefano, Cristina. *The Child Is the Teacher: A Life of Maria Montessori*. New York: Other Press, 2022.

Egan, Kieran. *Getting It Wrong from the Beginning: Our Progressivist Inheritance from Herbert Spencer, John Dewey, and Jean Piaget*. New Haven: Yale University Press, 2002.

Eissler, Trevor. *Montessori Madness!: A Parent to Parent Argument for Montessori Education*. Georgetown, TX: Sevenoff, 2009.

Kramer, Rita. *Maria Montessori: A Biography*. Reading, MA: Perseus, 1988.

Lillard, Angeline Stoll. *Montessori: The Science Behind the Genius*. 3rd ed. Oxford: Oxford University Press, 2017.

Lillard, Angeline S., Jessica Taggart, Daniel Yonas, and Mary Nia Seale. "An Alternative to 'No Excuses': Considering Montessori as Culturally Responsive Pedagogy." *Journal of Negro Education*, to be published in 2024.

Lillard, Angeline S., Megan J. Heise, Eve M. Richey, Xin Tong, Alyssa Hart, and Paige M. Bray. "Montessori Preschool Elevates and Equalizes Child Outcomes: A Longitudinal Study." *Frontiers in Psychology* 8 (October 30, 2017). https://www.frontiersin.org/articles/10.3389/fpsyg.2017.01783/full.

Loeffler, Margaret Howard, ed. *Montessori in Contemporary American Culture*. Portsmouth, NH: Heinemann Educational Books, 1992.

Loveless, Tom, ed. *The Great Curriculum Debate: How Should We Teach Reading and Math?* Washington, DC: Brookings Institution Press, 2001.

Mayer, R. E. "Should There Be a Three-Strikes Rule Against Pure Discovery Learning?" *American Psychologist* 59, no. 1 (2004):14–19.

Montessori, Maria. *The Absorbent Mind*. New York: Dell, 1984.

Montessori, Maria. *The Discovery of the Child*. New York: Ballantine Books, 1990.

Montessori, Maria. *Education and Peace*. Thiruvanmiyur, Chennai, India: Kalakshetra Press,1972.

Montessori, Maria. *The Formation of Man*. Amsterdam: Montessori-Pierson, 2007.

Montessori, Maria. *From Childhood to Adolescence*. Thiruvanmiyur, Chennai, India: Kalakshetra Press, 1973.

Montessori, Maria. *The Method of Scientific Pedagogy Applied to the Education of Young Children in the Children's House*. New York: Schocken Books, 1912. Reprinted as *The Montessori Method*. New York: Schocken Books, 1964.

Montessori, Maria. *Montessori Speaks to Parents: A Selection of Articles*. Amsterdam: Montessori-Pierson, 2017.

Montessori, Maria. *The 1946 London Lectures*. Amsterdam: Montessori-Pierson, 2012.

Montessori, Maria. *The 1913 Rome Lectures: First International Training Course*. Amsterdam: Montessori-Pierson, 2013.

Montessori, Maria. *The Secret of Childhood*. New York: Ballantine Books, 1972.

Montessori, Maria. *To Educate the Human Potential*. Thiruvanmiyur, Chennai, India: Kalakshetra Press, 1991.

Moretti, Erica. *The Best Weapon for Peace: Maria Montessori, Education, and Children's Rights*. Madison: University of Wisconsin Press, 2021.

Newsweek "Montessori: Madness over the Method." November 20, 1972.

Povell, Phyllis. *Montessori Comes to America: The Leadership of Maria Montessori and Nancy McCormick Rambusch*. Lanham, MD: University Press of America, 2010.

Rambusch, Nancy McCormick. *Learning How to Learn: An American Approach to Montessori*. Baltimore: Helicon Press, 1962.

Whitescarver, Keith, and Jacqueline Cossentino. "Montessori and the Mainstream: A Century of Reform on the Margins." *Teachers College Record* 110, no 12. (December 2008): 2571–2600.

INDEX

Absorbent Mind, The (Montessori), 142

absorbent minds, 23–25, 156, 198

abstract thinking skills, 25, 31, 50, 60, 168–169

accreditation, 130–136, 138, 174

active learning, 3, 47, 88

adaptability, 6–7, 13, 122–123, 156–157, 221–222

administrators. *See* heads of school; school principals; teaching directors

adolescents, 33–41, 119–121, 197, 198–200, 210–215

affordability, 154–155

age groupings, 52, 54–56, 162, 175

American Montessori Society (AMS), 64, 132–133, 134–136, 174

Association Montessori Internationale (AMI), 64, 81, 131–132, 133–134, 174

atmosphere, in Montessori classrooms, 51–52, 61–63, 82–83, 92–93, 144–145

authority, respect for, 194, 213

awareness, 26, 61, 65–66, 88

balance, of freedom and responsibility, 45, 47–48, 78–79, 91, 200–201

Binomial Cube, 60

boundaries, 78–79, 80, 91, 176, 200–216

brain development, 42, 44–46

branding issues, of Montessori approach, 124–126

Bruner, Jerome, 3

busy work, 148

Casa dei Bambini (Rome), 62

cell phone usage, 213–214

character development, 11–13, 87–88, 111, 201, 206

charter schools, 164

Chicago Public Schools, 157–158, 161–163

children with greater needs, 7–8, 94–95, 176–177, 181–182

Children's House, the (Rome), 62

choices
   in classroom work, 22, 69, 72–73, 83–85, 178
   freedom and responsibility with, 78–79, 91
   in home environments, 200–216
   in prepared environments, 80, 176

classrooms, Montessori
  age groupings in, 54–56
  anecdotal examples of, 96–103
  assistants in, 54, 76
  atmosphere in, 61–63, 82–83,
    92–93, 144–145
  classroom design for, 53
  conflict resolution, 175–176
  curriculum presentation in, 83–88
  evaluating, 144–150
  learning materials in, 50–51, 57–61
  ratio of teachers to class size in, 54
  specialists in, 176–177
  typical, 15
  work cycles in, 56
coaches, Montessori-trained, 138,
  163–164, 183
Coffee Discussions, 118–119
collaboration
  among teachers, 104–105, 108–114,
    139
  as character trait, 12, 224, 226
  communication skills for, 30–31
  competition and, 161
  elementary-aged children and,
    51–52
  in home environments, 191–192,
    199, 201, 204–207
  social development and, 25–26
communication
  collaborative skills for, 30–31
  between parents and teachers,
    109–122, 206
  teacher to teacher, 104, 108
"Communication in Signs," 26
competition, 12, 43, 161, 170–171
concentration skills, 18, 56, 148–150,
  205
confidence building, 33, 40, 158–159
conflict resolution, 175–176
Continuing Education Evenings,
  116–118
continuity
  in Montessori approach, 45, 60, 76
  in Montessori public schools,
    162–163, 180
  of teaching, 103, 138, 217

control of error, 60–61
conventional school model, 2–3, 4,
  30–31, 48–49, 73, 109, 154,
  161–162, 165–169, 173
cooking activities, 36–37, 113,
  207–208
cosmic education, 25, 226
Cossentino, Jacqueline, 187
Country Day schools/movement, 125
courage, 12, 34, 39–41, 55, 86, 150,
  186, 214
courtesy, 145–147
COVID-19, 217–218
Cox, Anne, 157, 175–176, 184, 185
creativity, 122, 140, 189–190, 223
critical thinking. See thinking skills
Csikszentmihalyi, Mihaly, 148
curiosity, 12, 26–27, 39, 83–84, 147,
  215, 229–231

Dewey, John, 3
dignity, 40, 103, 158
directors. See teaching directors
Directors' Meetings, 106–108
Directors' Week, 105–106
discipline. See self-discipline
division (mathematics), 86, 136, 172
downtime. See free time

education for life, 5, 11–13, 44–46,
  187
elementary-aged children
  classroom curriculum for, 83–87
  classroom presentation by, 69–78
  developmental stages, 24–33
  in home environments, 197–198,
    207–209
  learning environments for, 51–52
  parental modeling behaviors and,
    198
  teacher presentations to, 71–72,
    170–171
  See also Lower Elementary class-
    rooms; Upper Elementary
    classrooms
empathy, 26, 54, 65–66, 175–176,
  223, 226

engagement, 12, 17–18, 178, 195–
    198, 204–205, 208
equalization, of performance
    outcomes, 155–156
extrinsic motivation, 216

face-to-face meetings, 114–115
family and families. *See* home
    environments
farm programs, 34, 122, 211
field trips. *See* work trips
floors, in Montessori classrooms, 53
flow, state of, 18, 148
Flower Arranging, the, 67–68
focus, 12, 17–19, 25, 56, 67, 209
follow-up work, 72
Forest Bluff School, 90–94
fractions (mathematics), 110, 113,
    136
free time, 208–209
free will, 22–23, 144, 206
freedom
    boundaries and, 200–201
    individual, 140, 147, 223–224
    responsibility and, 45, 47–48,
        78–79, 91, 200–201
furniture, in Montessori classrooms,
    53

"go for it" attitude, 43
Golden Beads, 168
Goodwin, Virginia McHugh, 134
grace, acts of, 12, 51, 64–65, 114,
    145–147
grades and grading, 1, 2–3, 109–110,
    171
Grammar Box, 69–71
Great Lessons, 26, 32, 83, 86
groupings of units (mathematics), 59

heads of school, 105, 108, 120
home environments
    adolescents in, 197, 210–214
    choices and boundaries in, 200–216
    elementary-aged children in,
        197–198, 207–209

Montessori approach in, 188–196,
    202–203, 216–219
Montessori graduates and, 214–216
parental modeling behaviors and,
    198–200, 207
preparation of, 195–198
toddlers in, 196–197, 198, 203–207
human tendencies, 23, 24, 31, 45

imaginations, development of, 25, 26
imitation, 55, 67, 142, 175–176, 198
independence
    fostering, 74–76, 101–103, 113, 154,
        188–191, 195–196, 200
    in learning, 6, 22, 54, 60–61, 83–85
indirect preparation, 24, 74–75, 162
individuality, 63, 200, 223–224
infants, 48, 119
intellect
    growth of, 25–26, 62, 111, 166, 208
    integration with freewill, 22–23
    self-formation and, 48–49
internal liberty, 140, 147, 223–224
    See also freedom
internships, 34, 210
intrinsic motivation, 33, 216
Itard, Jean-Marc Gaspard, 7

Jessen, Lynn Lillard, 93–94
joy, 18, 87, 147–148, 154, 161

keys to the world, concept of, 50, 149

language learning activities, 32,
    69–71, 82
learning environments. *See*
    classrooms, Montessori;
    prepared environments
*Learning How to Learn: An
    American Approach to
    Montessori*, (Ramsbach), 132
learning materials. *See* materials,
    Montessori
lessons, 26, 32, 83, 86, 171
life skills and activities, 11, 22–23,
    34, 191, 204, 227

Lillard, Angeline, 155
Lillard, Paula Polk, 9, 10, 93–94, 118
Linari, Jane Sheehy, 93–94
Locke, John, 2
Lower Elementary classrooms, 24–33,
    51–52, 97–103
low-income families, children of, 8,
    153–159

magnet schools, 159–160, 164
manners. *See* courtesy
Maria Montessori Speaks to Parents
    (Montessori), 90
materials, Montessori, 57–61
  in classrooms, 50–51, 57–61
  display and arrangement of, 57
  interrelationship of, 59–60
  origin of, 6, 7–8, 57–58
  presentation of, 66–67
  purpose of, 58, 73–74
  unique features of, 60–61
mathematics, 59–60, 86, 168–169, 172
misbehavior, handling of, 76,
    141–144
Mission Meeting, 105–106
modeling behaviors
  adult to child, 64–65, 66, 73, 92,
    106, 198–199, 207, 225
  older to younger child, 55, 76–77
  peer-to-peer, 54
Montessomethings, 126–130
Montessori, Maria
  on adolescence, 33–41, 120, 211
  as advocate for underprivileged and
    marginalized people, 156
  background of, 7–9
  childhood development theory of,
    24–34
  criticisms of, 140
  early childhood development
    theory of, 17–24
  education of, 81–82
  on imitation, 142
  misinterpretations of, 131
  observations, 5–6, 11, 22–26, 44,
    49–51, 62–63, 87, 111, 140,
    188–189, 223

on peace, 187, 224–225
planes of development theory of,
    16–45
on play time, 209
post-adolescence development
    theory of, 42–44
on role of adults, 142–144, 227
terminology used by, 23–24, 25,
    34, 40, 48, 60, 74, 75, 144, 148,
    157, 224
Montessori, Mario, 81, 131, 132
Montessori Accreditation Council for
    Teacher Education (MACTE),
    174
Montessori approach
  adaptability in, 6–7, 221–222
  best practices in education and,
    150–151
  branding issues of, 124–126
  character traits fostered by, 11–13
  continuity in, 45, 60, 76
  curricular plan for, 81–88
  in home environments, 188–196,
    202–203, 216–219
  pillars of, 49–50
  in public education, 153–158. *See
    also* Montessori public pro-
    grams
  role of adults in, 49, 75–78, 89–90,
    227
Montessori classrooms
  evaluative measures in, 170–171
  toddlers in, 17–24
Montessori from the Start (morning
    lectures), 119
Montessori graduates, 9–13, 42–44,
    54, 210, 214–216
Montessori Method. *See* Montessori
    approach
Montessori Method, The
    (Montessori), 8–9
Montessori Public Policy Initiative
    (MPPI), 134, 174
Montessori public programs
  administrators in, 159–162,
    169–170, 178–181, 193
  advocating for, 182–187

benefits of, 153–158, 178, 185–186
challenges facing, 165–166, 179–180
history and growth of, 164–165
research support for, 155
varying levels of teacher training in, 160–161
Montessori schools
accreditation of, 130–136, 138
adaptability of, 122–123
culture in, 50, 85, 88, 104–105, 138
variations in, 126–130, 150–151
Moore, Katherine, 164
motivation to excel, 18, 33, 172, 215–218

National Center for Montessori in the Public Sector (NCMPS), 155, 163
No Child Left Behind Act of 2001, 2
notes and note-keeping, by teachers, 73, 95, 115
Number Rods, 59

organization, 12, 23, 31, 50–51, 86

parenting styles, 191–194
parents
as advocates for Montessori approach, 90, 182–187, 216–219
child's needs versus needs of, 195–198
collaboration between child and, 191–192, 199, 201, 204–207
communication with teachers, 109–121, 206
educational events for, 115–121
modeling behaviors by, 198–199, 207
See also home environments
peace, education for, 187, 223, 224–225
peer-to-peer teaching, 24, 54, 74–75, 76, 111
Piaget, Jean, 3
Pink Tower, 11, 61

planes of development, 16–45, 202–203, 225–226
play. See free time
potentiality, 144, 156–157, 226, 227
prepared environments, 50–63
age groupings in, 54–56
atmosphere in, 61–63
choices and boundaries in, 80, 176
classroom design for, 53
learning materials in, 57–61
spirit of, 61–63
work cycles in, 56
See also classrooms, Montessori
preschools, Montessori, 125, 155
Primary classrooms, 17–24, 54, 67–69, 82, 96–97, 158, 197
progressive school model, 3–4, 6, 31, 47
Promlee-Benz, Ta, 175–176, 177–178
Public Montessori in Action, 163
public school boards, working with, 166, 181
pushing, control of. See conflict resolution

questioning, 26, 49, 71, 185, 226

Race to the Top (2009), 2
Racks and Tubes, 172
Rambusch, Nancy McCormick, 132–133
reasoning, development of, 24–25, 32–33, 213
Red Rods, 58–59
resourcefulness
behavior examples of, 26–30, 77, 96–101, 102, 189–190
character trait of, 13, 16, 158
through work, 52, 74
respect, 12, 25, 39–41, 51, 144–147, 194, 224
See also self-respect
responsibility
freedom and, 45, 47–48, 78–79, 200–201
learning, 39–41, 210–211

school cultures
   conventional, 162, 167–173, 191
   Montessori, 50, 85, 88, 104–105, 138
school principals, 159–162, 169–170,
      178–181, 193
screen time. *See* technology, use of
Secondary Level Evenings and Teas,
      119–121
Seebeck, Elizabeth, 157, 176, 184,
      185, 187
Séguin, Édouard, 7
self-actualization, 225–226
self-awareness, 65–66, 88
self-discipline, 77–78, 147, 209, 224
self-formation, 5, 48–49, 94, 119–
      121, 226
self-motivation, 23–24, 215–218
self-regulation, 175–176
self-respect, 16–17, 34, 41, 158
   See also respect
sensitive periods, 23, 24, 45, 138
shelves, in Montessori classrooms,
      53, 57
simplicity, 22, 50, 90, 122, 224
social development, 25–26, 34, 40,
      111–112, 223
social newborns, 34
   See also adolescents
Spindle Boxes, 59
standardized tests and testing. *See*
      tests and testing
Stephenson, Margaret, 132–133
storytelling, 26–27, 32, 83

Table Washing, 18–21
teachers, in conventional school
      model, 2–3, 4, 47
teachers, Montessori
   accreditation and certification of,
      173–175
   challenges facing, 137–139
   classroom presentations by, 66–72,
      83–86
   communication with parents,
      109–121, 206
   flexibility and freedom allowed,
      177–178

goals of, 49
notes and note-keeping by, 73, 95, 115
ratio of, to class sizes, 54
roles of, 31–32, 72–78
team-approach to, 104–109, 151
training for, 63–66, 125, 132–135,
      159–160, 173–174
teaching directors, 105–108, 118
team-teaching, 104, 106–109, 151
technology, use of, 189, 199–200,
      211–213
tests and testing, 2, 3, 165–173
thinking skills, 11, 22, 25–26, 43–44,
      170, 185, 223
Thorndike, Edward, 2
Three Period Lesson, 171
three-year cycles, 52, 54–56, 94–95,
      162, 172–173
time management strategies, 101
Toddler classroom. *See* Primary
      classrooms
toddlers, 196–197, 198, 203–207
Trinomial Cube, 163

Ungerer, Rich, 134
United States, accreditation in, 130–136
universal child, concept of, 6–8, 156–157
Upper Elementary classrooms, 136,
      143, 163, 169

valorization, 17, 40–41
Verb Grammar Box, 69–71
verbalization, of knowledge, 58,
      170–172

walls, in Montessori classrooms, 53
Whitby School (Greenwich,
      Connecticut), 132
whole child approach, 49, 141
wilderness training, 34–41
work, concept of, 17–23, 60
work cycles, 53, 56, 85, 104, 163, 181
work trips, 34–41

young adults. *See* adolescents;
      Montessori graduates
Young Children's Community, 108

ABOUT THE AUTHOR

Paula Lillard Preschlack, ME, was born on July 8, 1969, in Cincinnati, Ohio, as the youngest of five girls. Two years later, her family moved to a Chicago suburb, where she attended Ronald Knox Montessori School and then Lake Forest Country Day School through the ninth grade. She attended Holderness School in New Hampshire for high school and acquired her bachelor of arts at Hampshire College in Massachusetts. After first wanting to be a writer and a horse trainer, she became interested in Montessori through her older sister, Lynn Lillard Jessen, and her mother, Paula Polk Lillard. Paula holds diplomas from the Association Montessori Internationale for three levels: Assistants to Infancy, Primary, and Elementary. She trained at the Montessori Institute in Denver and the Washington Montessori Institute in DC. In 2017 Paula audited The Orientation to Adolescents led by David Kahn. For twenty-five years she worked at Forest Bluff School, as a Primary teacher, an Elementary teacher, the assistant head, and the head of school. She now writes and speaks about Montessori education.

Paula lives in Lake Forest, Illinois, with her husband and two standard poodles, while their young adult children attend New York University and Skidmore College. Her hobbies are horseback riding and hiking. She wants to help others, and she loves to laugh!